MORE
HIGH SCHOOL
TALKSHEETS
ON THE NEW TESTAMENT
FOR AGES 14-18

52 READY-TO-USE
DISCUSSIONS

DAVID LYNN

youth specialties

ZONDERVAN.com/
AUTHORTRACKER
follow your favorite authors

ZONDERVAN

More High School Talksheets on the New Testament, Epic Bible Stories: 52 Ready-to-Use Discussions
Copyright © 2010 by David Lynn

YS Youth Specialties is a trademark of YOUTHWORKS!, INCORPORATED and is registered with the United States Patent and Trademark Office.

Requests for information should be addressed to:

Zondervan, *Grand Rapids, Michigan 49530*

ISBN 978-0-310-66869-5

Cover design: David Conn
Interior design: Brandi Etheredge Design

Printed in the United States of America

11 12 13 14 15 /DCI/ 23 22 21 20 19 18 17 16 15 14 13 12 11 10 9 8 7 6 5 4 3 2

For Amy:
Blessing #1

CONTENTS

THE HOWS AND WHATS
OF TALKSHEETS

about opinions, learn about themselves, and grow in their faith.

IMPORTANT GUIDING PRINCIPLES BEFORE USING NEW TESTAMENT TALKSHEETS

Let's begin by agreeing on two primary principles: (1) Faith is essentially caught, not taught, and (2) The Holy Spirit alone works best to establish faith within someone's life, changing someone from a knower to a believer and a church attendee to a lifelong follower of Jesus. If we can agree on these first principles, then it is easier to explain how NEW TESTAMENT TalkSheets are designed. It is not so much a teaching tool as a tool designed to engage real faith connections and encourage faith vocabulary in the lives of young people.

You are holding a very valuable book! No, it won't make you a genius or millionaire. But it does contain 52 instant discussions for high school youth. Inside you'll find reproducible NEW TESTAMENT TalkSheets that cover 52 stories from the birth of Jesus to the end of the book of Revelation; plus simple, step-by-step instructions on how to use them. All you need is this book, a few copies of the handouts, and some young people (and maybe a snack or two). You're on your way to touching on some serious issues in young people's lives today.

So many church attendees do not know how to articulate their faith, nor do they often see real, vital connections for their faith outside of the church building. NEW TESTAMENT TalkSheets exercises are designed to help young people make real-life connections between what they believe and their day-to-day lives, as well as develop a living faith vocabulary, as opposed to a church vocabulary used only in the God house to please adults and religious leaders. For faith to grow with us in ways that last a lifetime, all of us need to discover faith's vital connection in our day-to-day lives. We need to see where Jesus in our lives engages the real world we live in. And we need to have an ability to express this connection, or a "vocabulary of faith" that grows with us and goes with us, rather than merely a religious Christian-ese we speak in religious settings and on certain occasions.

These NEW TESTAMENT TalkSheets are user-friendly and very flexible. They can be used in a youth group meeting, a Sunday school class, or a Bible study group. You can adapt them for either large or small groups. And, they can be covered in only 20 minutes or explored more intensively in two hours.

You can build an entire youth group meeting around a single NEW TESTAMENT TalkSheet, or you can use NEW TESTAMENT TalkSheets to supplement other materials and resources you might be using. These are tools for you—how you use them is your choice.

High School NEW TESTAMENT TalkSheets are not your average curriculum or workbook. This collection of discussions will get your young people involved and excited about talking through important issues. The NEW TESTAMENT TalkSheets deal with epic stories and include interesting activities, challenging questions, and eye-catching graphics. They will challenge your young people to think

These NEW TESTAMENT TalkSheets exercises are aimed at engaging young people in real conversations where belief can be discovered, Christian words and notions can be unpacked, and faith can be connected with and expressed. In such settings the earliest Christians explored and expressed their faith. Our Lord Jesus used fishing with fishermen to connect his first followers with what he was doing, using words and images that were familiar to them. Creating settings where young people can talk about faith develops a faith vocabulary and deepens faith by connecting it to relevant life experiences.

NEW TESTAMENT TALKSHEETS AS AN ENGAGING TOOL RATHER THAN A TEACHING TOOL

We have often made a very fundamental mistake in how we assist young people in their faith development. We have hammered down on the obvious answers to questions that the young people are often not even asking. What you wind up with are young people who can answer the question "correctly" but don't see why the answer is relevant to their daily lives.

Take, for example, the primary question of faith: Who is your Lord and Savior? The right answer is "Jesus Christ is my Lord and Savior." I have heard young people answer this question correctly for many years. But when it comes to real life, I have also witnessed many young people get stumped on a valid understanding as to what "Lord" means in a culture where all people are their own sources of truth or as to why they need to be saved when all people are "basically okay." We often make the mistake of assuming that good information is enough. But the information needs to possess something vital for youth to attach to, and if the questions are not there, the information may not seem relevant.

When we teach young people answers to questions they are not asking, nor even know that they need to ask, we are leaving them with answers that don't fit and faith that will not stand up under pressure. This is why we believe that young people need to understand the tensions of life from which questions arise and struggle with how they answer those questions daily in their lives before they hear how God has addressed those questions in the person of Jesus Christ. Then we can ask, "If this is how life is, then who is YOUR Lord and Savior?"

By engaging young people inwardly and INNER-gizing young people into a real dialogue about their life, perceptions, and faith, we can make pathways where we can partner with them as they grow in their discipleship.

A COMMON PITFALL TO AVOID

Faith development is often a stepped process. Some things need to be set in place before other things can be embraced. We might say that a person moves from A to B before moving on to C and eventually arriving at D. A mistake many leaders may make is that the movement from A to D looks simple to them, and they are impatient for those they are working with to make that developmental leap. Good Christian leadership understands that we are often guides for encounters on the roadside as people make their way in following the Master.

A pitfall that is common in Christian leadership is to invite people to make a leap in faith development they're unable to sustain. Often young believers make a substitutional leap of faith and jump from A to D based on what the leader believes. People are very willing to do this because they might trust their leaders or might be afraid to express real doubts in an unsafe environment. They might also think it's a lack on their part to move so slowly in faith, which can make them feel guilty. There's also performance anxiety in our faith settings that can cause people to take on language that fits the situation but is essentially not a part of their day-to-day lives.

I have witnessed these conditions, where real faith is not deep enough to sustain the pressures of real life and substitutional faith is worn like a garment in the God house. Such followers who attend gatherings but cannot pray for themselves hold a secret sense of doubt and guilt and often defer to the religious leadership on all matters of faith.

Jesus spoke of such followers, who are like shallow soil on which the seed falls.

Essentially there are three roles a discussion leader can fulfill: An Instrument, a Thorn, or a Stage Director: (1) An Instrument can be a force in the hand of the Holy Spirit that works in the process of faith-building in the life of young disciples; (2) As a Thorn the leader can become an irritant in the life of disciples that alienates them from the faith community by creating an unsafe faith environment with unrealistic expectations and impatient discipleship methods; (3) A Stage Director leader is one who inoculates young people against catching real faith by creating an environment that encourages satisfying an expectation by taking on a mask of believing and a language of the church. This effectually insulates them from embracing real, vital faith expressed in a living language. As you can see, only one role serves well in the life of young followers, and that is the role of an Instrument.

NEW TESTAMENT TALKSHEETS HELPS US BE GOOD STEWARDS OF A SACRED PROCESS

But if we understand deep, rich soil may take time and much mulching if a seed is to take root, then we can as leaders trust that faith is not about ourselves achieving something in the life of a person, but about the Holy Spirit shaping a life into a follower. We can become stewards of a most sacred process. Young people can pick up useless notions of faith and life on their way to discovering real faith that rumbles deep with a vital discipleship. Patient and loving mentoring is needed if these useless notions are to be replaced with life-giving awareness in a living, vital faith in Jesus.

Remember that Thomas did not at first believe that Jesus was resurrected even though the other disciples expressed to him what they had witnessed. It is a great testimony of those early followers of Jesus that Thomas was still with them "in their midst" a week later when Jesus showed up and confirmed himself to Thomas. It is important to create a safe environment where young people can explore their faith and express themselves without the expectation of correct performance or the need to make the developmental leap that they are not ready to sustain as a disciple until, for them, Jesus shows up.

LEADING A NEW TESTAMENT TALKSHEET DISCUSSION

NEW TESTAMENT TalkSheets can be used as a curriculum for your youth group, but they are designed to be springboards for discussion. They encourage your young people to take part and interact with each other while talking about real life issues. And hopefully they'll do some serious thinking, discover new ideas for themselves, defend their points of view, and make decisions.

Youth today face a world of moral confusion. Youth leaders must teach the church's beliefs and values—and also help young people make the right choices in a world full of options. Teenagers are bombarded with the voices of society and the media—most of which drown out what they hear from the church.

A NEW TESTAMENT TalkSheet discussion works for this very reason. While dealing with the questions and activities on the NEW TESTAMENT TalkSheet, your young people will think carefully about issues, compare their beliefs and values with others, and make their own choices. NEW TESTAMENT TalkSheets will challenge your group to explain and rework their ideas in a Christian atmosphere of acceptance, support, and growth.

The most common fear of high school youth group leaders is, "What will I do if the young people in my group just sit there and don't say anything?" Well, when young people don't have anything to say, it's because they haven't had a chance or time to get their thoughts organized! Most young people haven't developed the ability to think on their feet. Since many are afraid they might sound stupid, they don't know how to voice their ideas and opinions.

The solution? NEW TESTAMENT TalkSheets let your youth deal with the issues in a challenging, non-threatening way before the actual discussion begins. They'll have time to organize their thoughts, write them down, and ease their fears about participating. They may even look forward to sharing their answers! Most importantly, they'll want to find out what others say and open up to talk through the topics.

If you're still a little leery about the success of a real discussion among your youth, that's okay!

YOUR ROLE AS THE LEADER

The best discussions don't happen by accident. They require careful preparation and a sensitive leader. Don't worry if you aren't experienced or don't have hours to prepare. NEW TESTAMENT TalkSheets are designed to help even the novice leader! The more NEW TESTAMENT TalkSheet discussions you lead, the easier it becomes. Keep the following tips in mind when using the NEW TESTAMENT TalkSheets as you get your young people talking.

BE CHOOSY

Each NEW TESTAMENT TalkSheet deals with a different story. Under the title of each of the NEW TESTAMENT TalkSheets is a simple subtitle heading that expresses the theme of the TalkSheet. Choose a NEW TESTAMENT TalkSheet based on the needs and the maturity level of your group. Don't feel obligated to use the NEW TESTAMENT TalkSheets in the order they appear in this book. Use your best judgment and mix them up however you want—they're tools for you!

MAKE COPIES

Young people will need their own copy of the TalkSheet. Only make copies of the youth side of the TalkSheet! The material on the reverse side (the leader's guide) is just for you. You're able to make copies for your group because we have given you permission to do so. U.S. copyright laws have not changed, and it is still mandatory to request permission from a publisher before making copies of other published material. It is against the law not to do so. However, permission is given for you to make copies of this material for your group only, not for every youth group in your state. Thank you for cooperating.

TRY IT YOURSELF

Once you have chosen a NEW TESTAMENT TalkSheet for your group, answer the questions and do the activities yourself. Imagine your young people's reactions to the NEW TESTAMENT TalkSheet. This will help you prepare for the discussion and understand what you are asking them to do. Plus, you'll have some time to think of other appropriate questions, activities, and Bible verses.

GET SOME INSIGHT

On each leader's guide page, you'll find numerous tips and ideas for getting the most out of your discussion. You may want to add some of your own thoughts or ideas in the margins.

INTRODUCE THE TOPIC

You may introduce the topic before you pass out the NEW TESTAMENT TalkSheets to your group, and then allow the topic to develop as you use the material. We have a simple format on the leader's guide that can help your introduction. First, there is the "Read Out Loud" section. Simply read the paragraph or two out loud, then ask a young person to read the story from the Bible. After the story is read, you can use the question in the "Ask" section to get the group primed for a discussion of the story.

NEW TESTAMENT TalkSheets work best with a strong concluding presentation rather than a strong teaching time prior to using the Talksheet. You can use the "Close" section to help guide your closing presentation. Depending on your group, keep your introduction short and to the point. Be careful not to over-introduce the topic, sound preachy, or resolve the issue before you've started. Your goal is to spark their interest and leave plenty of room for discussion, allowing the material to introduce the topic.

Pass out the NEW TESTAMENT TalkSheet and be sure that everyone has a pencil or pen. Now you're on your way! The following are excellent methods you can use to introduce any topic in this book—

- Show a related short film or video.
- Read a passage from a book or magazine that relates to the subject.
- Play a popular CD that deals with the topic.
- Perform a short skit or dramatic presentation.
- Play a simulation game or role-play, setting up the topic.
- Present current statistics or survey results, or read a current newspaper article that provides recent information about the topic.
- Use an icebreaker or other crowd game, getting into the topic in a humorous way.
- Use posters, videos, or any other visuals to help focus attention on the topic.

There are endless possibilities for an intro—you're limited only by your own creativity! Keep in mind that a clear and simple introduction is a very important part of each session.

SET BOUNDARIES

It'll be helpful to set a few ground rules before the discussion. Keep the rules to a minimum, of course, but let the youth know what's expected of them. Here are suggestions for some basic ground rules:
- What's said in this room stays in this room. Emphasize the importance of confidentiality.

Some young people will open up; some won't. Confidentiality is vital for a good discussion. If your youth can't keep the discussion in the room, then they won't open up.
- No put-downs. Mutual respect is important. If your young people disagree with some opinions, ask them to comment on the subject (but not on the other person).
- There's no such thing as a dumb question. Your group members must feel free to ask questions at any time. The best way to learn is to ask questions and get answers.
- No one is forced to talk. Let everyone know they have the right to pass or not answer any question.
- Only one person speaks at a time. This is a mutual respect issue. Everyone's opinion is worthwhile and deserves to be heard.

Communicate with your group that everyone needs to respect these boundaries. If you sense that your group members are attacking each other or getting a negative attitude during the discussion, do stop and deal with the problem before going on.

ALLOW ENOUGH TIME

Pass out copies of the NEW TESTAMENT TalkSheet to your young people after the introduction and make sure that each person has a pen or pencil and a Bible. There are usually five or six activities on each NEW TESTAMENT TalkSheet. If your time is limited, or if you are using only a part of the NEW TESTAMENT TalkSheet, tell the group to complete only the activities you assign.

Decide ahead of time whether or not you would like the young people to work on the NEW TESTAMENT TalkSheet individually or in groups.

Let them know how much time they have for completing the NEW TESTAMENT TalkSheet and let them know when there is a minute (or so) left. Go ahead and give them some extra time, and then start the discussion when everyone seems ready to go.

SET THE STAGE

Create a climate of acceptance. Most teenagers are afraid to voice their opinions because they don't want to be laughed at or look stupid in front of their peers. They want to feel safe if they're going to share their feelings and beliefs. Communicate that they can share their thoughts and ideas—even if they may be different or unpopular. If your young people get put-downs, criticism, laughter, or snide comments (even if their statements are opposed to the teachings of the Bible), it'll hurt the discussion.

Always phrase your questions—even those that are printed on the NEW TESTAMENT TalkSheets—so that you are asking for an opinion, not an answer. For example, if a question reads, "What should Bill have done in that situation?" the simple addition of the three words "do you think" makes the question less threatening and a matter of opinion, rather than a demand for the right answer. Your young people will relax when they feel more comfortable and confident. Plus, they'll know that you actually care about their opinions and they'll feel appreciated!

LEAD THE DISCUSSION

Discuss the NEW TESTAMENT TalkSheet with the group and encourage all your young people to participate. Communicate that it's important for them to respect each other's opinions and feelings! The more they contribute, the better the discussion will be.

If your youth group is big, you may divide it into smaller groups of six to 12. Each of these small groups should have a facilitator—either an adult leader or a youth member—to keep the discussion going. Remind the facilitators not to dominate. If the group looks to the facilitator for an answer, ask him or her to direct the questions or responses back to the group. Once the smaller groups have completed their discussions, combine them into one large group and ask the different groups to share their ideas.

You don't have to divide the groups up with every NEW TESTAMENT TalkSheet. For some discus-sions, you may want to vary the group size and/or divide the meeting into groups of the same sex.

The discussion should target the questions and answers on the NEW TESTAMENT TalkSheet. Go through them one at a time and ask the young people to share their responses. Have them compare their answers and brainstorm new ones in addition to the ones they've written down. Encourage them to share their opinions and answers, but don't force those who are quiet.

AFFIRM ALL RESPONSES—RIGHT OR WRONG

Let your young people know that their comments and contributions are appreciated and important. This is especially true for those who rarely speak during group activities. Make a point of thanking them for joining in. This will be an incentive for them to participate further.

Remember that affirmation doesn't mean approval. Affirm even those comments that seem wrong to you. You'll show that everyone has a right to express their ideas—no matter how controversial they may be. If someone states an opinion that is off base, make a mental note of the comment. Then in your wrap-up, come back to the comment or present a different point of view in a positive way. But don't reprimand the person who voiced the comment.

DON'T BE THE AUTHORITATIVE ANSWER

Some young people think you have the right to answer to every question. They'll look to you for approval, even when they are answering another group member's question. If they start to focus on you for answers, redirect them toward the group by making a comment like, "Remember that you're talking to everyone, not just me."

Your goal as the facilitator is to keep the discussion alive and kicking. It's important that your young people think of you as a member of the group—on their level. The less authoritative you are, the more value your own opinions will have. If your young people view you as a peer, they will listen to your comments. You have a tremendous responsibility to be, with sincerity, their trusted friend.

LISTEN TO EACH PERSON
God gave you one mouth and two ears. Good discussion leaders know how to listen. Although it's tempting at times, don't monopolize the discussion. Encourage others to talk first—then express your opinions during your wrap-up.

DON'T FORCE IT
Encourage all your young people to talk, but don't make them comment. Each member has the right to pass. If you feel that the discussion isn't going well, go on to the next question or restate the question to keep them moving.

DON'T TAKE SIDES
You'll probably have different opinions expressed in the group from time to time. Be extra careful not to take one side or another. Encourage both sides to think through their positions—ask questions to get them deeper. If everyone agrees on an issue, you can play devil's advocate with tough questions and stretch their thinking. Remain neutral—your point of view is your own, not that of the group.

DON'T LET ANYONE (INCLUDING YOU) TAKE OVER
Nearly every youth group has one person who likes to talk and is perfectly willing to express an opinion on any subject. Try to encourage equal participation from all the young people.

SET UP FOR THE TALK
Make sure that the seating arrangement is inclusive and encourages a comfortable, safe atmosphere for discussion. Theater-style seating (in rows) isn't discussion-friendly. Instead, arrange the chairs in a circle or semicircle (or sit on the floor with pillows).

LET THEM LAUGH!
Discussions can be fun! Most of the NEW TESTAMENT TalkSheets include questions that'll make them laugh and get them thinking, too.

LET THEM BE SILENT
Silence can be scary for discussion leaders! Some react by trying to fill the silence with a question or comment. The following suggestions may help you to handle silence more effectively:

- Be comfortable with silence. Wait it out for 30 seconds or so before responding. You may want to restate the question to give your young people a gentle nudge.
- Talk about the silence with the group. What does the silence mean? Do they really not have any comments? Maybe they're confused or embarrassed or don't want to share.
- Answer the silence with questions or comments like, "I know this is challenging to think about…" or "It's scary to be the first to talk." If you acknowledge the silence, it may break the ice.
- Ask a different question that may be easier to handle or that will clarify the one already posed. But don't do this too quickly without giving them time to think the first one through.

KEEP IT UNDER CONTROL
Monitor the discussion. Be aware if the discussion is going in a certain direction or off track. This can happen fast, especially if the young people disagree or things get heated. Mediate wisely and set the tone that you want. If your group gets bored with an issue, get them back on track. Let the discussion unfold, but be sensitive to your group and who is or is not getting involved.

If a young person brings up a side issue that's interesting, decide whether or not to pursue it. If discussion is going well and the issue is worth discussion, let them talk it through. But, if things get way off track, say something like, "Let's come back to that subject later if we have time. Right now, let's finish our discussion on…"

BE CREATIVE AND FLEXIBLE

You don't have to follow the order of the questions on the NEW TESTAMENT TalkSheet. Follow your own creative instinct. If you find other ways to use the NEW TESTAMENT TalkSheets, use them! Go ahead and add other questions or Bible references.

Don't feel pressured to spend time on every single activity. If you're short on time, you can skip some items. Stick with the questions that are the most interesting to the group.

SET YOUR GOALS

NEW TESTAMENT TalkSheets are designed to move along toward a goal, but you need to identify your goal in advance. What would you like your young people to learn? What truth should they discover? What is the goal of the session? If you don't know where you're going, it's doubtful you will get there. As stated earlier, there is a theme for each of the NEW TESTAMENT TalkSheets. You will find this theme in smaller type in the heading of each of the TalkSheet titles.

BE THERE FOR YOUR YOUNG PEOPLE

Some young people may want to talk more with you (you got 'em thinking!). Let them know that you can talk one-on-one with them afterward.

Communicate to the young people that they can feel free to talk with you about anything with confidentiality. Let them know you're there for them with support and concern, even after the NEW TESTAMENT TalkSheet discussion has been completed.

CLOSE THE DISCUSSION

There is a "Close" section at the end of each of the leader guides with a paragraph or two of closing comments. Present a challenge to the group by asking yourself, "What do I want the young people to remember most from this discussion?" There's your wrap up!

Sometimes you won't need a wrap-up. You may want to leave the issue hanging and discuss it in another meeting. That way, your group can think about it more and you can nail down the final ideas later.

A FINAL WORD TO THE WISE— THAT'S YOU!

Some of these NEW TESTAMENT TalkSheets deal with topics that may be sensitive or controversial for your young people. You're encouraging discussion and inviting your young people to express their opinions. As a result, parents or others in your church may criticize you—they may not see the importance of such discussions. Use your best judgment. If you suspect that a particular NEW TESTAMENT TalkSheet will cause problems, you may not want to use it. Or you may want to tweak a particular NEW TESTAMENT TalkSheet and only cover some of the questions. Either way, the potential bad could outweigh the good—better safe than sorry. To avoid any misunderstanding, you may want to give the parents or senior pastor (or whomever else you are accountable to) copies of the NEW TESTAMENT TalkSheet before you use it. Let them know the discussion you would like to have and the goal you are hoping to accomplish. Challenge your young people to take their NEW TESTAMENT TalkSheet home to talk about it with their parents. How would their parents, as young people, have answered the questions? Your young people may find that their parents understand them better than they thought. Also, encourage them to think of other Bible verses or ways that the NEW TESTAMENT TalkSheet applies to their lives.

1. Everyone in Bethlehem who listened to the shepherds' report was amazed. What do you think amazed them the most? What amazed you the most when you first heard about Jesus?

2. Finish this sentence: The one thing that makes me happiest about the good news that the shepherds heard is…

3. The shepherds rushed to find Jesus in Bethlehem. What are you in a rush to find this Christmas? (You may check more than one.)

❏ Pleasure
❏ Freedom
❏ The perfect gift
❏ A great meal
❏ The best Christmas tree
❏ A break from school
❏ Peace with God

❏ The right girlfriend/boyfriend
❏ The real Jesus
❏ The purpose for my life
❏ Freedom from worry
❏ Something more than I have now
❏ A home with no fighting
❏ Money

4. The shepherds experienced God's presence in their worship together. If you could be in charge of your congregation's worship for one Sunday, what would you do so that everyone in attendance would experience God's presence?

5. Who are you most like in the story?

❏ The worshiping shepherds
❏ Mary, who wondered what lay ahead
❏ Joseph, who did exactly what God wanted and supported Mary
❏ The surprised townspeople who heard the shepherds' story
❏ The manager of the inn who was nowhere to be found

READ OUT LOUD

The Roman Empire was experiencing *Pax Romana*, or Roman Peace, that was brought about by the brutal force of the Roman military. Violently crushing any rebellion on the part of its subjects, Rome ruled supreme. The Roman Empire's few citizens enjoyed this peace while the majority of those living under Roman rule were slaves. In this context comes the announcement of the angels (a hymn called "Gloria in Excelsis Deo")—"Glory to God in the highest, and on earth peace to men on whom his favor rests." You can read the story in Luke 2:8-20.

ASK

What celebrity *don't* you admire? What celebrity *do* you admire?

DISCUSS, BY THE NUMBERS

1. Use this item to begin a faith conversation about what amazed the shepherds the most. Then move your discussion to today—"What amazed you the most when you first heard about Jesus?"
2. Listen to your group members' completed sentences. Ask, "How is the good news that the shepherds heard the same good news that is told about Jesus today?" "Why do you think so many people view God as a mean, punishing God and don't see the good news of God's love as good?" What can you do to correct that misperception of God?"
3. Tally the top three responses by your group members. The band U2 has a song in which they declare that they still haven't found what they're looking for. Ask, "Have you found what you are looking for in Jesus Christ?" "Have you experienced God's forgiveness? God's loving presence?"

4. Let your group describe what they would do the same and different in worship so that everyone is drawn deeper into the experience of knowing God.
5. Find out who each of your group members see themselves as most like in the story. Share who you see yourself most like. Encourage honesty rather than Sunday school answers. Talk about where your group members see their growth areas to be (stronger faith; more wonder and awe of God; surprised by God).

CLOSE

Part of worship is experiencing God's presence. We do that together as a congregation and individually throughout the week in our everyday relationship with God. The shepherds experienced God's presence as they worshiped just like Joseph and Mary, the angels, and probably some of the townspeople.

God is always present in our lives—whether or not we "feel" God close to us. Let us worship God as we become aware of God's presence!

1. Zechariah was pumped about the coming birth of Jesus Christ. What excites you the most when you think of Jesus' birth? (If you're not excited, describe why.)

2. Luke 1:67-75

JESUS IS COMING SOON

Getting ready to celebrate Jesus' birth

2. What do you think is the biggest obstacle to thinking about Jesus at Christmastime?

3. Do you **A (agree)** or **D (disagree)** with each of these statements?

_____ Christmas is a reminder of the hope we have in Jesus.
_____ At Christmas we should think about the stuff we want.
_____ Forgiveness is the message of Christmas.
_____ Christmas reminds us that everyone will go to heaven.
_____ During the Christmas season we should remember that God is alive and working in the world.

4. What is the best way for you to get ready to celebrate Christ's birth? What is the best way for your family to get ready to celebrate Christ's birth?

5. Do you think these statements are **T (true)** or **F (false)**?

_____ Our physical world is temporary.
_____ Christ is coming again soon.
_____ I look forward to Christ's coming again.
_____ Christ's second coming makes little difference in how Christians live today.
_____ The second coming of Christ motivates me to live a holy life.

READ OUT LOUD

The father of John the Baptizer was none other than Zechariah, the hero in today's story. Zechariah was a Jewish priest at the time of Christ's birth. He was visited by the angel Gabriel and told of the coming birth of his son John (called John the Baptist or John the Baptizer). Because Zechariah didn't believe Gabriel, he was unable to speak until his son's birth. At the birth of John the Baptizer, Zechariah prophesied about Jesus. This prophecy—in the form of a hymn called the "Benedictus"—prepares us to celebrate Christ's birth. Read the prophecy found in Luke 1:67-75.

ASK

What is the shortest time it has taken you to get ready for school in the morning?

DISCUSS, BY THE NUMBERS

1. Use this item to start a faith conversation about getting ready to celebrate the birth of Jesus. Listen to the group's responses to the question. Then ask, "How excited are your friends about Christ's birth?"
2. Create a list of answers. Then create a list of ways to get around these obstacles.
3. See commentary in bold after each statement.
   - Christmas is a reminder of the hope we have in Jesus. **Ask, "How often do we reflect on the hope we have in Christ?"**
   - At Christmas we should think about the stuff we want. **Debate this one. Look at the pros and cons of focusing on "stuff" during the Christmas season. Ask, "What would Christmas be like if we bypassed gift-giving and focused exclusively on the birth of Christ through prayer, fasting, Bible reading, worship, and other spiritual disciplines?"**
   - Forgiveness is the message of Christmas. **Again, debate this one. Ultimately, Christ and the salvation he brings to us is the reason for the season.**
   - Christmas reminds us that everyone will go to heaven. **Will everyone go to heaven? The Bible is clear that only those who repent and believe in Jesus are saved.**
   - During the Christmas season we should remember that God is alive and working in the world. **Christmas is a great reminder of what God did over 2,000 years ago and what he is doing now!**
4. Create two lists, one that describes the best ways for your group members to get ready to celebrate Christ's birth and another that describes the best ways for your group's families to ready themselves to celebrate.
5. See commentary in bold after each statement.
   - Our physical world is temporary. **True. A house fire proves this.**
   - Christ is coming again soon. **True. When we don't know, but the Bible tells us soon! Could be 100 years from now or 100 days. Christ is coming again. He came first as a baby. His second coming will be deliverance to those who have been saved, and judgment to those who have rejected him.**
   - I look forward to Christ's coming again. **Sometimes true and sometimes not so true—especially for young people who have not yet experienced much of life.**
   - Christ's second coming makes little difference in how Christians live today. **Talk about the difference it should make. Ask, "Does it make a difference to most Christians?"**
   - The second coming of Christ motivates me to live a holy life. **Ask, "If your parents left you alone for the weekend, and you knew they were coming back at 8 p.m. on Sunday, what would you do?" Ask again, "If your parents left you alone for the weekend, but you didn't know when they would return, what would you do?" Ask, "What made the difference in your response?" We don't know when Christ will come again. Hopefully the anticipation of his imminent return motivates us to holy living.**

Read and discuss 2 Peter 3:10-11.

But the day of the Lord will come like a thief. The heavens will disappear with a roar, the elements will be destroyed by fire, and the earth and everything in it will be laid bare. Since everything will be destroyed in this way, what kind of people ought you to be? You ought to live holy and godly lives. (2 Peter 3:10-11)

CLOSE

As Christmas quickly approaches we need to be reminded of the words of Zechariah's song. God rescued us in Jesus Christ. God provided the way of salvation so that we can serve him.

Read Luke 1:74-75. "To rescue us from the hand of our enemies, and to enable us to serve him without fear in holiness and righteousness before him all our days."

1. **Do you think there are more or fewer people in the United States seeking Jesus today? In the world?**

THE WISE MEN LOOK FOR JESUS

Everyone is seeking something

2. **What do you think the Magi were seeking as they followed the star to Bethlehem?**

   - ❑ Knowledge and power they could use to manipulate others
   - ❑ Relief from sadness and pain
   - ❑ Pleasure to enjoy their lives more
   - ❑ Purpose to give their lives meaning
   - ❑ Popularity and prestige
   - ❑ Wealth so they could feel more secure
   - ❑ Peace from the troubles in the world

3. **The star led the wise men to Bethlehem. Rank the following things that lead you from most (1) to least (10).**

   ___ A teacher at school
   ___ Advertising
   ___ My friends
   ___ An adult at my church
   ___ My pastor's sermons
   ___ Parents/grandparents
   ___ The Bible
   ___ My music
   ___ My appearance
   ___ Achievement (in class, in sports)

4. **Worldly philosophies and religions distract people from seeking Christ. Which of the following do you think distracts people in the United States the most?**

   - ❑ Religions like Islam, Hinduism, or Mormonism say people must work their way into heaven.
   - ❑ Hedonism says pleasure is the ultimate purpose in life.
   - ❑ Materialism says the person with the most stuff wins.
   - ❑ New Age beliefs say people are in control of the universe (in other words, people play the role of God).
   - ❑ Atheism says there is no God (or gods); people are on their own.
   - ❑ Other: _____

5. **What are you seeking from Christ?**

   - ❑ Best friend
   - ❑ Moral guide
   - ❑ Get-out-of-hell-free card
   - ❑ Spiritual coach
   - ❑ A Santa Claus
   - ❑ Comfort
   - ❑ A sense of belonging
   - ❑ Forgiveness/right relationship with God
   - ❑ Love
   - ❑ Hope

READ OUT LOUD

The wise men—the Bible never says how many—were educated men from what is now the area of Saudi Arabia, Iraq, and Iran. They were schooled in astronomy, philosophy, religion, and medicine. And they were searching for Jesus. Read the story found in Matthew 2:1-12.

ASK

When you were a kid, where was the best place to hide when you played hide-n-seek?

DISCUSS, BY THE NUMBERS

1. In the United States church attendance has declined. The United States appears to be taking the road Great Britain and Europe have taken by becoming more and more secular. While church attendance is not the only indicator of interest in Jesus, it is the best data we have and probably does indicate less interest in Jesus in the United States. Central and South America, Africa, and parts of Asia are showing much more interest in Jesus and Christianity.

2. Scripture tells us that the Magi both sought and worshiped the baby Jesus. Ask, "What do you think Herod was seeking?"

3. Take this opportunity to discuss those things that lead us in good and bad directions. Ask, "Which of these things can lead you astray?" "Which will lead you to Jesus?"

4. Worldly philosophies and religions often distract people from seeking Christ. Which of the following do you think distracts people in the United States the most? Mormonism is growing in the United States, as is Islam. Materialism continues to deceive in spite of the Great Recession and its consequences. New Age beliefs have grown in popularity since the 1960s—people have a menu of beliefs that center around finding the "god inside you," your innate wisdom, your "true self," and the like. Atheism has grown, but most people still believe in some sort of god or higher power.

5. This item can spark a healthy faith conversation about what your group members seek from Jesus. Spend time talking with your group about how the forgiveness we have in Christ sets our relationship right with God so that we can be friends with God.

CLOSE

No matter your social status, your family background, or your education, everyone is seeking something. Some seek pleasure. Others power. Others spiritual enlightenment. The Bible clearly points to Jesus as the only one who will satisfy the spiritual vacuum that exists in our souls.

JOHN THE BAPTIZER PREPARES THE WAY

God wants us to introduce others to Jesus

1. What happens when you talk with people about Jesus?

- ❏ I never talk with the people I know about Jesus unless they are already committed Christians.
- ❏ If I dropped a "J" bomb on my friends, they would think I'm a religious nut.
- ❏ I talk often with people about Jesus.
- ❏ I never talk about Jesus or politics with my friends because I don't want to offend them.
- ❏ I don't know anyone who is not already a Christian.
- ❏ None of the people I know want to hear about Jesus.
- ❏ I believe all religions lead to God, so I don't need to talk about Jesus.

2. Which of the following people are you most like?

- ❏ John the Baptizer
- ❏ The crowds
- ❏ The tax collectors
- ❏ The soldiers
- ❏ Herod

3. If John the Baptizer were to come to your school, how do you think he would present the gospel to young people? To school staff? To parents?

4. If someone asked me about Jesus, I would—

- ❏ Act like I didn't hear them and talk about something else
- ❏ Tell them I wasn't that into Jesus
- ❏ Say, "Read the Bible if you want to know."
- ❏ Tell them that Jesus is the guy sending them to hell
- ❏ Ask them why they would want to know about Jesus
- ❏ Talk with them about what Jesus has done for me
- ❏ Laugh and shake my head

5. Choose the top two ways you feel are the best ways to introduce your friends to Jesus.

- ❏ Live like Jesus makes a difference in your life
- ❏ Invite your friends to church
- ❏ Pray for your friends
- ❏ Talk often with your friends about Jesus
- ❏ Carry your Bible everywhere you go
- ❏ Wear T-shirts that have a Christian message
- ❏ Put a Christian bumper sticker on the family car
- ❏ Give each of your friends a Bible
- ❏ Share the good news with your friends
- ❏ Give your friends a Christian comic book

In many different ways John preached the good news to the people. (Luke 3:18, CEV)

6. Challenge Question: What is one new thing you could do to introduce your friends to Christ?

READ OUT LOUD

John the Baptist (or Baptizer, as some have called him) was Jesus' cousin. The Old Testament predicted that John would come before Jesus to get people ready for Jesus' ministry. Read about John the Baptizer from Luke 3:1-20.

ASK

What do you say when you introduce a good friend to an acquaintance?

DISCUSS, BY THE NUMBERS

1. One thing you can say about John the Baptizer—he wasn't shy when it came to talking about God. Your group, if it's like most, doesn't talk often to nonbelievers about Jesus. Use this item to discuss the importance of introducing others to Christ.

2. See which of the boxes was checked most and least. Reread the story as you talk about each of the people. Ask, "Why do you think God wants us to introduce others to Jesus?"

3. Brainstorm creative ways John might present the gospel in your world. Ask, "What if John presented the gospel today the same way he did nearly 2,000 years ago?" Talk about why the message needs to stay the same but the presentation can change to fit the culture of today.

4. Get a faith conversation going about your group's readiness to give an answer to questions about Jesus.

5. Luke 3:18 tells us that John the Baptizer shared the good news of Christ's love and forgiveness in many different ways. There are great and not-so-great ways to tell others about Jesus. Let your group identify the top three or four strategies that would work to introduce their friends to Jesus.

In many different ways John preached the good news to the people. (Luke 3:18, CEV)

6. Use this item to challenge your group members to try one new way to introduce their friends to Christ.

CLOSE

Sharing Christ is all about getting people interested in Jesus. It may mean you pave the way for someone else to talk with them about Jesus. It may mean you talk directly about the gospel with them. It may mean you and your Christian friends, together and over time, introduce someone to Jesus. John the Baptizer did what he was called to do—introduce Jesus to a lost world in pain. We are called to do the same.

JESUS GETS BAPTIZED

Getting going in ministry

1. **Which *one* of the following would be the *most* difficult thing for you to volunteer to do for Christ?**

   ❑ Become a full-time pastor or worship leader
   ❑ Take a purity pledge
   ❑ Fast from texting one day each month
   ❑ Do a summer mission trip
   ❑ Volunteer in a homeless shelter four hours a week
   ❑ Write a weekly spiritual blog on how to live as a teenager for Jesus
   ❑ Delete all inappropriate songs from my Mp3 player

2. **Are you more like John the Baptizer (helping others in their ministry) or Jesus (the leader of a ministry)?**

   ❑ John the Baptizer   ❑ Jesus

3. **Jesus' baptism was not to repent of his sins because Jesus was sinless. Rather, Jesus' baptism set him apart to do what God wanted him to do. It was the beginning of his ministry. Have you been baptized? If so, when? Why did you get baptized? What does your baptism mean to you today? How are you living out your baptism?**

4. **John didn't want to baptize Jesus because he didn't feel worthy or holy enough to do so. Yet, Jesus told him, "For now this is how it should be, because we must do all that God wants us to do" (Matthew 3:15, CEV). So John agreed to baptize Jesus. Are you ready to do all that God wants you to do with your life?**

   ❑ Most definitely   ❑ Probably   ❑ Maybe   ❑ No way

5. **Do the statements below describe you? Write Y (yes, that's me) or N (no, that's not me).**

   ___ I pray often about the ministry God wants me to have.
   ___ I try not to think about the ministry God wants me to have.
   ___ I like to think of new things I can do for God.
   ___ I'm not a strong enough Christian to have a ministry.
   ___ I would be willing to work with someone on a ministry.
   ___ I have no interest in participating in a ministry.
   ___ I'm too young to do a ministry.

READ OUT LOUD
Ministry. Every Christian has one. John the Baptizer had one. You have one. Maybe you don't know what it is yet. Read about John the Baptizer helping Jesus get started in his ministry. Read Matthew 3:13-17.

ASK
What is the best time of day for you to get up and get going?

DISCUSS, BY THE NUMBERS
1. See which of the activities were checked the most and the least. These items get your group started talking about ministry.
2. See which of your group members view themselves as leaders or helpers in ministry. Both are important and need to be encouraged.
3. The purpose of this *TalkSheet* is to talk about ministry rather than the doctrinal distinctions regarding baptism. But this can be a good time to talk about your congregation's or denomination's theological perspective on baptism.
4. Talk about what it means to do all God wants us to do without being judgmental of those who are not yet ready to fully commit their lives to service.
5. See comments in bold after each statement.
- I pray often about the ministry God wants me to have. **Luke 3:21 tells us that Jesus prayed while he was being baptized. Prayer is essential for any ministry to be effective.**
- I try not to think about the ministry God wants me to have. **This describes many people "sitting in the pew" today. By not thinking about it they don't have to commit to any ministry.**
- I like to think of new things I can do for God. **This is cool and should be encouraged.**
- I'm not a strong enough Christian to have a ministry. **All Christians, no matter where they are on their faith journeys, have ministries because they have been given spiritual gifts by God. They may not be doing the ministry, but they have one.**
- I would be willing to work with someone on a ministry. **This is great.**
- I have no interest in participating in a ministry. **Without being judgmental, encourage those who don't have an interest to do something, even the smallest something. They may think they are too busy or too hurt from a prior church or too something else.**
- I'm too young to do a ministry. **Not at all. Even babies have a ministry in our congregations—to remind us of the childlike faith we need to come to Christ.**

CLOSE
John the Baptizer helped Jesus begin his ministry. Each of us has a ministry, whether it is leading or helping. Pray for those who are doing ministry presently. Pray for those who are willing to explore a ministry as they get going!

1. Check the following boxes if you've ever—

- ❏ been tempted
- ❏ given in to temptation
- ❏ resisted temptation

2. Do you agree (A) or disagree (D) with the following statements?

___ If you are doing God's work, you will experience opposition and resistance from the devil.

___ Satan can take advantage of situations in which we find ourselves.

___ After a spiritual high, Satan often tempts us.

___ God tempts you to sin.

___ Satan's temptations often seem reasonable.

___ Every temptation you face is from Satan.

3. Jesus quoted Scripture for each of the three temptations Satan aimed at him. Why do you think the Bible is an effective weapon with which to fight temptation? (Check your top answer.)

- ❏ The Bible reminds us of God's love for us.
- ❏ Our feelings can't be trusted.
- ❏ Scripture tells us what God wants us to do and not do.
- ❏ The Bible lists every possible temptation.
- ❏ The Bible gives us principles to live by.
- ❏ The Bible reminds us that God doesn't want us to have any fun.
- ❏ Scripture reveals the truth.

4. Satan twisted the Scripture when he quoted Psalm 91:11 to Jesus. What was Satan trying to accomplish by this? Why do you think it is important for us to correctly interpret the Scriptures?

5. Underline one of the following five verses. Read the verse. Decide how this passage of Scripture could help you say no to temptation.

Proverbs 3:5-6 • Romans 12:9 • Ephesians 2:10 • 1 Thessalonians 4:3-5 • 1 John 2:16

From *More High School TalkSheets on the New Testament: 52 Ready-to-Use Discussions* by David Lynn. Permission to reproduce this page granted only for use in buyer's youth group. Copyright © 2010 by Youth Specialties. www.youthspecialties.com

READ OUT LOUD

Jesus was tempted—tempted like you and me. All of us have been tempted in the past and will be tempted again and again in the future. The temptation faced by Christ nearly 2,000 years ago can teach us how best to handle any of the temptations we may face in the future. Read what Christ did in Matthew 4:1-11.

ASK

Do you think young people face more temptations than adults?

DISCUSS, BY THE NUMBERS

1. This activity shows your group members the extent of temptation's effect on us. We've all been tempted, given in to temptation, and resisted temptation.
2. See commentary in bold after each statement.
   - If you are doing God's work, you will experience opposition and resistance from the devil. **Most likely. No resistance from the Evil One means you are not a threat.**
   - Satan can take advantage of situations in which we find ourselves. **Yes. Talk about what these vulnerable situations might be, like hanging out with someone who smokes dope or putting yourself in a comprising situation while out on a date.**
   - After a spiritual high, Satan often tempts us. **Yes, Jesus had been fasting, one of the spiritual disciplines that's not often practiced today (at least by Christians in the U.S.) when Satan came to tempt him.**
   - God tempts you to sin. **No. See James 1:13-15.**
   - Satan's temptations often seem reasonable. **Yes, that's why they are so tempting.**
   - Every temptation you face is from Satan. **No. Again see James 1:13-15. Sometimes it is our own selfish desires.**
3. Jesus quoted Scripture for each of the three temptations Satan aimed at him. Why do you think the Bible is an effective weapon with which to fight temptation? (Check your top answer.)

See commentary in bold after each statement.
- ❑ The Bible reminds us of God's love for us. **Yes, which we need to remember when we are tempted.**
- ❑ Our feelings can't be trusted. **Feelings aren't good or bad, they are just there, and as such they do not give us accurate data on which we can make healthy decisions.**
- ❑ Scripture tells us what God wants us to do and not do. **Yes, more than most Christians realize. When people say, "I don't know what God's will is for my life," they often haven't yet searched the Bible for direction.**
- ❑ The Bible lists every possible temptation. **No, and it was never meant to.**
- ❑ The Bible gives us principles to live by. **Yes, which can help us deal with the temptations we face.**
- ❑ The Bible reminds us that God doesn't want us to have any fun. **No, God wants us to have all kinds of fun. This is why God gave basic rules like the Ten Commandments, so that we are protected from those things that don't give us long-lasting fun.**
- ❑ Scripture reveals the truth. **Yes, and we want to live by the truth.**

4. Twisting Scripture is carried out by cults, atheists trying to put down believers, and even naive Christians who don't know any better. Satan quotes Psalm 91:11 but leaves out the second half of the verse. Jesus reminds him of the whole truth.
5. Use one of the Bible verses to spark a faith conversation about how to say no to temptation.
   Proverbs 3:5-6 • Romans 12:9 • Ephesians 2:10 • 1 Thessalonians 4:5 • 1 John 2:16

CLOSE

Say yes to Jesus. Say yes to the Bible. Say yes to prayer. And you can say no to temptation.

JESUS TALKS WITH NICODEMUS

Sharing the good news at the right time and place

1. **What do you think John 3:16 means to people who do not believe in Jesus Christ?**

   ❏ They ignore it.
   ❏ They think it's a silly superstition.
   ❏ They have never read it.
   ❏ They think they are in control of their own lives and don't need God.
   ❏ They believe that all paths lead to God.
   ❏ They believe one must work one's way to God.
   ❏ It's just a saying from a prophet that may or may not be true.

2. **Why do you think Nicodemus, a Pharisee and member of the ruling council, came to Jesus under the cover of darkness?**

3. **Nicodemus was looking for truth when he came to Jesus. What are you looking for from Jesus?**

4. **Read the statements and decide if you A (agree) or D (disagree):**

   ___ The best time to talk with others about their relationships with Jesus Christ is when they are by themselves.
   ___ Most people are curious about spiritual things.
   ___ There are friends of mine who would put their faith in Christ if I talked with them about Christ's love and forgiveness.
   ___ As Nicodemus saw God in Jesus (John 3:2), people can see God working in my life.
   ___ I know how to talk with my friends and relatives about God's grace available through Jesus Christ.

5. **How would you explain salvation to someone who doesn't understand it?**

6. **Do you think Nicodemus put his faith in Jesus Christ even though he remained a member of the religious ruling council who opposed Jesus?**

   YES   NO   MAYBE SO

READ OUT LOUD

What do you think of when you hear John 3:16? A popular Bible verse? Big banners at football games? Nicodemus? Yes, Nicodemus! He was a religious leader who came to Jesus at night. And he was the recipient of that most famous verse, John 3:16. But you probably never think of him when you see the John 3:16 banners held up by fans during extra-point kicks. Well, now, maybe you will. Read his story in John 3:1-21.

ASK

Why do you think John 3:16 is such a popular Bible verse in the United States?

DISCUSS, BY THE NUMBERS

1. Here's a great faith conversation starter to get your group talking about sharing the good news found in John 3:16.
2. After talking about Nicodemus' possible fear of being seen with Jesus, ask, "How embarrassed are you to be known as a follower of Christ's?"
3. Possible answers could include—
   • Hope
   • A get-out-of-hell-free card
   • The meaning and purpose of life
   • How to have a right relationship with God
   • Love
   • Help for my problems
4. Use this item to talk about how to share the good news at the right time and place.
5. Here is a simple explanation you can use with your group:

   God created us with the freedom to choose to live a self-centered life or to obey God. Since we chose our selfish way of wrongdoing, we are separated from God. No matter what we do—how good we try to be, what self-help books we read, or what religion we try to follow—we can't reach God.

   But God has reached out to us through Jesus Christ. God made a way for us to be forgiven of our self-centered ways. Jesus died on a cross and came back from the grave. His death paid the price for our wrongdoing, our sin, and now we can have a friendship with God and experience the promised new life. So how should we respond to God's offer of Jesus Christ?

God loved the people of this world so much that he gave his only Son, so that everyone who has faith in him will have eternal life and never really die. God did not send his Son into the world to condemn its people. He sent him to save them!
(John 3:16-17, CEV)

You need only to put your trust in Jesus Christ. It's as easy as **A-B-C**. First, you need to **A**dmit that you need Jesus, that you are a sinner separated from God. Second, you need to **B**elieve in Jesus Christ, that he died, came back to life so that your sins could be forgiven, and is your only hope for a relationship with God. Third, **C**ommit your life to Jesus Christ so that he controls your life rather than your selfish desires.

Are you ready for these **ABCs**? Here is a prayer you can pray to get you started:

*Dear Jesus, I **A**dmit that I am a sinner, that I need you. I **B**elieve you died for my sins. I give my sins to you and ask for forgiveness. I **C**ommit my will and my life to you so that you take control. I want to follow you as my Savior and Lord. In Jesus' name I pray. Amen.*

6. Nicodemus, still one of the religious leaders, defended Jesus before his arrest (John 7:50-52). He also retrieved Christ's body for burial along with Joseph, a wealthy follower of Jesus who used his tomb in which to bury him (John 19:39-42). You decide.

CLOSE

Telling others about the good news is as easy as **A-B-C**. So let's review. First, you need to **A**dmit that you need Jesus, that you are a sinner separated from God. Second, you need to **B**elieve in Jesus Christ, that he died, came back to life so that your sins could be forgiven, and is your only hope for a relationship with God. Third, **C**ommit your life to Jesus Christ so that he controls your life rather than your selfish desires.

THE WOMAN AT THE WELL

Jesus cares about our spiritual emptiness

1. Jesus used his thirst as an opportunity to start a faith conversation with the woman at the well. How do you start faith conversations with your family or friends?

   ❑ I just start talking about Jesus.
   ❑ I never start faith conversations with my family or my friends.
   ❑ I use drive time to bring up faith issues with my family or my friends.
   ❑ I tell my personal story of what Jesus has done for me.
   ❑ I invite my friends and family members who don't know Jesus to my church.
   ❑ I don't think it's good to talk about politics or religion with my family or friends.
   ❑ I tell my family or friends that they are going to hell, and this starts a healthy faith conversation.

2. The woman at the well was spiritually ignorant. Jesus said she had no idea what God wanted her to have—to experience God's grace through Christ that leads to eternal life.

   ❑ I have thoroughly experienced God's grace.
   ❑ I have kind of experienced God's grace.
   ❑ I have no idea what it is like to experience God's grace.

3. Do you think each of these statements is T (true) or F (false)?

   ___ People who haven't experienced God's love and forgiveness are missing out.
   ___ Most people want to know more about Jesus.
   ___ People who haven't put their faith in Christ are doomed.
   ___ I owe it to my friends to tell them about Jesus.
   ___ My friends distort what Christians believe.
   ___ I need to know more about what it means to follow Christ.
   ___ It often takes time and lots of conversation before someone is ready to accept Christ by faith.

4. Before the woman at the well was ready to give her life to Christ, she had to see that she was spiritually empty and needed Jesus. How could you point out to your friends the emptiness they face apart from Christ?

   ❑ I could show genuine concern for the problems they experience.
   ❑ Maybe my friends aren't spiritually empty without Christ.
   ❑ I have no clue.
   ❑ I'm not old enough to understand spiritual emptiness.
   ❑ I could talk about how empty my life was without Christ.
   ❑ My friends pretend their lives are great, so it's impossible to point out their emptiness apart from Christ.
   ❑ I could tell how Christ gives meaning and purpose to my life.

5. Why do you think the woman ran to tell those she knew about Jesus? Why do you think the people she knew came back to talk with Jesus? How do you think she got them interested in Jesus? What got you interested in Jesus? What do you think would get your friends who aren't followers of Christ interested in Jesus?

READ OUT LOUD

She was a woman, in biblical times considered a second-class citizen at best. And a Samaritan, hated by the Jews. Jesus talked with her. Cared about her spiritual emptiness. Read the story found in John 4:3-30.

ASK

What do you think is the best way for others to show they care about you?

DISCUSS, BY THE NUMBERS

1. Jesus used his thirst as an opportunity to start a faith conversation with the woman at the well. Have a faith conversation about how to start faith conversations. Look at each of the statements as a potential faith conversation-starting technique.

2. When you experience God's grace you find it much easier to share the good news with others. Tell a story from your life about your experience with grace.

3. See commentary in bold after each statement.
   - People who haven't experienced God's love and forgiveness are missing out. **Ask, "What are they missing out on?"**
   - Most people want to know more about Jesus. **Debate how true this is with your group members' friends.**
   - People who haven't put their faith in Christ are doomed. **According to Scripture they have doomed themselves if they have heard and rejected Jesus.**
   - I owe it to my friends to tell them about Jesus. **This is a great one to debate. If Jesus cares about their spiritual emptiness, shouldn't we?**
   - My friends distort what Christians believe. **Check this one out to see the kinds of friends your group members have.**

   - I need to know more about what it means to follow Christ. **This is part of our spiritual growth.**
   - It often takes time and lots of conversation before someone is ready to accept Christ by faith. **Often true. Ask why this is so often the case.**

4. Jesus used the emptiness the woman experienced in her marriages to show her that she was spiritually empty. This item gives you plenty of information to start a faith conversation about spiritual emptiness. Talk about what it takes before someone is ready to confess sins and turn to Jesus.

5. Take each question and listen to your group's responses. Focus attention on how to get your group members' friends interested in Jesus.

CLOSE

Every human being on the planet is spiritually empty without Christ. Religions (and there are many around the world) strive to fill that spiritual void. The religion of atheism explains away the void by saying it doesn't exist. But it does—and this void can only be filled by a relationship with Jesus Christ.

1. The government official urgently needed Jesus to perform a miracle of healing for his son. How much do you need Jesus?

```
1    2    3    4    5    6    7    8    9    10
◆○○○○○◆○○○○◆○○○○◆○○○○◆○○○○◆
```
I urgently   I don't need
need Jesus   Jesus at all

2. When have you had the easiest time relying on Jesus (E=easiest)? When have you had the most difficult time relying on Jesus (D=difficult)?

___When I have a big test
___When I'm not getting along with my best friend
___When I have no worries
___When I might fail a class
___When I'm on vacation
___When I don't feel good about myself
___When I'm healthy
___When I lose my job
___When my family has enough money
___When I've had a fight with my mom
___When I try to talk to someone about Jesus
___When my parents are getting along

3. The government official faced a serious family illness before he turned to Jesus. Why do you think it takes a major crisis for people to turn their lives over to Christ?

4. Do you agree (A) or disagree (D) with these statements?

___ Jesus heals people today.
___ There is a difference between a cure and healing.
___ Jesus heals everyone who prays for healing.
___ If you aren't healed, it's because you lack faith.
___ People are fooled into thinking they are healed.

5. The government official (and everyone in his household) put his faith in Christ after experiencing the healing miracle. The miraculous healing convinced them that Jesus was who he said he was. What did it take for you to realize that Jesus is who he says he is? When did you put your faith in Christ?

READ OUT LOUD

The people of Galilee—that region of the country where Jesus grew up—saw him perform miracles in Jerusalem during the Passover. Many put their faith in him as the Messiah. When Jesus was returning to Galilee, a government official hurried to him and begged that he come heal his sick son. The man had enough faith to know that Jesus could make his dying son well. Read the story from John 4:45-54.

ASK

What friend can you count on to always be there for you?

DISCUSS, BY THE NUMBERS

1. Re-create the line scale and ask your group members to place their X on that line. Ask, "What does it mean to urgently need Jesus?" "Why do some people think they don't need Jesus at all?"

2. Explore why we so often turn to Jesus when in a crisis but then neglect our relationship with him when things are going well. Ask, "What might happen if you deepened your relationship with Christ during the good times so that when the bad times arrived you could more easily count on Christ?" "Can you name a crisis time that brought you closer to Christ?"

3. Tell a story of someone you know (it could be you) who put his/her faith in Christ as a result of a major life crisis.

4. See commentary in bold after each statement.
   - Jesus heals people today. **You can debate the honesty of "faith healers" if you choose. The point here is not that you need a faith healer to pray over you for healing but that Jesus does heal. Ask, "Have you ever prayed for someone who was healed of cancer or another major illness?"**

   - There is a difference between a cure and healing. **One can be cured of a disease by a physician but not healed spiritually. And one can be healed spiritually but die because the person was not cured of a specific disease.**
   - Jesus heals everyone who prays for healing. **Jesus heals spiritually, which readies us for eternal life even if we're not cured of physical disease.**
   - If you aren't healed, it's because you lack faith. **The apostle Paul had a "thorn" in his side that he prayed God would take away—and God did not. Do you think that means Paul didn't have faith? Good. Same goes for you.**
   - People are fooled into thinking they are healed. **Yes, this can happen. There is a phenomenon called a "placebo effect" in which people get better, or seem to get better, because they want to get better.**

5. Discuss people's responses to the question, "What did it take for you to realize that Jesus is who he says he is?" Tell the story of when you put your faith in Christ.

CLOSE

The government official believed that Jesus could heal his son from the serious illness that was killing him—if only Jesus would come to his home. The man seemed to think that Jesus had to be with his son for the healing to occur. The man had not yet put his faith in Jesus as the Messiah. Jesus stretched the man's faith by healing the boy from a distance. And it was that action that led the man to put his faith in Jesus as his Savior. The man learned that he could count on Jesus whether he was present or far away. And we learn that we too can count on Jesus every day!

1. **Every day you receive hundreds of suggestions from friends, commercials, parents, teachers, coaches, the Internet, the Bible, and more, on how you should live. How do you tell which are godly and which are not?**

   ❏ There is no way to know.
   ❏ Test what you hear against what the Bible says.
   ❏ If it feels right, then it must be right.
   ❏ Ask an adult.
   ❏ Do what your friends do.
   ❏ It doesn't matter.
   ❏ Go with what your first impression tells you.

2. **I hear what Christ has to say when—**

3. **What do you think—do you A (agree) or D (disagree)?**

   ___ We can be close to Jesus like he was with his family.
   ___ If you are from a dysfunctional family, Jesus can help you learn what it means to live in a healthy family.
   ___ You must be good to get close to Jesus.
   ___ Communion is like a family meal with Jesus.
   ___ The church is like Jesus' family.

4. **Label each statement with M (that's me) or N (that's not me).**

   ___ I choose worship or Bible studies with my congregation over other activities.
   ___ I have asked God to give me a love for the Bible.
   ___ I like helping others whenever I can.
   ___ Quiet time with God is a priority.
   ___ Talking about my faith is something I do frequently.
   ___ I honor my parents in everything I do.

5. **Question Bombardment: How willing are you to obey what Christ tells you to do? How much of what Christ says will you obey? How will you know that you're being obedient? How will your life be better or worse because you're obedient?**

READ OUT LOUD

Jesus loved his family, especially his mother. His first miracle was in response to a concern his mother had. And yet he seemed to brush off his family in today's story. Read the story found in Luke 8:19-21.

ASK

Which of your great-grandparents had the biggest family?

DISCUSS, BY THE NUMBERS

1. See commentary in bold after each statement.
- There is no way to know. **God gave us minds that can discern what choices we should make. And God asked that we love him with our hearts, minds, and souls. So let's use our brains to glorify God.**
- Test what you hear against what the Bible says. **Yes, the Bible is a compass that guides the Christian in decision-making.**
- If it feels right, then it must be right. **Not at all. Emotions come and go. Feelings can't accurately guide us. We can listen to them and ask questions about them (e.g., Why do I feel guilty? Can I trust this person?). They may help us come to some conclusions, but feelings can't be our ultimate guide.**
- Ask an adult. **Hopefully your young people know trustworthy adults to whom they can go for direction.**
- Do what your friends do. **Friends can help guide you if they are the right kind of friends and have your best interest in mind.**
- It doesn't matter. **Yes it does. We don't want to let hundreds of unfiltered messages into our minds.**
- Go with what your first impression tells you. **Ask, "Where is this first impression coming from— my conscience, indigestion, the Holy Spirit?"**
2. Listen to your group members' completed sentences. **Talk about listening for the voice of Christ through reading the Gospels (Matthew,**

Mark, Luke, and John), regular prayer, devotional books, a weekly Bible study, sermons, and worship.
3. See commentary in bold after each statement.
- We can be close to Jesus like he was with his family. **As a Christian you're part of the family of God and can grow closer to Christ just like you can grow closer to your parents or siblings.**
- If you are from a dysfunctional family, Jesus can help you learn what it means to live in a healthy family. **The unconditional love that is needed for a healthy and strong family can be learned from Jesus.**
- You must be good to get close to Jesus. **No, only God is good. You must be humble and aware of your brokenness to get close to Jesus.**
- Communion is like a family meal with Jesus. **Yes, it is.**
- The church is like Jesus' family. **The Bible says so (see Ephesians 2:19).**
4. Each of the statements addresses hearing and obeying God. Talk about how you and your group members can make each of these statements true in your lives.
5. This *Question Bombardment* gets at your group's commitment to obedience. Give time for each of your group members to respond to the questions.

CLOSE

Though Jesus seemed to brush his family aside, that was not the case. A look at his life shows that he loved them. Jesus used an interruption by his mom and brothers to teach the crowd a life lesson. Read Luke 8:21. Jesus invites everyone to follow him and to be part of his family by hearing and obeying what he says.

"My mother and brothers are those who hear God's word and put it into practice."
Jesus, in Luke 8:21

11. Luke 9:18-22

"WHO DO YOU SAY I AM?"

Who is Jesus to you?

1. People in the United States go through life not really thinking about who Jesus is...

   ❏ All of the time
   ❏ Most of the time
   ❏ Some of the time
   ❏ They know who Jesus is all of the time but don't want to admit it.

2. Do you **A (agree)** or **D (disagree)** with each of these statements?

   ___ If Jesus is who he says he is, then I am in big trouble.
   ___ Christ makes life exciting.
   ___ When you know who Jesus really is, your life changes dramatically.
   ___ You can believe in Jesus without appearing strange to other people.
   ___ Jesus is a way, a truth, and a life.

3. Can Jesus be one's Savior without being one's Lord?

   ❏ Yes
   ❏ Maybe
   ❏ No way

4. Why should you be grateful that you know the truth about the identity of Jesus? Answer either **Y (yes)** or **N (no)**.

   ___ By faith I can now accept Christ's forgiveness.
   ___ Because the truth will set me free.
   ___ I now have the answer to a trivia game question.
   ___ So I won't be fooled by other religions.
   ___ I don't have to go to hell.
   ___ I no longer have to live in sin.
   ___ So I can get the answer right in Sunday school.

5. Jesus didn't want the crowds that came to hear him to know his true identity because—

6. In today's short story we found Jesus praying alone. Why did he do this so often? How often do you do this?

READ OUT LOUD

After the feeding of 5,000-plus people, Jesus goes off for some alone time with the disciples and to pray. While away from the crowds, he asks his disciples the most important question of all time. Read the short story from Luke 9:18-22.

ASK

Who would you say knows you the best?

DISCUSS, BY THE NUMBERS

1. Get your group's opinion. Ask, "How can people go through life, living in the United States, without thinking about who Jesus really is?"
2. See commentary in bold after each statement.
- If Jesus is who he says he is, then I am in big trouble. **If Jesus is God and has a claim on our lives, then we must submit to that claim. If we refuse, then we are in big trouble.**
- Christ makes life exciting. **Does he ever! You can't go wrong committing your life to Christ.**
- When you know who Jesus really is, your life changes dramatically. **If it doesn't change, then you don't know who Jesus is.**
- You can believe in Jesus without appearing strange to other people. **Many Christians are not crazy or weird; still the Bible says the world won't understand the Christian message.**
- Jesus is a way, a truth, and a life. **No, he is the only way, truth, and life.**
3. Yes, a person can be saved (Savior) but not totally committed to Christ (Lord). But why would you want to live like that?
4. Discuss each statement as a reason for being grateful (with some better than others).
5. Jesus didn't want the crowds that came to hear him to know his true identity because 1) the crowds didn't yet know enough about Jesus; 2) Jesus didn't want his timetable to be disturbed—if the people knew, then their reactions would interfere with God's plans; and 3) the resurrection of Christ would be the proof that people needed to believe in Jesus as Savior and Lord.
6. We often find Jesus praying alone or with the disciples. Ask, "How is Jesus a model for us?"

CLOSE

The disciples told Jesus that the crowds who listened to his teaching believed Jesus was someone important, like a prophet. So Jesus, in Luke 9:20, asked the disciples, *"Who do you say I am?"* Peter—the unofficial spokesman for the disciples—said, "The Christ of God." Jesus is still asking that very same question of us today— "Who do you say I am?"

1. Put an arrow ➜ by the one that's true for you—

It's easier for me to follow the ways of this world than to follow Christ.

It's just as easy for me to follow Christ as it is to follow the ways of this world.

It's easier for me to follow Christ than to follow the ways of this world.

THE COST OF CHRIST-FOLLOWING

What will it cost you to follow Jesus?

2. Which statement is most true for you?

❏ I think about what Jesus Christ wants me to do more than I think about what I want to do.

❏ I think about what I want to do more than I think about what Jesus Christ wants me to do.

3. Rank the following from easiest (1) to most difficult (7) for you.

___ To have a heartfelt desire to be a Christ-follower

___ To say no to selfish ambitions

___ To say yes to whatever Christ puts in my life

___ To let Jesus walk through life's troubles with me

___ To be willing to suffer for Christ if I must

___ To sacrifice for the cause of Christ

___ To act like Christ in all that I do

4. How do you choose to "take up your cross daily and follow Christ"?

❏ I don't.

❏ I wish I knew.

❏ I consciously say to myself, "Today, I will give all of my life to Jesus."

❏ I try really hard to follow what the Bible tells me.

❏ I remember the sermon from Sunday.

❏ I go to church every day.

❏ I pray all the time.

5. Which of the following are examples of losing your life for Christ so that you can save it?

❏ Finding a bracelet at school and keeping it

❏ Working an extra shift for an older employee whose child is ill

❏ Back-talking your teacher

❏ Taking credit for someone else's idea at work

❏ Serving breakfast at a homeless shelter when you could be sleeping in

❏ Listening to someone's pain when you would rather listen to your music

❏ Cursing out your boss the last day on the job

❏ Controlling your temper when you want to blow up

❏ Showing kindness to a neighbor when you have your own work to do

❏ Judging others for things they are doing wrong

6. What do you think it means for Jesus to be ashamed of those who are ashamed of him?

"If anyone is ashamed of me and my words, the Son of Man will be ashamed of him when he comes in his glory and in the glory of the Father and of the holy angels." —Jesus, in Luke 9:26

12. THE COST OF CHRIST-FOLLOWING—What will it cost you to follow Jesus?
(Luke 9:22-26)

READ OUT LOUD
Jesus is about to teach his followers something hard to understand. But before he begins he tells the disciples he will soon pay the biggest price he can for their salvation—he will die for them. Then he teaches the people what it will cost to follow him. Read the story found in Luke 9:22-26.

ASK
Where in the world would you want to go no matter what the cost?

DISCUSS, BY THE NUMBERS
1. Encourage honesty, not the Sunday school answer. Talk about the ways of Christ and how they differ from the ways of this world.
2. The first answer is about self-denial while the second describes self-indulgence. The Bible teaches us to deny ourselves while the world promotes self-indulgence. The Bible teaches Christ-esteem while the world promotes self-esteem. The Bible teaches us to give so that it will be given to us while the world says get all you can for yourself.
3. All of these statements describe denying self. Talk about each, asking for practical ways to practice each of them.
4. Ask, "Why daily?" Answer: This is not a salvation passage but a discipleship passage. This is a daily decision to make Christ the Lord of every aspect and corner of our lives.
5. The checked statements are examples of losing your life while the unchecked are examples of trying to gain the world.
   - ❏ Finding a bracelet at school and keeping it
   - ✔ Working an extra shift for an older employee whose child is ill
   - ❏ Back-talking your teacher
   - ❏ Taking credit for someone else's idea at work
   - ✔ Serving breakfast at a homeless shelter when you could be sleeping in
   - ✔ Listening to someone's pain when you would rather listen to your music
   - ❏ Cursing out your boss the last day on the job
   - ✔ Controlling your temper when you want to blow up
   - ✔ Showing kindness to a neighbor when you have your own work to do
   - ❏ Judging others for things they are doing wrong
6. Talk about this question by asking more questions: "Does being ashamed of Christ mean you won't go to heaven?" "Are you walking away from Christ when you are ashamed of him?" "Is being ashamed of Jesus the same as rejecting him?"

CLOSE
Condemned criminals carried the crossbeam to the place where they would be crucified. We are like those criminals in that we should die for our sins. But because we place our faith in Jesus, we are then crucified with Christ, and we belong to him. Jesus now asks us to forget about ourselves and live a life of sacrifice. So we denounce ourselves and our sin and walk with Jesus in sacrificial love.

1. How do you think Jesus preached the gospel about himself?

One day as [Jesus] was teaching the people in the temple courts and preaching the gospel... (Luke 20:1)

2. Why were the religious leaders trying to trick Jesus into saying something that would hurt his credibility with the people? (Check your top two.)

- ❏ Jesus was hurting their income.
- ❏ They honestly believed that Jesus was wrong.
- ❏ The religious leaders didn't want to submit to Jesus as their Messiah.
- ❏ They had not given Jesus permission to make the changes he was making at the temple.
- ❏ Jesus was not one of them.
- ❏ Belief in Jesus by the people was eroding their power.
- ❏ If Jesus was right, then they were wrong.

3. The religious leaders were amazed at the answers Christ gave to their questions. Why do you think they refused to believe in Christ in spite of what they heard? Why do you think some people refuse to listen to what Christ has to say today?

They were unable to trap [Jesus] in what he had said there in public. And astonished by his answer, they became silent. (Luke 20:26)

4. What do you think about each of the following statements? Do you SA (strongly agree), A (agree), D (disagree), or SD (strongly disagree)?

- ___ Followers of Christ should do everything he asks.
- ___ People only read the things Jesus said that they agree with and skip over the rest.
- ___ Most Christians have no idea what Jesus requires of them.
- ___ What the Bible says about Jesus is true.
- ___ It is easier to be a Christian than a follower of another religion like Mormonism, Islam, Buddhism, or Hinduism.
- ___ It is easy to twist what Jesus said to make it mean what you want it to mean.

5. Like the religious leaders of Jesus' time, many people today attempt to find loopholes in what Christ said. They re-interpret what Jesus said so they don't actually have to do it. Therefore, to these people…

"Love your enemies" (Matthew 5:44) really means—

"Do not judge" (Matthew 7:1) really means—

"You cannot serve both God and money" (Matthew 6:24) really means—

6. Check the boxes before the statements that are not found in the Bible.

- ❏ "God helps those who help themselves."
- ❏ "To thine own self be true."
- ❏ "Money is the root of all evil."
- ❏ "And ye shall know the truth, and the truth shall make you free."
- ❏ "And as ye would that men should do to you, do ye also to them likewise."
- ❏ "Neither a borrower nor a lender be."
- ❏ "God will not give you more than you can handle."
- ❏ "Beggars can't be choosers."
- ❏ "Man shall not live by bread alone."
- ❏ "Charity begins at home."

13. Luke 20:1-26

DISCOUNTING JESUS

Finding a way around what Jesus tells us

READ OUT LOUD

The religious leaders were trying to discredit what Jesus had to say. Jesus was teaching the day after he cleaned out the money-hungry vendors in the temple. Read the story found in Luke 20:1-26.

ASK

What class do you most wish you could avoid?

DISCUSS, BY THE NUMBERS

1. Did Jesus yell and scream? Ask for lots of money? Play the organ? Jesus told stories, showed compassion, and said to the people that they should turn from their sins, put their trust in him, and follow him.
2. See commentary in bold after each statement.
   - Jesus was hurting their income. **Yes, especially since they probably received a cut from the salespeople in the temple courtyard selling sacrificial animals and exchanging foreign currencies.**
   - They honestly believed that Jesus was wrong. **They knew his miracles were real but didn't seem to care.**
   - The religious leaders didn't want to submit to Jesus as their Messiah. **Yes, most definitely.**
   - They had not given Jesus permission to make the changes he was making at the temple. **Yes, and they wanted to control all things religious.**
   - Jesus was not one of them. **Jesus was an outsider to their religious world but popular with the people.**
   - Belief in Jesus by the people was eroding their power. **Yes, because so many people were putting their faith in Christ.**
   - If Jesus was right, then they were wrong. **Yes, and they didn't want to be wrong.**
3. These questions can get a good faith conversation going.
4. These statements can spark a great faith conversation.
5. See example re-interpretations in bold.

   "Love your enemies" (Matthew 5:44) really means—**Be nice to them at church only.**

   "Do not judge" (Matthew 7:1a) really means—**No matter how bad or dangerous others' behavior is, don't form an opinion without hanging around them for a while.**

   "You cannot serve both God and Money" (Matthew 6:24b) really means—**If you give a little of your money to God, then technically you are not serving money—just God. You can do whatever you want with the rest of the money.**
6. See commentary in bold after each statement.
   - ✔ "God helps those who help themselves." **Not in the Bible. A popular saying of Benjamin Franklin, a deist, who believed that there was a God out there somewhere who did not intervene in our lives. Benjamin Franklin believed people were left alone to help themselves. This is contrary to the biblical view, which says people can't help themselves but need God's grace. God helps those who admit they are helpless and broken.**
   - ❑ "And ye shall know the truth, and the truth shall make you free." **Found in John 8:32. This passage refers to John 8:31, which tells us that we must not merely receive God's truth but also obey that truth in our daily lives. As we live out God's word, we are set free from the slavery of sin.**
   - ✔ "Beggars can't be choosers." **Not in the Bible. A saying that excuses us from giving the proper help to those in need.**
   - ✔ "To thine own self be true." **Not in the Bible. Found in Shakespeare's play *Hamlet*. Biblically we are to be wary of the sinful, natural self. Instead, we are to be controlled by the Spirit of God (Romans 8:8-9).**
   - ❑ "Man shall not live by bread alone." **Deuteronomy 8:3; Matthew 4:4**
   - ✔ "Money is the root of all evil." **Not in the Bible. This is Scripture twisting. The Bible says in 1 Timothy 6:10 that "the love of money is the root of all evil." Money is neither good nor evil. It is your attitude toward money that makes the difference.**
   - ✔ "Charity begins at home." **Not in the Bible. This saying is often used as a self-centered excuse for not helping others.**
   - ❑ "And as ye would that men should do to you, do ye also to them likewise." **Luke 6:31. This is the Golden Rule.**
   - ✔ "Neither a borrower nor a lender be." **Not in the Bible. Found in Shakespeare's play *Hamlet*, another self-centered excuse for not helping others.**
   - ✔ "God will not give you more than you can handle." **Not in the Bible. This is a distortion of 1 Corinthians 10:13 which talks about temptation. We often find ourselves in situations that overwhelm us (finances, work, studies), and they are much more than we can handle. That's why we need God!**

CLOSE

Why do we try, like the religious leaders in Jesus' time, to find a way around what Jesus tells us? Because we don't like what he said or we don't want to do what he wants us to do. Yet, if we want to follow Jesus, we must stop looking for the loopholes and start living like him.

14. John 7:37-52

THE PEOPLE TAKE SIDES

Whose side are YOU on?

1. Answer these three questions:

Why do you think the Pharisees were so annoyed by Jesus?

What do you think impressed the soldiers the most about Jesus?

Why do you think Jesus so easily divided the crowd?

2. The people in the story debated Jesus' identity. Who do people say Jesus is today?

❏ My friends say Jesus is—

❏ My parents say Jesus is—

❏ The average person on the street says Jesus is—

3. The Pharisees distorted the message of the Old Testament so they would not have to accept Jesus as God. How does this happen today?

❏ People believe what they want to believe.
❏ People believe what they think the Bible says even though they have never studied it.
❏ People believe what others tell them without checking it out.
❏ People don't believe in absolute truth.
❏ People believe whatever is trendy at the time.
❏ People will believe almost anything they read or hear except for the Bible.
❏ People want to believe that there are many ways to God other than Jesus.

4. Nicodemus was a Pharisee who was on Jesus' side. He defended Jesus to a point. Why do you think Nicodemus was afraid to come right out and say he had put his faith in Christ as the Messiah? How are you like Nicodemus? How are you unlike Nicodemus?

5. If you want to follow Christ, there is a long list of things you can't do.

TRUE   FALSE   DON'T KNOW

6. Place an X on the line scale below, indicating whom you are following—the world or Christ.

```
1        2        3        4        5        6        7        8        9        10
◆○○○○○○○○◆○○○○○○○◆○○○○○○○◆○○○○○○○◆○○○○○○○◆
Follower                                                      Follower
of the world                                                 of Christ
```

READ OUT LOUD

Because Jesus stood to preach in the middle of a ceremony in which the priest drew water from the Siloam Pool, Jesus' words of spiritual thirst and living water would have had special significance to those in attendance at this religious ceremony. In fact, it was so significant that his message divided the large crowd. Read the story found in John 7:37-52.

ASK

Whose side are you usually on when you play a game—the winning or losing side?

DISCUSS, BY THE NUMBERS

1. You may need to read the story twice to help your group members better answer these three questions. Use your group members' answers to begin a faith conversation about why Jesus was so controversial. Ask, "Why do you think Jesus is still controversial today?"
2. Like the people in the story who debated Jesus' identity, people today have varying opinions as to who Jesus really was (and is). Who do people say Jesus is today? There is enough evidence to prove that Jesus Christ did, in fact, exist. We are left to decide if he is God, as he said; a liar; or a lunatic. Listen to the completed sentence stems. Ask your group to draw some conclusions about what people today think about Jesus.
3. See which of the statements was most identified as the reason people distort Scripture today. Use this opportunity to begin a faith conversation about how easily we can be fooled if we begin listening to others rather than the Bible. The Pharisees accused the temple guards of being deceived by Jesus' message. Ask, "Why do you think people today would see Jesus' message as deceptive rather than the truth?"
4. Ask your group to determine when they are most like Nicodemus and most unlike Nicodemus. Ask, "When are you most likely to stand up for Jesus?"
5. The Pharisees had a long list of dos and don'ts that were to be followed so that God could accept us. See what perception your group has of rules for Christian living by tallying up the TRUE, FALSE, or DON'T KNOW responses to the statement, "If you want to follow Christ, there is a long list of things you can't do." The reality— Christ frees us rather than keeps us in bondage. Because of the promises we have in Christ, we can live holy lives rather than be obligated to keep a list of rules.
6. Recreate the line scale on a whiteboard or easel pad paper. Have your group members place their X on the line. Have an honest faith conversation about "taking sides"—following the world or following Christ.

CLOSE

Read John 7:43 to your group. Say, "Jesus has been causing divisions for the past 2,000 years. As followers of Jesus we struggle with how to live in the world without letting the world live in us. There are no easy answers or simple steps we can take to successfully follow Christ 100 percent of the time. But we do know that Jesus walks with us as we submit our lives to him one day at a time."

The people started taking sides against each other because of Jesus. (John 7:43, CEV)

1. The Jewish people participating in the holiday celebration wanted to know who Jesus was. Most of the people I know think Jesus is—

2. Who do you think Jesus is? When did you first hear about Jesus? Who told you? How did you respond?

3. Do you **agree (A)** or **disagree (D)** with the following statements?

____ Jesus is a mythical figure to most people.
____ People reject Jesus because they want to run their own lives.
____ Christianity has too many dos and don'ts, so people reject it.
____ People believe Jesus is for the weak.
____ People don't put their faith in Christ because they don't know how.
____ The biggest reason people don't put their trust in Jesus is because they don't want to give up their immoral way of living.
____ Following Jesus and being a Christian are two different things.
____ If you put your faith in Jesus, you must get involved in a church to grow.
____ Jesus is the only way to a right relationship with God.
____ Hypocritical Christians keep people from accepting Christ as their Savior.

4. Do you think that each of these statements is **T (true)** or **F (false)**?

____ I know for a fact that Jesus is coming again.
____ Jesus is Lord of my life.
____ My congregation is an important part of my life.
____ I pray every day for God to guide my life.
____ I talk often to others about what Jesus has done for me.
____ I know that Jesus is God.
____ The Bible has authority over my life.

5. Darrien wore his new T-shirt to school today. He got it at the Christian concert he went to with his youth group last night. It was an amazing concert, and he really liked the shirt.

   At lunch a guy from his English class sat down beside him. "Nice shirt," he said. "So what's up with this Jesus guy?"

   Darrien took a deep breath. "Well," he said, searching for the right words...

   If you were Darrien, what would you say?

15. NOT A GUESSING GAME—Jesus is who he said he is
(John 10:22-42)

READ OUT LOUD
Today's story occurred during the Feast of Dedication or Lights (called Hanukkah today). This winter holiday commemorated Israel's rescue from an oppressive Roman emperor, Antiochus Epiphanes, by the Jewish leader, Judas Maccabeus. Once again, the Jewish people were facing oppression by the Roman Empire. So on the minds of many Jewish people that day was the identification of the long-awaited Messiah. *Who was he? How would he deliver them from the oppression they now faced?* Read the story found in John 10:22-42.

ASK
What kind of identification do you have? A library card? A school ID? A social security card? A birth certificate? What does your identification say about you?

DISCUSS, BY THE NUMBERS
1. Listen to the completed sentences. Create from these responses a composite (i.e., combined from different elements) description of Jesus.
2. Create a new composite of Jesus from your group members' responses to the questions. Compare this composite to the one created in Item #1. Tell the group that the reason the Jewish people wanted to stone Jesus was because he said he was God. The crime of blasphemy was death by stoning. Either Jesus is God, as he said, or he deserved to be stoned to death. That is the decision before your group today—is Jesus who he said he is?
3. See commentary in bold after each statement.
   - Jesus is a mythical figure to most people. **Some people believe that Jesus never existed. He is nothing more than a creation of the imaginations of religious nuts. To others Jesus was a real human being but nothing more than a moral example. And to Christians he is the living Son of God.**
   - People reject Jesus because they want to run their own lives. **To declare that Jesus is God means that he has a claim on our lives. And that means we can't run our lives the way we want to run them.**
   - Christianity has too many dos and don'ts, so people reject it. **This is a misperception of Christianity. The opposite is true—Christianity frees one from slavery to sin. Rules for living protect one from the consequences of sin.**
   - People think Jesus is for the weak. **Jesus said that he came for the sick, not the healthy (see Matthew 9:12). By that Jesus meant he came for those who know they are broken and need a Savior rather than those who believe they can live on their own. So yes, Jesus did come for the weak. The reality is—we are all weak…but some of us don't want to admit it.**
   - People don't put their faith in Christ because they don't know how. **Get a good faith conversation going on this one.**
   - The biggest reason people don't put their trust in Jesus is because they don't want to give up their immoral way of living. **Yes, there are many who want to live on their own terms rather than submit to God.**
   - Following Jesus and being a Christian are two different things. **This is a great one to debate.**
   - If you put your faith in Jesus, you must get involved in a church to grow. **Yes, although many want to go it alone. The church was instituted by Jesus as a faith community in which Christians grow their faith.**
   - Jesus is the only way to a right relationship with God. **Jesus clearly says again and again that he is the only way.**
   - Hypocritical Christians keep people from accepting Christ as their Savior. **We are all hypocrites!**
4. Today's story looked at the unbelief of some of the Jews. **The purpose of this activity is to allow your group members to affirm their faith in Christ.**
5. Talk about the pros and cons of the different responses.

Note: When Jesus replied to the Jewish people about them being "gods," he was referring to Psalm 82:6. In this context Jesus was saying that the word god means a leader chosen by God for a certain task. He then goes on to imply that he is God's son, chosen by God the Father for a specific task. Jesus was not saying that they are, or would become, a "god." That is a gross misinterpretation of Scripture.

CLOSE
Remember, Jesus told the Jewish people that he is God. Here's the question before us today: *Is Jesus who he said he is?* The answer to that question makes all the difference in the world. It shapes our very lives, guides all our decisions, and greatly influences how we think and act on a daily basis!

JESUS CALMS A STORM

No matter the circumstances, Jesus is in control.

1. **The disciples obeyed Christ and started off across the lake. How often do you obey Jesus?**

   ❏ All of the time   ❏ Most of the time
   ❏ Some of the time   ❏ None of the time

2. **Question Bombardment: Why do you think other boats followed the boat Jesus and the disciples were in? How many people follow Christ because of you? How many people follow you because of Christ in you? What do you think people see in you that's like Jesus?**

3. **What do you think would have happened if the disciples had trusted that Christ could handle the storm even while asleep?**

4. **The disciples, unable to trust in Christ while he was asleep in the middle of the storm, panicked. When do you have the toughest time relying on Christ?**

   ❏ All the time   ❏ When I can't see a solution to my problem
   ❏ When I am feeling down   ❏ Monday through Saturday
   ❏ At school or work   ❏ During sports practice
   ❏ At home   ❏ Mostly when I am anxious
   ❏ Anytime things get tough   ❏ When I'm with friends who are not Christ-followers

5. **What do you suppose those in the boats following Jesus did when the storm began?**

   ❏ They headed back to shore.
   ❏ They started fishing to see if anything was biting during the storm.
   ❏ They jumped overboard.
   ❏ They cried out to Jesus.
   ❏ They panicked just like the disciples.

6. **What do you think—A (agree) or D (disagree)?**

   ___ It doesn't feel like Jesus is in control of the circumstances in my life.
   ___ Jesus is in control of most of the situations that I face.
   ___ Jesus can't possibly understand the circumstances that exist in my life.
   ___ I play a part in helping Jesus solve the problems in my life.
   ___ I have seen Jesus take care of problems in my life.
   ___ I have a tough time trusting Jesus to take care of the storms in my life.
   ___ Jesus knows about the situations I face before I face them.
   ___ I often turn the worries I experience over to Jesus.

7. **Why do you think the disciples were more afraid after Jesus calmed the storm?**

They were terrified and asked each other,
"Who is this? Even the wind and the waves obey him!" (Mark 4:41)

READ OUT LOUD

After teaching a large crowd of people from a boat on the Sea of Galilee, Jesus asked his disciples to take him across the lake. The storms that plague the Sea of Galilee are well known. Through the mountainous ravines around the lake blow winds that produce violent storms. Let's pick up the story in Mark 4:35-41.

ASK

What kind of music gets you out of control? In which of your classes do you feel out of control? In which sport?

DISCUSS, BY THE NUMBERS

1. Find out which of the four responses was most common for your group. Ask, "How easy is it for you to obey Jesus?" "How ready are you to obey Jesus?"
2. Go through each of the questions. Christ drew others to himself by who he was and how he lived. Without guilting or shaming your group members, talk about the influence Christ will have on others if we allow Christ to live through us.
3. When we trust in Christ, our lives are dramatically changed. While we can't say with certainty what would have happened if the disciples had trusted Christ to take care of the storm, even while he was asleep, we can assume that Jesus would have calmed it. Obviously, Jesus would not have allowed the boat to sink and all on board to die. Use this as an opportunity to have a faith conversation about what we are missing out on by *not* trusting in Jesus.
4. See if there was a common answer given by your group members. Talk about those tough times they face. Point out that they are in good company, since the disciples had tough times relying on Christ. Ask, "What storms or problems in your life have caused you to panic?" "What gets you to turn to Jesus?"
5. We can assume the passengers in the boats following Jesus had a similar response to that of the disciples. Ask, "Do you think any of them trusted that Jesus would calm the storm?"
6. See commentary in bold after each statement.
   - It doesn't feel like Jesus is in control of the circumstances in my life. **Jesus is sovereign, meaning he** is ultimately in control. While Christ may allow certain things to happen, nothing surprises him or catches him off guard. It may feel like our lives are out of control sometimes, but we can trust that Jesus has our best interests in mind. We need only to submit to his will and to his control.
   - Jesus is in control of most of the situations that I face. **Jesus is in control of all situations.**
   - Jesus can't possibly understand the circumstances that exist in my life. **Hebrews 4:15-16 tells us that Jesus does understand.**
   - I play a part in helping Jesus solve the problems in my life. **God has given us a free will that can work with God. Philippians 2:12 encourages us to do our part in working out our sanctification.**
   - I have seen Jesus take care of problems in my life. **Tell what Jesus has done in your life.**
   - I have a tough time trusting Jesus to take care of the storms in my life. **Tell your story of trusting in Jesus through some tough times.**
   - Jesus knows about the situations I face before I face them. **Jesus is never surprised by our life circumstances.**
   - I often turn the worries I experience over to Jesus. **1 Peter 5:7 tells us we can do this.**
7. Read Mark 4:41 out loud. **Ask one or more of your group members to answer the question. Ask, "What do you think the disciples learned from the miracle of Christ calming the storm?"**

> *They were terrified and asked each other, "Who is this? Even the wind and the waves obey him!" (Mark 4:41)*

CLOSE

Jesus calmed the storm and the disciples saw that he controlled nature! They learned a great lesson that day, as did all of the passengers in the boats following Christ. As the followers of Christ learned more and more about Jesus, they were able to rely on him more easily. Challenge your group members to get to know Jesus more intimately. Ask, "How would knowing more about Jesus help you to know what he can do in your life?"

1. Many of the religious leaders in Jesus' time were selfish. Instead of teaching the truth, they said things that made them look good. They didn't seem to really care much about the people under their spiritual guidance. Whom do you trust to tell you the truth?

JESUS FEEDS MORE THAN 5,000

Jesus gives proof of his divinity

- ❑ My family
- ❑ Friends at school
- ❑ The newspaper
- ❑ Salespeople at the mall
- ❑ Adults at my school
- ❑ Adults in my congregation
- ❑ Television news programs
- ❑ My best friend
- ❑ My pastor
- ❑ Advertisements
- ❑ The Bible
- ❑ Magazines

2. Jesus was worried about the people who had been following him. He knew they were tired and hungry and needed rest. He showed compassion toward them. Is it difficult for you to show compassion to people in today's world?

- ❑ Always difficult
- ❑ Most of the time difficult
- ❑ Sometimes difficult
- ❑ Rarely difficult
- ❑ Never difficult

3. The disciples were probably more than a little surprised when Jesus asked them to feed all those people. They didn't have food or any money to buy food. What do you think Jesus wanted to teach the disciples through this situation? Do you think they "got it"?

4. Jesus performed a miracle before the eyes of the people. He took a small amount of food and turned it into more than enough food for the crowd of 5,000 men, their wives and children, and others in their extended families. Yet there were probably people in the crowd who didn't believe that Jesus was who he said he was. Just as in those days, there are people today who refuse to believe that Jesus is who he said he is. If Jesus just did more miracles today, would people believe in him?

DEFINITELY YES   NOT NECESSARILY

5. Do you **A (agree)** or **D (disagree)** with each of these statements?

____ I know for certain that Jesus is God.
____ If Jesus is not God, then there is no hope for this world.
____ Jesus is still showing people that he is God.
____ The miracles Jesus performed don't prove that he is God.
____ If Jesus is God, then other religions are wrong.

17. JESUS FEEDS MORE THAN 5,000—Jesus gives proof of his divinity
(Mark 6:30-44)

READ OUT LOUD

The disciples were exhausted from their ministry work. They hadn't yet had a chance to eat. So Jesus and the disciples made private plans to get away and rest. The book of Matthew tells us that Jesus and the disciples headed out on a boat to cross the Sea of Galilee. Surprisingly, the people figured out those plans and rushed ahead to meet Jesus. Christ felt sorry for them because they were "like sheep without a shepherd." Read the rest of the story found in Mark 6:30-44.

ASK

How does someone prove that they are friend "material"?

DISCUSS, BY THE NUMBERS

1. Ask, "Why do you think the truth is so important?" "Why do you think the truth is in such short supply today?" "Who today is pushing lies?" "How important do you think the truth is for you?"
2. Jesus felt sorry for the people following him. Ask your group members why they find it difficult (or easy) to feel sorry for hurting people. Ask, "Why does Jesus want us to love our neighbors as we love ourselves?"
3. The disciples were probably more than a little surprised when Jesus asked them to feed all those people. They didn't have any food or any money to buy food. Ask group members to share their responses to the two questions: "What do you think Jesus wanted to teach the disciples through this situation?" "Do you think they 'got it'?" Ask, "What do you think Jesus wants us to take away from his miraculous feeding?"

4. The miraculous feeding, like the other miracles Jesus performed, was proof of his divinity. Debate this statement: "If Jesus just did more miracles today, people would believe in him." Ask, "Why do you think there seems to always be a group of people who refuse to believe in Jesus no matter what they hear, read, or see about him?"
5. Each of the statements is related to the divinity of Christ. Ask, "Why is it important that Jesus is who he says he is?" (Christianity and our eternal salvation depend upon Jesus being God, dying for our sins, and coming back to life. Without the resurrection Christianity offers no hope.)

CLOSE

Jesus is God. He proved his divinity not only by the words he spoke, but by the miracles he performed. He healed the sick and those who couldn't walk. He restored the sight of the blind. He raised the dead to life. Jesus is God.

1. **Why do you think Jesus frequently went off by himself to pray?**

   - ❏ So he could focus on what he was praying about.
   - ❏ The disciples were driving him crazy.
   - ❏ He didn't want the disciples to hear what he was talking about.
   - ❏ He felt closer to God when he was by himself.
   - ❏ He needed the quiet time.

2. **Do you A (agree) or D (disagree) with these statements?**

   - ___ The disciples were angry with Jesus for abandoning them on the lake during a storm.
   - ___ The disciples sailed off without Jesus as he requested because they wanted to obey him.
   - ___ Jesus sent the disciples out on the lake knowing there would be a storm.
   - ___ The disciples were relying on Jesus during the storm even though he was on the mountain praying.
   - ___ The disciples were wimps.
   - ___ Jesus didn't really walk on water. He walked on a sandbar just under the water.

3. **Sometimes Jesus uses the storms or difficult times that we have in our lives to help us grow stronger in our faith. Circle any storms that you have lived through that Jesus used to help make your faith stronger.**

   - • A loved one's death
   - • Death of a pet
   - • Betrayal by a friend
   - • Fear of the future
   - • Failing a class
   - • Parent losing a job
   - • Illness
   - • Money problems
   - • Parents divorcing
   - • Moving
   - • Not fitting in
   - • Break up with girlfriend/boyfriend

4. **Just like the disciples who were afraid of the storm, we face fearful situations and need to know that Jesus is near. Which do you need to hear from Jesus—**

   "Do not be afraid" or "Do not worry"?

5. **Peter quit looking at Jesus and began to sink. What has happened to you when you've taken your eyes off Christ?**

6. **It must have been very scary for Peter to obey Jesus and step out of the boat and walk on the water. He would have had to fight that little voice in his head that said, "You know you are going to drown, don't you?!" But Peter trusted Jesus enough to do it. What in your life do you need to trust Jesus to help you do?**

   - ❏ Talk to someone about my faith
   - ❏ Stop hanging around friends I know who are bad for me
   - ❏ Stop playing games that promote the wrong values
   - ❏ Get more involved in my church
   - ❏ Think about what I am going to do when I get older
   - ❏ Stop doing things that are physically bad for me
   - ❏ Find a job
   - ❏ Speak up for myself when I feel uncomfortable
   - ❏ Study harder
   - ❏ Be friendlier to the "uncool" people at my school

READ OUT LOUD

The disciples are again on the Sea of Galilee, and it's about to get bumpy in the boat. The winds, raging through the mountain ravines, have kicked up another violent storm—only in this storm, they are without Jesus. They experienced Jesus calming the waters in a previous storm. What a miracle! They just saw Christ feed more than 5,000 people. Another amazing miracle. And now here they are, caught in another storm. What will they do? Read the story found in Matthew 14:22-33.

ASK

How much sleep do you need to get you through the day?

DISCUSS, BY THE NUMBERS

1. See which reasons your group members chose. Ask, "Why would it be good for you to pray alone?" "What kind of list could you use to help you pray?"

2. See commentary in bold next to each statement.
   - The disciples were angry with Jesus for abandoning them on the lake during a storm. **The disciples could have experienced all kinds of emotional responses to the storm—anger, fear, abandonment, betrayal. All things we feel at times when we think God has abandoned us. Feelings are neither good nor bad. Feelings are just there. They happen. It's what you do with those feelings that matters.**
   - The disciples sailed off without Jesus as he requested because they wanted to obey him. **Ask, "What are you willing to do to show your obedience to Christ?"**
   - Jesus sent the disciples out on the lake knowing there would be a storm. **Yes, he did. He wanted the disciples to continue to learn about faith without him being there.**
   - The disciples were relying on Jesus during the storm even though he was on the mountain praying. **Maybe. But the terror they felt seems to show otherwise. Ask, "Can you rely on Christ and worry at the same time?"**
   - The disciples were wimps. **If the disciples were wimps, then we are also.**
   - Jesus didn't really walk on water. He walked on a sandbar just under the water. **Some have postulated this theory. Does it seem a realistic explanation?**

3. Listen to your group members' faith-strengthening stories. Tell one of your own stories that can encourage your group members.

4. The terrified disciples screamed when they saw Jesus walking on the water. Talk about what your group members need to hear from Jesus when they face fearful situations.

5. Listen to the stories your group members tell about what has happened to them when they have taken their eyes off Jesus. Ask, "What happens when you keep your eyes on Jesus?"

6. See which of the situations your group members checked. Ask, "How do you fight that same voice that told Peter he was going to drown?" Ask, "What is Christ asking you to do that scares you?"

CLOSE

The power of Christ is available to us daily. We need not fear what comes our way. We need only to have the faith to step out of the boat and keep our eyes on Jesus.

1. Jesus was teaching, probably in the home of his disciple Peter. The roof broke open. What do you think the crowd was thinking? What do you think Jesus was thinking? How about Peter?

19. Mark 2:1-12

JESUS RESPONDS TO FRIENDS WITH FAITH

Every Christian needs friends with faith

2. Do you **A (agree)** or **D (disagree)** with each of these statements?

____ The man's paralysis was caused by his sins.

____ Jesus proved that he was God again and again in the Gospels.

____ People today don't think they need forgiveness of sins because they don't see themselves as sinners.

____ The paralyzed man's health was deteriorating. He had serious problems.

____ The actions of the four men carrying the paralytic showed that they had put their trust in Christ.

3. **Question Bombardment:** Like the paralyzed man, we all need friends with faith—Christian friends. How many Christian friends do you have? How strong is their faith? How many Christian friends do you need? How are your Christian friends different than your friends who aren't followers of Christ? How many non-Christian friends do you have?

4. The paralyzed man lay on a mat often used by the poor. Why do you think Jesus reached out so often to the poor?

❑ Jesus was born and grew up poor.
❑ The poor had nowhere else to turn.
❑ Jesus tried to help the poor win the lottery.
❑ The poor knew they needed a Savior while the rich relied only on themselves.
❑ Jesus knew that the poor were more likely to see their sinfulness.
❑ The poor had the humility needed to put their faith in Christ.
❑ The poor were receptive to Jesus' message.

5. Both the teachings and miracles of Jesus amazed the crowds of people who witnessed them.

What's your opinion?

The thing that amazes people today about Jesus is—

READ OUT LOUD

Jesus was in his disciple Peter's home. This is where Jesus hung out when he was in Capernaum (see Mark 1:29). People quickly learned where Jesus was and jammed into Peter's place to hear Jesus preach. Read what happens next from Mark 2:1-12.

ASK

What is something you know for certain that your friends would do for you?

DISCUSS, BY THE NUMBERS

Note: Daniel 7:13-14 began the tradition of calling the Messiah "the Son of Man." Jesus calls himself the Son of Man.

1. These three questions will get the conversation going.
2. See commentary in bold after each statement.
- The man's paralysis was caused by his sins. **No. Jesus said, "Your sins are forgiven," to illustrate the point that he had the authority to forgive sins. Since he was God, Jesus could also heal the man.**
- Jesus proved that he was God again and again in the Gospels. **He said it and proved it through performing miracles. Jesus said he was God when he forgave the paralyzed man of his sins. Why? Because only God had the power to forgive sins. Jesus then proved he could forgive sins by healing the man.**
- People today don't think they need forgiveness of sins because they don't see themselves as sinners. **Jesus can forgive sin just as he did with the man he healed in today's story. There are many who compare their sins to the sins of others and think they are okay. They have failed to compare their sins to God's standard of holiness, which brings them up short.**
- The paralyzed man's health was deteriorating. He had serious problems. **Probably true, as evidenced by the rush of his friends to get him in front of Jesus.**
- The actions of the four men carrying the paralytic showed that they had put their trust in Christ. **Probably true. Why else would they have worked so hard to get their friend to Jesus?**
3. Ask, "Do you have four friends like the paralyzed man had? What are these Christian friends willing to do for you? What are you willing to do for them? Do they help or hinder your relationship with Christ?"
4. Jesus spoke often about helping the poor. The Old Testament also commands us to care for the poor. Jesus was interested in justice, something the poor rarely received. Ask, "How are you looking out for the poor as Jesus did?"
5. Listen to the completed sentences of your group members. Ask, "What surprises you most about Jesus?"

CLOSE

Read Mark 2:12 out loud. What was amazing about this story? Jesus' miracle? Jesus' forgiveness of sin? Jesus proving to the teachers of the law that he was the long-awaited Messiah? All of the above. What's also amazing is that a poor man in ill health had four friends with faith in Jesus who were willing to help their friend find healing and forgiveness. If you don't remember anything else from today's true story, remember this—we need friends with faith to walk with us, and sometimes even carry us, on our journey of faith.

[The paralyzed man] got up, took his mat and walked out in full view of them all. This amazed everyone and they praised God, saying, "We have never seen anything like this!" (Mark 2:12)

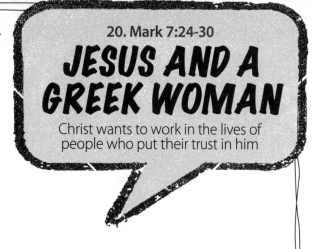

20. Mark 7:24-30

JESUS AND A GREEK WOMAN

Christ wants to work in the lives of people who put their trust in him

1. The Greek woman was in pain because of her daughter's situation. What do young people do that brings pain to their parents? (Circle the top three.)

Lie	Use drugs
Violate curfew	Get body piercings
Hang with bad friends	Drop out of church
Waste money	Talk back
Shoplift	Have premarital sex
Flunk a class	Dress provocatively
Drink alcohol	Text & drive
Drive under the influence	
Get suspended from school	

Other: _____

2. Place an X on the line scale below that best describes what most people do when they suffer.

◆○○○○○○○○○○◆○○○○○○○○○○◆○○○○○○○○○○◆○○○○○○○○○○◆

Attempt to find relief   Cry out to Jesus
in worldly pleasures

3. The pain and suffering that I sometimes experience in my life—

❑ brings me closer to God.
❑ does nothing to my relationship with God.
❑ pushes me farther away from God.

4. The disciples requested Jesus get rid of the woman as she persisted to beg for mercy. Who tries to keep you from following Christ?

5. What do you think? **T (true)** or **F (false)**—

___ Like the woman, we should keep praying and praying until our request is answered.
___ Christ honors the exercising of our faith in him.
___ Jesus is like Santa Claus.
___ Like the woman, we should put our faith in Christ rather than get discouraged and down.
___ People should blame Christ when their prayers are not answered the way they wish them answered.
___ Christ doesn't answer my prayers because I'm not good enough.
___ One way God teaches us to pray is by requiring us to pray again and again for the same thing.

6. The woman asks Jesus for mercy but never tells Jesus how to help her. Are you willing to ask God for help and then rely on him to decide how to help?

READ OUT LOUD

A Greek woman approaches Jesus with her daughter's sad story of demon possession. Here we have a Gentile, someone outside the Jewish faith, wanting help from the Messiah sent to the Jews. This story is a picture of what is to come—the Jewish nation rejecting Jesus, who then opens up salvation to everyone, Jew and Gentile. This daughter was under the influence of Satan. The Bible doesn't say how or why her life was opened to this demonic influence—just that it happened. The mother desperately wanted to help her daughter but was powerless to do so. The pain she experienced over her daughter's situation brought her to Jesus. Read the story found in Mark 7:24-30.

ASK

What sport would require persistence on your part to be great at it?

DISCUSS, BY THE NUMBERS

1. The Greek woman seemed to be aware of the fact that Jesus came to the Jews first. Yet, her faith kept her persistent. And the pain she felt for her daughter also seemed to motivate her reliance on Jesus as the only hope for her daughter's demonic condition. Use this time to talk about the love most parents have for their children even when their young people are bringing pain into the family through bad choices. Ask, "Why do you think some young people bring pain to their families?" "How does doing this affect their relationship with their parents?"

2. When people experience pain and suffering, they look for relief—often in destructive behaviors such as substance abuse or shopping sprees. The Greek woman in this story turned to Jesus. In fact, she cried out to him again and again. Ask, "When have you cried out to Jesus for mercy?" "How did Christ respond?"

3. Pain and suffering bring people closer to or push them farther away from Jesus. Ask, "Why do some people push God away when life gets painful?" "Why is putting your faith in Christ a more appropriate response?"

4. Ask, "Were you surprised the disciples of Christ wanted to get rid of the woman?" Talk about what keeps your group members from including other believers.

5. See commentary in bold after each statement.

    • Like the woman, we should keep praying and praying until our request is answered. **Yes, if we believe our request is honoring to God. Praying for a new toy that we don't need is not honoring God. The** woman's request that Christ cast the demons out of her daughter was God-honoring. When our will and Christ's will are the same, then our prayers are answered with a "yes."

    • Christ honors the exercising of our faith in him. **If you mean you always get what you want, then no. If you mean that God will satisfy your longing for a relationship with him, then yes! Christ wants to work in the lives of people who put their trust in him.**

    • Jesus is like Santa Claus. **God is not a heavenly Santa Claus who indiscriminately gives us whatever we want. God provides for our needs in the way that is best for us.**

    • Like the woman, we should put our faith in Christ rather than get discouraged and down. **Everyone gets discouraged, but our faith helps us move past discouragement. Turn things over to Christ rather than let discouragement get you down.**

    • People should blame Christ when their prayers are not answered the way they wished them to be answered. **The woman never blamed Jesus. She kept requesting that he have mercy on her. We ought to do the same, for it is not the fault of God when we are the victims of evil. Ask, "Why do you think we often blame God for the pain and suffering we see in the world?"**

    • Christ doesn't answer my prayers because I'm not good enough. **No one is good enough. All of us fall short of God's standard of holiness. Goodness has nothing to do with our prayer life.**

    • One way God teaches us to pray is by requiring us to pray again and again for the same thing. **Yes, God wants us to be persistent. When we are persistent in prayer, we learn more about God's will for our lives and how to more effectively pray.**

6. So often we pray with a solution already in mind instead of giving God our need and letting him come up with the best solution. **After all, God knows and wants what's best for us.**

CLOSE

Jesus rewarded the faith and persistence of the Greek woman. What she asked for—mercy—was within God's will, and Jesus helped her daughter. God is *not* a flighty higher power who arbitrarily hands out goodies to some while striking others with pain and suffering. Our God is love. God waits for us to call on him, asking in faith for mercy. God wants to work in the lives of people who put their trust in him.

1. **Many of the people of Bethsaida refused to follow Christ even when they saw him perform miracle after miracle. Why do you think there are those who stubbornly refuse to follow Jesus, regardless of what they have seen him do in the lives of others?**

❏ They want to be in control of their own lives.
❏ They don't think the miracles they have seen will last.
❏ They are afraid of such power.
❏ They only believe in modern medicine.
❏ They think only fools believe that people's lives can change.
❏ They don't want to change they way they live.
❏ They think that what they have done is too bad for God to forgive.
❏ Other: _____

> ### 21. Mark 8:22-26
> # A BLIND MAN LEARNS ABOUT FAITH
> Our situation in life can be used by Christ to grow our faith

2. **Wherever Christ went, he helped others. What opportunities for helping others do you seek out, no matter where you are?**

3. **The blind guy's friends trusted in Christ so much that they believed Jesus needed only to touch the man to cure his blindness. Who do you know who is spiritually blind and needs Christ's touch of faith? How often do you pray for them? What else are you doing to bring them to Jesus?**

4. **Rank the following thoughts, from (1) most likely to (10) least likely, to indicate what the blind man might have been thinking as Christ led him by the hand away from Bethsaida.**

___ Curiosity—about what Christ might do
___ Fear—that he was going to trip
___ Doubt—if he could trust in Jesus
___ Anger—at his friends for bringing him to Jesus
___ Confidence—that he would be healed of his blindness
___ Anticipation—that it could really work
___ Regret—that it hadn't happened sooner
___ Love—for friends who cared about him so much
___ Concern—that Jesus would hurt him
___ Joy—that someone cared enough to help

5. **This gradual healing was not the normal way Christ healed people. Which statement do you think is true?**

❏ Christ prepared the blind man to put his trust in him through this gradual healing process.
❏ Through this gradual healing process, Christ strengthened the faith of the blind man.

6. **Jesus asked the healed man *not* to return to Bethsaida. Since the townspeople had rejected Christ, perhaps he felt that the people would be a bad influence on the man. How many people do you know who are a bad influence on your faith?**

❏ Nobody ❏ One person in particular ❏ A few people ❏ Lots of people

READ OUT LOUD

Christ came to Bethsaida, a town where he performed many miracles, yet the people stubbornly refused to turn to God (Matthew 11:20-21). A few of the people, however, seemed to put their faith in him. They believed that Jesus' touch would heal a blind friend. Interestingly, the blind man does not ask for healing, but his friends beg for Jesus' touch on his behalf. Read the story from Mark 8:22-26.

ASK

What would your life be like if you were blind?

DISCUSS, BY THE NUMBERS

1. Create a list of responses. Talk about the stubbornness some people express toward a relationship with Christ in the midst of evidence like miracles or changed lives.
2. Like Christ, we all have opportunities to help others. And as Christians we are compelled by Christ to love our neighbor as ourselves. See what kind of opportunities your group members are taking advantage of.
3. There are many spiritually blind people around us. Our job is to get them in front of Christ. It is the Holy Spirit's job to do the rest. Encourage your group members to pray for their friends who are not Christ-followers by listing their names and praying for them daily.
4. Christ prepared the man for his healing by walking him out of town; this action prepared the guy to receive the healing by faith and taught him to rely on Christ. Talk about the checked statements.
5. Christ used the man's blindness and the gradual healing process to grow the man's faith. The blind guy either put his faith in Christ during the healing process or was already a believer in Jesus and the process strengthened his faith.
6. This item gives you the chance to talk about the negative influence some people can have on a person's faith. Your group members have friends and acquaintances who—like the faithless people of Bethsaida—may negatively influence their faith development.

CLOSE

Christ used a man's blindness to teach him about faith. In the same way, Christ can use whatever situation in which you find yourself to grow your faith. Ask him today to develop your faith through the situations in your life.

1. **Check your response to each of the following statements.**

	Totally True	Mostly True	Not True
Jesus is the source of all life.	❑	❑	❑
Death in today's world is downplayed.	❑	❑	❑
Death will never defeat those who follow Christ.	❑	❑	❑
Everyone has to die because of sin.	❑	❑	❑
Death should be feared.	❑	❑	❑

"I am the resurrection and the life. He who believes in me will live, even though he dies."—Jesus, in John 11:25

2. **Check the response(s) to the following statement you believe is true: I believe my body will be resurrected at the end of time.**

   ❑ Not really. This body and this life is all there is. Once you die, that's it.
   ❑ Maybe, but it's all speculation. No one really knows.
   ❑ It depends on how good you were when you were alive.
   ❑ The Bible is clear. Believers who have placed their faith in Christ will be resurrected to new bodies for eternal life with God.

"Do you believe this?"—Jesus, in John 11:26

3. **Mary and Martha were grieving the death of their brother who was a believer in Jesus. Christ also grieved for Lazarus. Do you think Christians grieve differently if they know the person who died was a Christian?**

Jesus wept. (John 11:35)

4. **Check the statements you believe are true.**

   ❑ The resurrection of Lazarus could have been easily faked by the disciples.
   ❑ Jesus proved his divinity without question when he brought Lazarus back from the dead after four days in the grave.
   ❑ This is a made-up story.
   ❑ The resurrection of Lazarus clearly showed that Jesus could do anything.
   ❑ Resurrection is not that big of a deal today. Doctors bring people back to life all the time.

"Take away the stone," [Jesus] said. "But, Lord," said Martha, the sister of the dead man, "By this time there is a bad odor, for he has been there four days." (John 11:39)

5. **What's your opinion? I need God to do great things in my life because—**

*"Did I not tell you that if you believed, you would see the glory of God?"
—Jesus, in John 11:40*

6. **Lazarus' resurrection increases my faith in Jesus.**

   ❑ I agree   ❑ I disagree   ❑ I'm not sure

Therefore many of the Jews who had come to visit Mary, and had seen what Jesus did, put their faith in him. (John 11:45)

22. AN UNBELIEVABLE MIRACLE—Jesus raised Lazarus from the dead and can do impossible things in your life as well *(John 11:17-45)*

READ OUT LOUD

Lazarus, Jesus' good friend and brother to Martha and Mary, died four days before Jesus went to his hometown. Jesus purposely waited two additional days to come to Lazarus' aid. This way there would be no question that he had, in fact, died. Read what happens in John 11:17-45.

ASK

When did you first realize that your parents weren't perfect and couldn't do the impossible?

DISCUSS, BY THE NUMBERS

1. See commentary in bold after each statement.
   - Jesus is the source of all life. **Yes, and Jesus *is* life!**
   - Death in today's world is downplayed. **Often we hide death and try to keep people away from it. We try not to think about its reality. See Ecclesiastes 7:2.**
   - Death will never defeat those who follow Christ. **That's right. Death ultimately loses because Christians will be resurrected in the last days.**
   - Everyone has to die because of sin. **Everyone, including Christians, must die because everyone has sinned.**
   - Death should be feared. **Christians need not fear death. See Psalm 23:4.**
2. See commentary in bold after each statement.
   - **Not really. This body and this life is all there is. Once you die, that's it. The Sadducees of Jesus' time didn't believe in the resurrection (that's why they were Sad-you-see). Many believe this today.**
   - Maybe, but it's all speculation. **No one really knows. But we can know. We have a reliable document called the Bible that recorded Jesus' resurrection.**
   - It depends on how good you were while you were living. **Remind your group that grace is a free gift—it's not about how "good" you are because no one will ever be perfectly good.**
   - The Bible is clear. **Believers who have placed their faith in Christ will be resurrected to new bodies for eternal life with God. The Bible teaches that Christians will be raised to new life after we die (1 Corinthians 15:12-21). Even those who haven't put their faith in Christ will be brought back from**

the dead for judgment (Hebrews 9:27).

3. Grief happens when we lose something, especially a loved one, to death. It is normal and healthy. But when a believer in Jesus dies, the Bible teaches us that our grief is different because of the hope we have in everlasting life (See 1 Thessalonians 4:13).
4. See commentary in bold after each statement.
   - The resurrection of Lazarus could have been easily faked by the disciples. **No. He had been dead four days.**
   - Jesus proved his divinity without question when he brought Lazarus back from the dead after four days in the grave. **Yes, as well as through the other miracles he performed.**
   - This is a made-up story. **If so, then it's possible that the whole Bible is made up.**
   - The resurrection of Lazarus clearly showed that Jesus could do anything. **A resurrection was considered impossible except by the hand of God. Jesus can do the impossible.**
   - Resurrection is not that big of a deal today. Doctors bring people back to life all the time. **Near-death experiences are controversial and not easily provable. They are most likely chemical reactions in the brain due to lack of oxygen. Out-of-body experiences are also probably chemical reactions in the brain.**
5. Listen to the completed sentences of your group members. **Prayer requests will come out of these stories. Take time in your group to pray. Encourage your group members to expect to see the resurrection power of Christ at work in their lives.**
6. Talk through various responses with group members who are willing to share. **(There is no "correct" answer from the TalkSheet.) Focus on specific things about Jesus that increase their faith in him.**

CLOSE

Today's story is yet another reminder that God can do the impossible—even in our own lives. But as with Martha, Jesus asks us to believe in him for that to happen. We must live like we expect to see the resurrection power of Christ working in our lives.

AN UNBELIEVABLE EXPERIENCE

A taste of heaven can happen here on earth

1. Peter, James, and John developed a closer friendship with Christ than the other nine disciples. What kind of relationship do you have with Jesus?

❏ I have a really close relationship with Christ like Peter, James, and John.

❏ I have a close relationship with Christ like the other eight disciples (excluding Judas).

❏ I have a relationship with Christ like those in the crowds who put their trust in him.

❏ I am curious about what it would be like to have a relationship with Christ like that of those who listened to him.

❏ I don't have a relationship with Christ.

2. On the mountaintop Jesus' appearance is changed—what theologians call the transfiguration. The disciples can now see Jesus as he will be seen in heaven.

What do you think the disciples were thinking when they saw this?

❏ Wow!
❏ I have to tell more people about Jesus!
❏ I must be dreaming.
❏ How did he do that?
❏ He really is who he says he is!
❏ I knew I shouldn't have eaten that day-old fish!
❏ I'm scared.
❏ I believe.
❏ I'm still not sure.

3. Miraculously, Moses and Elijah appear on the mountaintop. Luke 9:30 tells us they talked about Jesus' upcoming death on the cross. Do you A (agree) or D (disagree) with these statements?

___ The disciples realized that their little taste of heaven on the mountaintop required the cross.
___ The presence of Moses and Elijah meant that the resurrection of believers was true.
___ Peter, James, and John received glorified bodies.
___ The disciples learned that ghosts were real.

4. Peter wanted to continue this little taste of heaven by building shelters for Moses, Elijah, and Jesus. If you had been there, what question would you have asked Moses? How about Elijah?

5. If I were on that mountaintop and heard God say "Listen to him [Jesus]!" this would have—

❏ Strengthened my faith
❏ Confused my faith
❏ Made me give up my faith

6. The disciples fell on their faces when they realized they were in the presence of God. What usually happens in order for you to become aware of God's presence? What do you do when you experience the awe of God's presence?

READ OUT LOUD

Jesus climbs to a mountaintop with the three disciples closest to him—Peter, James, and John. There he is transformed into his heavenly state and talks with Moses and Elijah about his coming death and resurrection. The whole experience is a little taste of heaven here on earth for the three disciples. Read the story in Matthew 17:1-8.

ASK

What is the most unbelievable thing you have ever seen?

DISCUSS, BY THE NUMBERS

1. Jesus chooses to share the moment of his transfiguration with his three closest disciples. Use this item to talk about the kind of relationship your group members have with Jesus.

2. Get a faith conversation going about what it will be like to see Jesus in heaven. Your group members may talk about what their glorified bodies will be like—bodies that will last through eternity. They may want to talk about their family and friends who will also be in heaven. There are some of your group members who will talk about family and friends who haven't put their faith in Christ and will wonder what becomes of them. Use this as an opportunity to talk about sharing Christ with family and friends who aren't Christians. For a good explanation of our heavenly bodies, read 1 Corinthians 15:35-58.

3. See commentary in bold after each statement.
   - The disciples realized that their little taste of heaven on the mountaintop required the cross. **Hearing Moses and Elijah talk with Jesus about his impending death would have forced the disciples to think about what would be happening to Jesus. They probably would have been confused, sad, scared, and excited as they anticipated the upcoming events in Jerusalem.**
   - The presence of Moses and Elijah meant that the resurrection of believers was true. **What an eye-opener for the disciples to realize that they would one day be resurrected—that death would not triumph.**
   - Peter, James, and John received glorified bodies. **No, they were only able to witness Jesus, Moses, and Elijah in their glorified bodies.**
   - The disciples learned that ghosts were real. **No, Moses and Elijah were not ghosts.**

4. Ask, "Would you have wanted to keep this little taste of heaven going if you were Peter?" Create a list of the questions your group members would want to ask Moses and Elijah. See what kinds of answers your group members come up with.

5. Hearing the voice of God certainly affected the three disciples. Talk about what it would do to the faith of your group members. Ask, "Why do you think God, the Father, repeats what he said to Jesus at the beginning of his ministry, here on the mountaintop, as Jesus' ministry on earth is drawing to a close?" One possible answer: To strengthen the faith of the three disciples so they could lead the other disciples in spreading the good news after Christ's death and resurrection.

6. Talk about those times when your group members experience God's presence (during worship, in prayer, while reading the Bible).

CLOSE

The bodies we have now are deteriorating due to sin that began with Adam and Eve. But at the end of time, everyone who died in Christ will be resurrected and receive new bodies that will last forever. Until then we receive glimpses of heaven here on earth as we do our Lord's work.

AN UNBELIEVABLE STORY

God's love for us is immeasurable

1. What could have been the son's reasons for wanting his inheritance, packing up, and leaving?

- ❏ There was no good reason for leaving since he had everything he needed.
- ❏ His dad liked his older brother the best.
- ❏ He wanted to be free of the family rules—to do anything he wanted.
- ❏ He was tired of being a farmer.
- ❏ He wanted to do God's will.

"There was a man who had two sons. The younger one said to his father, 'Father, give me my share of the estate.' So he divided up his property between them."—Jesus, in Luke 15:11-12

2. Why do you think God allows us to make bad, even disastrous, decisions, like the younger son made?

- ❏ God wants humankind to suffer.
- ❏ God has given us free will to choose between good and evil.
- ❏ God wants a good laugh now and then.
- ❏ God's too busy with the workings of the universe to worry about our decisions.
- ❏ God wants you to enjoy wild living like the younger son.

"Not long after that, the younger son got together all he had, set off for a distant country and there squandered his wealth in wild living."—Jesus, in Luke 15:13

3. The natural consequences of wild living are—

- ❏ usually you get away with it and pay no consequences.
- ❏ loss of money, friendships, possessions.
- ❏ injury.
- ❏ experimentation with wilder and wilder things.
- ❏ arrests.
- ❏ death.
- ❏ Other: _____
- ❏ harm to your family.
- ❏ a bad reputation.
- ❏ your future in jeopardy.

"After he had spent everything, there was a severe famine in that whole country, and he began to be in need." —Jesus, in Luke 15:14

4. What could be "working with the pigs" in your life?

- ❏ Get grounded
- ❏ Get arrested
- ❏ Lose my license
- ❏ Crash my parents' car
- ❏ Flunk a class
- ❏ Get pregnant
- ❏ Get fired
- ❏ Disappoint my dad
- ❏ Lose my mom's trust
- ❏ Get thrown off a sports team

"So he went and hired himself out to a citizen of that country who sent him to his fields to feed pigs." —Jesus, in Luke 15:15

5. After each of the following statements, write in your response—Y (yes), N (no) or MS (maybe so).

____ Repentance is a big deal with God.
____ Saying you're sorry shows that you're weak.
____ Telling someone you're sorry for something wrong you did is not enough to repair a hurt relationship.
____ You only need to repent when you have committed really big sins.
____ God always forgives those who repent.

"I will set out and go back to my father and say to him: 'Father, I have sinned against heaven and against you.'" —Jesus, in Luke 15:18

6. Finish this sentence: God's love is like the father's love in this story because—

"So he got up and went to his father. But while he was still a long way off, his father saw him and was filled with compassion for him: He ran to his son, threw his arms around him and kissed him."—Jesus, in Luke 15:20

7. Are you more like the older or younger son?

- ❏ I am more like the older son.
- ❏ I am more like the younger son.

READ OUT LOUD

In today's story, a younger son demands his inheritance from his father. With his wealth in hand, he heads off as far as he can from his family to a foreign country where he can party guilt-free apart from their presence. You can read the story from Luke 15:11-32.

ASK

How do you think love should be measured?

DISCUSS, BY THE NUMBERS

1. The younger son represents sinners who want to separate themselves from God's loving presence and live like they, instead of God, are in control of their lives. Use this item to discuss how you and your group members are like the youngest son.

2. The father never protested his younger son's departure. He freely gave him his share of the wealth and let him go on his way. Our Father in heaven created us with a free will to make moral choices that lead to life or death—our decision.

   See commentary in bold after each statement.

   • God wants humankind to suffer. **No, but because of sin, suffering in this world is sure to happen.**

   • God has given us free will to choose between good and evil. **Yes, beginning with Adam and Eve and extending down to us.**

   • God wants a good laugh now and then. **God is sad over our disastrous, sinful decisions.**

   • God's too busy with the workings of the universe to worry about your decisions. **No, God wants to be intimately involved in our lives if we will only allow him.**

   • God wants you to enjoy wild living like the youngest son. **No. But neither does God want us to be cold, uncaring, and judgmental like the oldest son.**

3. Listen to the checked consequences of your group members. Talk about the consequences that we pay for our sins; the unwillingness of Hollywood and pop culture to accurately portray consequences (notice that in the movies the natural consequences of sin are often downplayed); and the grace available to us from God.

4. Item #3 addresses the consequences of sin in general terms. This item focuses on consequences possibly experienced by your group members.

   Interesting note: In the Old Testament, God forbade the Israelites to eat pig meat. This was for their own protection. In warm climates like that of the Middle East, pork often carried diseases and parasites. When humans consumed the diseased meat it often led to severe sickness and physical disorders (see Leviticus 11:7). This fact makes "working with pigs" all the more poignant. Jesus' Jewish audience would've certainly picked up on the pig reference and taken it as evidence regarding just how far this young man had fallen from the good life he knew with his father.

5. See commentary in bold after each statement.

   • Repentance is a big deal with God. **Saying you're sorry, and meaning it, shows brokenness, the necessary prerequisite for salvation.**

   • Saying you're sorry shows that you're weak. **Just the opposite is true. To admit you're wrong, that you sinned, shows humility of character—a strength.**

   • Telling someone you're sorry for something wrong you did is not enough to repair a hurt relationship. **Sometimes it is, while other times it's necessary to do more to make amends, like pay back the money you stole, for example.**

   • You only need to repent when you have committed really big sins. **God's holiness requires that you repent of all sin.**

   • God always forgives those who repent. **Fortunately for us, YES!**

6. Listen to the completed sentences of your group members.

7. The younger son represents the sinners in Jesus' day—the ones rejected by the Pharisees and religious leaders. The older son represents the Pharisees—outwardly righteous, but inwardly unrepentant and rejecting the love of the father.

CLOSE

The story of the *Prodigal Son* could have been called *A Father's Incredible Love*. The focus of today's story is on God's readiness to freely accept those who are lost, those who are sinners, those who are ready to admit their brokenness. Each of us is the younger son, far away from home until we come to our senses, humbly come before our Father in heaven, and beg forgiveness. God is ready to accept everyone, no matter what their past, into his loving arms.

While we are all like the younger son, we often act like the older son, too—unwilling to accept and forgive those who need God's grace the most. We believe we are somehow better than others, not needing to ask for God's grace.

So we are both the younger and the older sons, depending upon the day of the week or maybe even the hour of the day. And for both sons, God's love is immeasurable!

1. **Can you remember your first Communion? How old were you? Did you know why you were taking your first Communion?**

2. **What do you think of these statements —do you A (agree) or D (disagree)?**

___ Communion reminds Christians that they belong to God's family.
___ Communion lets the church tell what Jesus has done.
___ Christ didn't expect the church to keep Communion going this long.
___ Communion can be served at home with one's family.
___ People should take Communion so that their sins will be forgiven by God.
___ Communion helps us get into heaven.
___ You don't have to take Communion if you are a Christian.

3. **Finish this sentence stem—**

During the serving of Communion, we should...

4. **The last supper Christ ate with his disciples was the Passover meal. This meal was eaten in remembrance of the Passover in Egypt when the Israelites were saved from death by painting lamb's blood on their doorposts. How is Jesus our Passover lamb? How is Communion like the Passover meal?**

5. **The cup of wine represented the new covenant, or agreement, God made with us through the death of Jesus. This agreement...**

a) is gross. What's up with drinking blood?
b) says your sins are forgiven if you realize your brokenness (sinfulness) and accept the forgiveness Christ freely gives to you.
c) means you have to be good enough to get into heaven.
d) implies other religions are wrong.
e) is for really religious old people.

6. **The disciples and Jesus ended their Passover meal by singing the Hallel Psalms (Psalm 115-118). Is any of this song familiar to you? Why do you think singing is an important part of worshiping God?**

READ OUT LOUD

The first Communion ever celebrated was the last meal Jesus had with his disciples before his death. The first Communion reminds us of the first Easter. The first Communion reminds us of all that Jesus has done for us. Read the story of the first Communion from Matthew 26:17-19, 26-30.

ASK

How often do you eat meals together with your family?

DISCUSS, BY THE NUMBERS

1. Begin your Communion discussion with these introductory questions that will prime the dialogue pump.
2. See commentary in bold after each statement.
   • Communion reminds Christians that they belong to God's family. **Yes, Communion celebrates our membership in the body of Christ.**
   • Communion lets the church tell what Jesus has done. **Agree. Communion is an outward sign of an inward spiritual reality. As such, Communion proclaims the good news of salvation in a visible way.**
   • Christ didn't expect the church to keep Communion going this long. **Disagree. Christ wants us to celebrate Communion until he returns (1 Corinthians 11:26).**
   • Communion can be served at home with one's family. **Talk about your doctrinal perspective on this issue with a reason why.**
   • People should take Communion so that their sins will be forgiven by God. **Disagree. Communion celebrates the forgiveness of our sins, but the act does not obtain forgiveness for us.**
   • Communion helps us get into heaven. **Communion has nothing to do with a ticket to heaven.**
   • You don't have to take Communion if you're a Christian. **You don't have to, but why wouldn't you want to? Note: There may be times in life when you might not feel like taking Communion. Can you think of any good reasons? Maybe you're feeling guilty or not close enough to God? It doesn't quite make sense to you, so why do it? What do you think Jesus' response would be to those reasons?**
3. Listen to the completed sentences and talk about how we should conduct ourselves during

Communion. Should we pray? Reflect on our lives? Ask for forgiveness? Be grateful for God's grace?
4. Jesus is our Passover Lamb. Just as the angel of death passed over the homes of all Israelites, who painted their doorposts with lamb's blood, so, too, does Jesus' blood save us from sin and death. Communion is a celebration of how Jesus saves us, like Passover is a celebration of how God saved Israel in the past. Christians believe that Passover set the stage for the coming of Jesus as our Messiah and Passover Lamb.
5. See commentary in bold after each statement.
   a) is gross. What's up with drinking blood? **At first glance Communion does seem gross. But it's an object lesson that reminds us that death is required for the forgiveness of sins.**
   b) says your sins are forgiven if you realize your brokenness (sinfulness) and accept the forgiveness Christ freely gives to you. **This is the point of the agreement spoken of in Matthew 26:28.**
   c) means you have to be good enough to get into heaven. **Just the opposite. The agreement shows you can't be good enough. But Jesus was good enough (perfectly holy) to be the sacrificial lamb to pay for your sins. (Explain to your group how the sacrificial lamb offered for the forgiveness of Israel's sin had to be a lamb without blemish. Jesus fit the bill perfectly and became our once-and-for-all sacrifice.)**
   d) implies other religions are wrong. **It implies that we can only have a friendship with God if our sinfulness or brokenness is taken care of. And Jesus is the only one who can do that.**
   e) is for really religious old people. **No, it's for everyone who wants to have a right relationship with God.**
6. If you ask your group members to examine the Hallel Psalms (Palm 115-118), they may find parts that are included in contemporary worship songs.

CLOSE

Our church is like a family who cares for and needs each other. One of the traditions of our church family is Communion. This tradition, started by Jesus himself, is something we are to do in remembrance of him until his return (see 1 Corinthians 11:26).

JESUS WASHES THE DISCIPLES' FEET

Christ showed what it means to serve others

1. Today's story begins with John telling the reader of Christ's love for his disciples. Do you think Jesus loved Judas, the disciple who sold him out? How can you be certain that Jesus loves you?

2. Do you agree or disagree with this statement?

> Jesus meant for us to wash each other's feet just like he meant for us to take Communion until he comes again.

❏ I AGREE ❏ I DISAGREE ❏ I DON'T KNOW

3. The disciples had recently been arguing over who among them would be the greatest in God's heavenly kingdom—not much humility there. So Jesus, with towel in hand, takes on the humbling role of the household servant. What thoughts do you think went through their heads as Jesus acted like their servant?

❏ I'm in big trouble when he gets to me.
❏ I should be washing *his* feet.
❏ Why would God want to wash my feet?
❏ I'm not worthy!
❏ I hope Peter keeps his mouth shut.
❏ Other: _____

4. The foot-washing exercise was a symbolic act designed to teach the disciples humility. Why didn't Jesus just tell them to be humble?

5. Peter was *humble* in that he didn't want Jesus to wash his feet and arrogant in thinking he could tell Jesus what to do. Which part of Peter are you more like?

❏ I'm humble.
❏ I'm arrogant.
❏ I'm neither.
❏ I'm both.

6. Why is humility a lesson you will have to learn again and again throughout your life?

7. How was the foot-washing a picture of the cross? How often do you need this picture in your head?

From *More High School TalkSheets on the New Testament: 52 Ready-to-Use Discussions* by David Lynn. Permission to reproduce this page granted only for use in buyer's youth group. Copyright © 2010 by Youth Specialties. *www.youthspecialties.com*

READ OUT LOUD

Filled with pride, none of the 12 disciples volunteered to wash the feet of Jesus, or any other feet, for that matter. It was the custom of the day that the servant of the house would wash the dusty feet of guests. So guess who played house servant to the embarrassment of the disciples? Read the story found in John 13:1-17.

ASK

How much service do you like to receive while eating at a restaurant?

DISCUSS, BY THE NUMBERS

1. The question, "Do you think Jesus loved Judas, the disciple who sold him out?" is an interesting question to debate because the human answer is most often "no!" Yet, Jesus' answer would be "yes." The answer to, "How can you be certain that Jesus loves you?" can be found in the words of the children's song that says, "Jesus loves me, this I know, for the Bible tells me so."

2. There are some churches that practice foot-washing just like baptism and Communion. Let your group debate whether or not Jesus commanded foot-washing to be like Communion and baptism without putting down congregations who believe that Jesus did.

3. Ask, "Why do you think only Peter said anything to Christ?" "How did their thinking help shape them as future disciples of Christ?" "What do you think the disciples talked about when they discussed this foot-washing incident after Christ went back to heaven?"

4. Jesus used object lessons and stories rather than lectures because people learn better that way. If your group were to wash each other's feet, then discuss the experience, they too would learn more about humility than by simply saying, "Go forth and be humble."

5. Ask, "How can we sometimes be both at the same time?" "Which attitude usually wins out in your life—humility or arrogance?" "Which of the two is more prized in today's world?"

6. The question, "Why is humility a lesson you will have to learn again and again throughout your life?" is a good one to discuss. Humility is something that quickly leaves us because of our brokenness. We are self-centered by nature (sinful nature) and don't easily give up the self to let Jesus take over.

7. Discuss both questions to help your group members see that the foot-washing is a great picture of what Jesus did for you on the cross.

CLOSE

Jesus is the true servant-leader. Jesus is the ultimate picture of true humility. Jesus did what the disciples refused. And now we have a choice. Will we act like Jesus and demonstrate humility in our thoughts and actions?

1. **Put an X somewhere on the line below indicating the likelihood that you will temporarily abandon Jesus like the disciples did.**

```
      1   2   3   4   5   6   7   8   9   10
   ◆○○○○○○◆○○○○○◆○○○○○◆
   No Chance                      100% Chance
```

2. **Jesus tells the disciples that even though they will abandon him, he will still be there for them. ("After I have risen, I will go ahead of you into Galilee." —Matthew 26:32)**

   React to the following statement: It's okay for me to abandon Christ for a time because he will always be there.

   ❏ I strongly agree   ❏ I agree   ❏ I'm not sure   ❏ I disagree   ❏ I strongly disagree

3. **"Are you one of those church girls who loves Jesus?" a boy called from the back of the room.**

   Jessica answered a question her teacher asked about something that someone would be willing to die for. Jessica's response had been her faith. That was when the "church girl" question came up.

   Jessica knew that boy was asking if she was a Christian. She thought for a moment and then answered, "Yes, I am one of those 'church girls.'"

   Peter felt like he would never abandon Jesus, no matter what the other disciples did. Do you think Jessica felt like Peter? Have you ever felt like this?

4. **Instead of standing up for Jesus as they promised, the disciples said they didn't know him or fled the scene. What do you think—Y (yes) or N (no)?**

   ___ I've acted like I didn't know Jesus.
   ___ I'm not worried about my relationship with Christ.
   ___ My commitment to Christ is solid.
   ___ I try to avoid conversations about Jesus.
   ___ I think often about Jesus.
   ___ If I were Peter, I would have taken a stand with Jesus.
   ___ I'm ready to sacrifice for Jesus.

5. **How do you demonstrate your devotion to Christ by what you say? By how you act?**

6. **I rely on Christ rather than myself...**

   ❏ All the time
   ❏ Mostly
   ❏ Sometimes
   ❏ Rarely
   ❏ Never

READ OUT LOUD

In today's story, Jesus' prediction of Peter's denial is what's usually remembered. But the larger story is a picture of all the disciples' abandonment of Christ. It is also the story of our choice—what will we do with Jesus? Read the story from Matthew 26:31-35. This story is also told in Mark 14:27-31, Luke 22:31-34, and John 13:34-38.

ASK

What job do you predict you will have in 10 years?

DISCUSS, BY THE NUMBERS

1. Both Peter and the other 10 disciples temporarily abandoned Jesus during his trial and execution. See where your group members see themselves as compared to the disciples. Create a large line scale like the one in this item on flip chart paper. Mark an X where each of your group members stand, including yourself. Talk about the pattern that emerges.

2. Jesus encouraged the disciples by saying to them he would see them again after his death. He was saying, "Listen up, don't lose confidence in me. I will rise from the dead! I will allow myself to be crucified, but evil won't prevail." Take time to talk about the fact that Jesus is always there for us, but that is not an excuse for us to abandon him (even though there may be times in our lives that we will).

3. This item gets at Peter's confidence that, no matter what happened, he would not walk away from Christ, even if others did. Ask, "What can we learn from Peter's experience?"

4. Eventually, all the disciples except John and Judas died a martyr's death. Judas committed suicide soon after selling Jesus out. But John was left to take care of Mary, Jesus' mother. The disciples had told Jesus on the night of his arrest that they were ready to die for him. Yet, that commitment evaporated almost instantly. Ask, "How can we maintain and grow our relationship with Christ in times of adversity?"

5. Jesus, not confident at all in Peter's devotion to him, predicted that Peter would deny knowing him three times before morning. It happened just as Jesus said it would. Talk about how your group members can demonstrate their devotion to Jesus in both word and deed.

6. Ask, "How do you think Peter relied on himself and his own abilities to remain faithful to Christ rather than on God's strength? Talk about ways to let go of self, including the spiritual disciplines of prayer, Bible reading, service, regular corporate worship, and the like.

CLOSE

Through our actions and words we affirm our devotion to Christ. The disciples were willing to do the same until the moment of truth arrived. Relying on their own strength, they walked (and ran) away from Jesus; but after the resurrection and the coming of the Holy Spirit, their devotion to Christ in word and deed remained strong. We can do the same by relying on the Holy Spirit, the encouragement we receive from each other, and the spiritual practices of prayer, Bible reading, worship, and service.

1. What is the most physical pain you have ever experienced?

THE SOLDIERS MAKE FUN OF JESUS

You will be made fun of if people see Jesus in you

2. Why do you think the Roman soldiers chose to so harshly insult Jesus?

- ❏ The soldiers were afraid of Jesus.
- ❏ They wanted a few laughs.
- ❏ They wanted to show how powerful they were.
- ❏ They were sadists and enjoyed hurting others.
- ❏ Jesus was a threat to their Roman religious beliefs.
- ❏ The soldiers didn't care about human life.
- ❏ Torturing others was a sport to the soldiers.
- ❏ The soldiers were caught up in the anger of the religious leaders toward Jesus.

3. Finish this sentence stem—

Knowing that Jesus suffered so severely makes me...

4. Spitting on Jesus was considered a colossal insult in first-century Palestine—just as it is today in the Western world. How do we sometimes act like the Roman soldiers toward Jesus? Why do you think Jesus is so forgiving toward us? How can we avoid acting like the Roman soldiers?

5. What would be the worst way for you to be made fun of for being a follower of Christ?

READ OUT LOUD
After Pilate freed Barabbas, a known criminal, he had Jesus severely beaten and given to soldiers for execution by brutal crucifixion. While preparations were being made for Jesus' crucifixion, the soldiers, well…you can read the story found in Matthew 27:26-31.

ASK
What subject in school causes you the most suffering?

DISCUSS, BY THE NUMBERS
1. This item gets your group members to talk about the pain of physical suffering that they have experienced, which will lead into the discussion of the pain Christ experienced before he even went to the cross.
2. While all of these reasons motivated the Roman soldiers, see which one your group members think was the biggest. Use this to talk about the need for Christ to suffer in order to fulfill prophecy (Psalm 129:3; Isaiah 50:6; Isaiah 53:5).
3. Listen to your group members' completed sentences. This item helps your group members consider what their response should be to the severe suffering Jesus endured on their behalf.
4. Listen to your group members' responses and facilitate some discussion before interjecting your own responses. Focus on the grace that is available through Jesus in spite of how we treat him.
5. Talk about the fact that committed Christians will be made fun of at times for their faith in Jesus. The Bible promises this!

CLOSE
[Leader: Tell a story about a time you were made fun of for being a Christ-follower]. Today's story showed how Jesus was made fun of and suffered. And those of us who choose to live for Jesus will find ourselves in situations where we will be made fun of and suffer for our faith as well. Count it a blessing to suffer for Christ, given what he did for you.

ON THE CROSS
Jesus died for our wrongdoing

1. The sign affixed to the top of the cross read, "This is Jesus, King of the Jews." What "signs" do we put over Jesus? (Pick the most popular two.)

   ❏ This is Jesus, a really good guy.
   ❏ This is Jesus, a real fun-sucking buzzkill.
   ❏ There was no Jesus.
   ❏ This is Jesus, an historical figure.
   ❏ This is Jesus, my Savior and Lord.
   ❏ This is Jesus, my Santa Claus who gives me what I want.
   ❏ This is Jesus, a lunatic.

2. Do you A (agree) or D (disagree) with these statements?

   ___ If there are many ways to God (Christianity, Islam, Buddhism, New Age, etc.), then God was cruel to force Jesus to suffer and die by crucifixion.
   ___ Jesus had already demonstrated that he was God and didn't need to prove again his deity with another miracle.
   ___ The guilt and shame Jesus felt when he took on your sin hurt more than the physical pain.
   ___ Crucifixion was a gruesome way to die.
   ___ Jesus didn't have to go through with death on the cross.
   ___ The cross is no longer seen as a symbol of death.
   ___ Jesus created the wood from which the cross was made.

3. Jesus' claims of being God were well known, so much so that people passing by while he hung on the cross made fun of these claims. If what Jesus claimed is true, then...

   a) He should have avoided the pain of the cross.
   b) It doesn't really matter today.
   c) He has a claim on my life.
   d) Wait! What he claimed can't possibly be true.

4. John 19:30 tells us what Jesus cried out before he died: "It is finished." In Greek the word "finished" is teleo, found on many written receipts at the time of Christ. These receipts were given when a purchase was paid in full. So when Jesus said his work on the cross was "finished," what was paid in full?

   ❏ That one big sin I committed
   ❏ The sin of murder
   ❏ Any sin that broke the Ten Commandments
   ❏ The sins of Hitler
   ❏ The sins that I should have paid for with my life

5. God hates sin so much that Jesus felt abandoned. What do you think hell will feel like for those who reject the grace Jesus offers them?

6. The curtain that separated the most holy place from the rest of the temple ripped into two pieces when Jesus died. This most holy place, called the "Holy of Holies," was where the presence of God was believed to dwell. As such, only a priest could access this place in the temple on behalf of the people of Israel. We are now privileged to come directly into God's presence because Christ made it possible for us to no longer be separated from God. How do you sometimes abuse this privilege?

   ❏ I'm not serious enough when I come into God's presence in prayer, worship, or Bible reading.
   ❏ I didn't know I was able to come directly into God's presence.
   ❏ I often take it for granted that I can come directly before God.
   ❏ I sometimes don't give God the respect he deserves.
   ❏ I often forget to ask forgiveness for my sins.
   ❏ I need to remember more often how fortunate I am to be able to go directly before God.
   ❏ I sometimes treat God like he is my personal genie.

7. As a result of the earthquake, graves in the rocks were opened and the dead were raised to life. This was intended as a testament to Jesus' death for the sins of the world. What do you think of this phenomenon?

   ❏ That's creepy.
   ❏ Wow! What a unique way to spread the gospel.
   ❏ That didn't really happen.
   ❏ Cool!

READ OUT LOUD

Crucifixion was a gruesome punishment used by the Roman Empire to execute criminals. The cross was made of wood in the form of either a T or an X. The criminal was either nailed or tied to the wooden beams—and suffered sometimes for days before dying. Read the crucifixion story of Jesus from Matthew 27:35-54. The story is also told from different perspectives in the other three gospels.

ASK

Who, close to you, has died?

DISCUSS, BY THE NUMBERS

1. Criminals who were killed by crucifixion had their crimes written on a sign and posted above their heads. Use this item to talk about perspectives the friends and acquaintances of your group members may have concerning Jesus.
2. See commentary in bold after each statement.
   - If there are many ways to God (Christianity, Islam, Buddhism, New Age, etc.), then God was cruel to force Jesus to suffer and die by crucifixion. **If there were many ways to make peace with God, it would have been cruel. But Jesus is the only way. Other religions or philosophies don't give us what God requires—death for sin.**
   - Jesus had already demonstrated that he was God and didn't need to prove again his deity with another miracle. **Yes, Jesus spent his ministry demonstrating his deity. The cross was not the time for miracles but a time for atonement for sin. The Jews knew sin required atonement but didn't recognize Christ as the Messiah who was this atonement.**
   - The guilt and shame Jesus felt when he took on your sin hurt more than the physical pain. **This is a worthy statement to debate. Did the sins of the world cause such anguish in Christ that they dwarfed the physical pain?**
   - Crucifixion was a gruesome way to die. **Yes, because it wasn't instantaneous. It was a barbaric death by torture that took hours, sometimes days.**
   - Jesus didn't have to go through with death on the cross. **Hypothetically, no. He could have allowed us to remain separated from God. But before the creation of the world, Christ had this redemptive plan in mind (Ephesians 1:4).**
   - The cross is no longer seen as a symbol of death. **Is it? Debate what the symbol of the cross now stands for.**
   - Jesus created the wood from which the cross was made. **Yes, he did; and when he created it he knew what it would be used for.**
3. Jesus does have a claim on our lives because he is our Creator, our Savior, and our Lord. He does, however, give us the free will to reject that claim on us.
4. See commentary in bold after each statement.
   - That one big sin I committed. **Yes, this sin is paid in full.**
   - The sin of murder. **Yes, murder is included in the list of sins taken care of on the cross by Jesus.**
   - Any sin that broke the Ten Commandments. **Breaking all 10 is covered by Jesus.**
   - The sins of Hitler. **Yes, even Hitler's sins. But for Hitler to go to heaven, he would have had to repent of his sins and put his faith in Christ's saving grace, just like the rest of us.**
   - The sins that I should have paid for with my life. **Yes! That's what grace looks like, and that's why Jesus died.**
5. Jesus quotes Psalm 22:1 when he cries out to God for deserting him. Hell is separation from God!
6. What a privilege we have as believers in Jesus to have direct access to the presence of God. Yet we often take this access for granted and abuse it. Talk about all the ways this privilege is abused and what your group members want to do about it.
7. It's creepy. It happened. It's cool. And yes, it was a unique, attention-getting method for spreading the gospel. Imagine all the witnesses of Jesus' death and resurrection, both alive and those folks who were resurrected, who could tell of God's love and grace.

CLOSE

All of your sins—and trillions of other sins—contributed to the suffering Christ felt that made him cry out to God in verse 46, "My God, my God, why have you forsaken me?" Since Christ gave his life for you and me, how should we live for him?

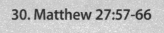

JESUS BURIED

Don't be deceived by the world

1. Joseph was an honest man who wanted to do the right thing for Jesus. He disagreed with the Sanhedrin, the Jewish Council of which he was a member, who wanted Jesus killed. He bravely stood up against those who hated Jesus. What could have happened to him for his stand? He could have lost his job as a member of the Sanhedrin, wealth, power and prestige, friends, and maybe even his life.

   What have Christians throughout history risked for Jesus? What have people you know risked for Jesus? What are you willing to risk for Jesus?

2. Pilate, most likely, gave Joseph the body of Jesus because of the guilt he felt for being talked into executing an innocent man. Put an X somewhere on the line below indicating your sense of guilt about the way you've treated Jesus.

```
  1       2       3       4       5       6       7       8       9      10
◆○○○○○○◆○○○○○○◆○○○○○○◆○○○○○○◆○○○○○○◆
No                                                        Overwhelming
Guilt                                                     Guilt
```

3. An Old Testament prophecy predicted the Messiah would be buried with the rich (Isaiah 53:9). Joseph's rock tomb fulfilled this prophecy.

   The prophecies fulfilled by Jesus should have alerted the Jews that Jesus was the promised Savior.
   ❏ I agree   ❏ I disagree   ❏ I'm clueless

   If the Old Testament prophecies had not been fulfilled by Jesus, he could have still been our Savior.
   ❏ I agree   ❏ I disagree   ❏ I'm clueless

   The Jews weren't looking for a Savior but a Warrior to get rid of their Roman oppressors.
   ❏ I agree   ❏ I disagree   ❏ I'm clueless

   Jews who rejected Jesus as their Messiah are still waiting for one to show up.
   ❏ I agree   ❏ I disagree   ❏ I'm clueless

   The Old Testament prophecies point to Jesus as our Savior.
   ❏ I agree   ❏ I disagree   ❏ I'm clueless

4. Choose a response to this statement: "People say that Jesus didn't rise in three days if he was put in the tomb by Joseph Friday afternoon and rose early Sunday morning. That's not even two full days. The Bible is wrong."

   ❏ I knew it. I knew the Bible was wrong.
   ❏ I'm confused, but there must be a good explanation.
   ❏ The Bible is correct, and I know why.

5. The Jewish religious leaders who went before Pilate remembered that Jesus predicted his own resurrection on the third day, so they got permission for Roman soldiers to seal and guard the tomb from Friday through Sunday. If they didn't believe this would happen, why did they do it? Because (circle one answer)...

   a) they knew that Christ would come back from the dead, and they wanted to kill him again.
   b) they wanted to have a front row seat with the soldiers of Jesus' resurrection.
   c) they didn't want the disciples to steal the body and fake a resurrection.
   d) they were wanting to get Pilate in trouble when the resurrection did, in fact, happen.

READ OUT LOUD

The world loves to be deceptive when it comes to the truth. And since Jesus is the truth, there will be deception by those who don't want to hear or believe that truth. So they make up their own truth—like calling Jesus a liar or, well, you need to read the story for yourself found in Matthew 27:57-66.

ASK

What is the scariest thing about going to a funeral?

DISCUSS, BY THE NUMBERS

1. Jesus was dead. The Sabbath, a day of rest, would be starting at sundown. Joseph, and his helper Nicodemus of John 3 (see John 19:39), needed to get Jesus in the tomb before nightfall so his body would not be burned or buried in the criminals' cemetery. Joseph stepped up and bravely took responsibility for Jesus' remains. Use this as a backdrop to talk about what you and your group members are willing to risk for Jesus. For more information on Joseph see Luke 23:50-51.

2. Create a large line scale on flip chart paper. Mark off where each of your group members saw themselves on the line. Talk about ways you and your group members have been guilty of treating Jesus badly. Ask, "What did you do with your guilt over treating Jesus badly?"

3. See commentary in bold after each statement.
   - The prophecies fulfilled by Jesus should have alerted the Jews that Jesus was the promised Savior. **Agree, and there are many Jews who see Jesus as their Messiah—their Savior and Lord.**
   - If the Old Testament prophecies had not been fulfilled by Jesus, he could have still been our Savior. **Disagree. The thing about prophecies—they must be fulfilled 100 percent of the time, or the prophet is a liar.**
   - The Jews weren't looking for a Savior but a Warrior to get rid of their Roman oppressors. **Agree. They wanted Rome defeated! This distorted their interpretation of what the Old Testament says about Jesus.**
   - Jews who rejected Jesus as their Messiah are still waiting for one to show up. **Agree. Some of them are. Others are Christians. And some of them are** secular Jews who have dropped their religious beliefs but maintain their cultural identity as Jewish.
   - The Old Testament prophecies point to Jesus as our Savior. **Agree. You are encouraged to look at Isaiah 53 with your group members.**

4. The Bible is correct, and here's why. The Jews counted part of a day as one day. The new day started at sundown, which means Friday afternoon when Jesus died and was placed in the tomb was considered Day One. Saturday was Day Two. And Sunday morning when Jesus rose from the dead was Day Three. Don't let the world deceive you into thinking that the Bible is wrong. Check out the facts.

5. The Jewish religious leaders who went before Pilate remembered that Jesus predicted his own resurrection on the third day, so they got permission for Roman soldiers to seal and guard the tomb from Friday through Sunday because... *(c.) they didn't want the disciples to steal the body and fake a resurrection.*

CLOSE

Many in the world want Jesus' resurrection to be untrue. Some believe he never existed or, if he did, he was just a good, moral person or a prophet sent from God—but not God in the flesh. So you will hear things like, "The resurrection was faked!" But how could it have been faked? Jesus had to have died on the cross. The soldier stabbed him in the side to make sure Jesus' heart had stopped beating. That's why water and blood poured out of his side—his heart was not working to circulate the blood. And because the soldier saw that Jesus was already dead, he did not need to break Jesus' legs to speed up the dying process. The tomb was sealed and guarded by Roman soldiers. There is no way the scared disciples would have dared approach the tomb—not to mention fight and overpower deadly soldiers. Jesus died. Jesus was in a guarded tomb. Jesus is no longer in the tomb. So yes, Jesus rose again. Jesus is alive.

ON THE ROAD

Jesus is everywhere if we only open our eyes

1. **Question Bombardment:** The custom of the Jews was to talk about the Old Testament while they traveled. Why do you think it was important for them to talk often about Scripture? How do you think it helped them? How could frequent discussions about the Bible with your friends and family help you? How many times during the week do you talk about Jesus or the Bible with someone else? Do you talk more with your peers or adults about Jesus?

2. The guys on the road were disappointed and couldn't figure Jesus out. "Why had he been crucified?" "Wasn't he the Son of God?" "What should they do now?" Finish this sentence—

   Jesus is a disappointment if...

3. Jesus walked along with the two men on the road to Emmaus, talking, explaining the Scriptures, and helping them understand their lives. How is your walk?

	Always	Sometimes	Rarely/Never
• My walk with Christ is improving.	☐	☐	☐
• My walk with Christ gives me encouragement.	☐	☐	☐
• My walk with Christ helps me get through the day.	☐	☐	☐
• My walk with Christ is my own rather than my mom's or dad's walk with Christ.	☐	☐	☐
• My walk with Christ is confusing.	☐	☐	☐

4. It seemed that Jesus was not going to stop in the village of Emmaus. But the two men wanted to hear more of what he had to say and asked him to stay. Why do you suppose Jesus refuses to force himself on us? Why do you think we need to invite Jesus to spend time with us?

5. Read the statements and decide if you **A (agree)** or **D (disagree)**.

   ___ Jesus is working throughout my community.
   ___ Christ is present in my church.
   ___ Jesus is visible in my family.
   ___ You can see Jesus at my school.
   ___ The presence of Christ is not as evident as it used to be in the United States.

6. Jesus disappeared when the two men finally recognized him. Jesus left them to reflect on what he had told them about himself. What do you think they learned from listening to Jesus? How often do you listen to Jesus through the Scripture?

READ OUT LOUD

The Sunday of Jesus' resurrection, two men were walking along the road to Emmaus, a town outside of Jerusalem. One was a follower of Christ named Cleopas, and the other, many scholars believe, was Luke. Neither of them were members of the original 12 disciples. But just as you are a disciple of Christ because you are a follower of Christ, they too were both disciples. See what happens by reading the story from Luke's account in chapter 24:13-35.

ASK

What do you think is the most remote place in the world?

DISCUSS, BY THE NUMBERS

1. Use this item to discuss how and why community is the best environment in which to grow in our faith. Christianity is not something we do by ourselves. We really do need each other for worship, encouragement, growth in God's Word, fellowship, and the like.

2. Jesus is a disappointment only when we try to play God and put him in a box. It's like we create a Jesus to conform to our image of who Jesus should be and what he should do for us. But Jesus isn't a disappointment when we accept Christ as he has been revealed to us in Scripture.

   The two men on the road felt Jesus didn't save Israel from the Romans (Luke 24:21). That's what they wanted him to do. But Jesus had a different plan. He wanted to give them a new life, a new relationship with God, a new way to live that included forgiveness of their sins.

   But we had hoped that he was the one who was going to redeem Israel. And what is more, it is the third day since all of this took place. (Luke 24:21, NIV)

3. Use this item to talk about the "walk" your group members have with Jesus. Do they understand what it means to "walk" with Jesus (to have a relationship with him where he guides their lives, encourages them, helps them deal with their sins)?

4. Jesus never forces himself on anyone. If you want Jesus, you must ask for him. Talk about what it means to invite Jesus into your life—to have a relationship with him.

5. Use each of these statements to talk about how your group members see Jesus working in each of the settings. Ask, "How do you see yourself fitting in where Jesus is working?"

6. Like the two men who were left to meditate and reflect on what Jesus had said to them, we need to listen to Scripture. Here is a simple strategy that your group members can use to listen to Scripture. It is the Read-Reflect-Reread-Rest method.

#1 Read a passage of Scripture. For example,

I am the way, and the truth, and the life. No one comes to the Father except through me.
—Jesus, in John 14:6

#2 Reflect on the passage by spending a few minutes silently focusing on the words and what they mean for people today.

#3 Reread the passage with authority in your voice (because Scripture has authority over our lives).

#4 Rest in the passage for the remainder of the day.

CLOSE

Jesus is everywhere if we only open our eyes. Jesus was present with the two men on the road to Emmaus even when they didn't recognize him. Jesus is present at the soup kitchen. Jesus is present in the White House. Jesus is working in our lives and in the lives of others. Jesus invites us to join him in all that he is doing around the world.

32. John 20:18-23

JESUS APPEARS TO 10 DISCIPLES

Christ is our living hope

1. Mary Magdalene, the first person to see the resurrected Jesus, tells the 10 disciples (Thomas was absent) what she saw and what Jesus had said. The disciples didn't believe her story. What could you do when people don't believe your Jesus story?

2. It's Sunday night. When Jesus first appeared to the disciples, they may have expected Jesus to yell at them for leaving him the previous Thursday night. Instead, Jesus surprised them by saying "Peace be with you!"

    • How has Jesus surprised you?

    • How has Jesus excited you?

    • How has Jesus calmed your fears?

3. The 10 disciples were now fully convinced that Jesus had come back to life.

    • What did this reality mean for their past?

    • What did this reality mean for their present?

    • What did this reality mean for their future?

4. The disciples were incredibly joyful that Jesus came back from the dead. It was one of those "too good to be true" moments. Can you identify a time you were this joyful about Jesus?

    ❑ Never happened to me
    ❑ One time
    ❑ A couple of times
    ❑ Many, many times

5. Rank the following statements from **most important (1)** to **least important (7)**.

    ___ Telling others about Christ's love and forgiveness
    ___ Assuring people their sins are forgiven if they turn their lives over to Jesus
    ___ Giving Bibles to people who don't have them
    ___ Inviting friends to church
    ___ Praying with those who are hurting
    ___ Sending missionaries to places outside this country
    ___ Helping the poor

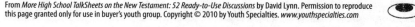 

READ OUT LOUD

The 10 disciples were losing hope in the promises of Jesus. Locked away behind (most likely) bolted or barricaded doors, they huddled in fear without a plan for their future. Thinking, perhaps, that the last three years of their lives were wasted on a hoax, they… (well, read it out loud from John 20:18-23).

ASK

What career do you hope to pursue when you complete your education?

DISCUSS, BY THE NUMBERS

1. First ask, "Who in our group has a Jesus story?" A Jesus story is about what Jesus has done in your life and the lives of those you know.

   Second ask, "Why might people not believe your Jesus story?"

   Third ask, "How can you show love to those who don't buy your Jesus story?"

2. Share how Jesus surprised, excited, and/or calmed your fears. Then let volunteers tell their stories. While the disciples may have expected Jesus to be angry with them for their abandonment, he instead offered forgiveness. Ask, "What can we learn from the way Jesus treated the disciples?"

3. The reality of the resurrection is that Jesus is our living hope. The crucified and risen Christ redeems our past, our present, and our future. Ask, "What does it mean to you that Christ is your living hope?" Read 1 Peter 1:3 out loud.

4. Use this item to talk about how easy it is for us to take for granted the joy that comes from experiencing Jesus in our lives. Share some experiences of joy that have arisen out of your relationship with Christ.

5. Use this item to talk about the importance of (1) telling others about Christ's love and forgiveness and (2) assuring people their sins are forgiven if they turn their lives over to Jesus. Christ talked about both of these in John 20:21, 23.

CLOSE

The resurrected Christ is our living hope—a hope that will never disappoint. Our money and stuff will disappoint. Worldly philosophies will disappoint. Our friendships and jobs will disappoint. Even church will disappoint. Christ is the only thing that can give us a living hope that lasts for eternity. Even now Christ is saying to you, "Peace be with you!"

JESUS GOES FOR THE DOUBTER

Followers of Christ can have their doubts

1. I doubt the existence of God when...

- ❏ it's storming outside.
- ❏ my parents are fighting.
- ❏ I am alone.
- ❏ my prayers aren't answered the way I wished they would be.
- ❏ I am ill.
- ❏ I can't figure out my future.
- ❏ I am having difficulty in a class at school.
- ❏ I am feeling down.
- ❏ I don't like the way I look.
- ❏ my boyfriend/girlfriend dumps me.
- ❏ someone starts a rumor about me.
- ❏ my parents expect too much.
- ❏ I wake up late for school.
- ❏ my dad loses his job.
- ❏ I don't have the right clothes.

2. Thomas didn't believe the other 10 disciples had seen Jesus risen from the dead. Why wouldn't Thomas have trusted his 10 friends after spending more than three years together with them and Jesus? (Check what you think is the biggest reason.)

- ❏ Thomas always thought the other 10 disciples weren't the sharpest tools in the shed, and so he didn't believe their eyewitness account.
- ❏ Thomas never believed Jesus would rise from the dead.
- ❏ Thomas missed the meeting where Jesus had shown up because he lost faith in Jesus as the Son of God.
- ❏ Thomas thought that God had abandoned him when Jesus died.
- ❏ Thomas took matters into his own hands, believing what he wanted to believe rather than the evidence Jesus had already given the other ten disciples.
- ❏ Thomas was drinking too much wine.
- ❏ Thomas suffered from an anxiety disorder that made it difficult to put his trust in Christ.

3. Thomas was gone when Jesus first appeared to the disciples. Answer these questions to help you better understand the consequences of Thomas' absence.

a) How did Thomas' absence hurt his relationship with Christ? How does your absence from church hurt your relationship with Christ?

b) How did Thomas' absence from the disciples' meeting hurt them? How does your absence from church hurt your church?

c) Why do you think it was important for Thomas to be with the other disciples? Why is it important for you to be with your church family on a regular basis?

d) If Thomas quit meeting with the other disciples altogether, what would have happened to his faith? What would happen to your faith if you stopped going to church?

e) If Thomas never saw Jesus after his resurrection, do you think he would have abandoned his faith in Christ? What would have to happen for you to abandon your faith in Christ?

4. What would a Good Friday but no Easter do to your faith? (Check only one.)

- ❏ My faith in Christ would be useless.
- ❏ I don't understand.
- ❏ My faith in Christ would still be key to my salvation.

5. Finish this sentence stem—

Thomas sees the resurrected Jesus and...

READ OUT LOUD

Christ, back from the dead, had shown himself to 10 of the disciples. Thomas was conspicuously the only disciple missing at their meeting. And was he in for a surprise. Read the story from John 20:24-31.

ASK

Which of your friends do you think will never doubt you?

DISCUSS, BY THE NUMBERS

1. Doubting is normal. Everyone does it to one degree or another. And doubting is something that can occur throughout life. Some of the disciples doubted Jesus to the end, yet they still believed (Matthew 28:16-17). Doubting is good because it causes you to reflect on what you really believe. It helps you ask questions about your faith in Christ. Encourage your group members to keep coming back and keep asking the hard questions that arise from their doubts.

2. Use these statements to get your group talking about the reasons Thomas was so untrusting of his fellow disciples. Talk about the need to develop a trusting community with those in your church. Ask, "What are the benefits of trusting the people who belong to your faith community?"

3. There are consequences for our lack of involvement and commitment to regularly meet with our church (worship, Bible study, etc.). Use these questions about Thomas and ourselves to talk about the importance of being an active part of the family of God, the body of Christ, the church. Talk about the different reasons your group members gave for *not* missing church.

4. As 1 Corinthians 15:17 teaches, our faith is meaningless without the resurrection. Everything we, as Christians, believe hangs on the truth of the resurrection.

5. Listen to the completed sentence stems. This is a time to talk with your group about what it means to make Jesus our Savior (forgives our sins) and Lord (in charge of our lives).

CLOSE

It's been a tough week or so for the disciples. Their best friend, Jesus, was crucified. They've dealt with grief, disappointment, and fear that later turned into shock, amazement, and joy at Jesus' resurrection and appearances to them. It's no surprise with the roller coaster ride they've all been on that Thomas would struggle to believe all that the other disciples told him about Jesus. But Thomas' personal encounter with the risen Lord banished every doubt. Thomas went from doubt to 100 percent belief. We will doubt, and doubt again. But we will ultimately choose to walk away or believe!

JESUS EXITS WITH A PLAN

Christ gives a strategy for spreading the gospel

1. **Why do you think Jesus gave abundant proof of his resurrection before returning to heaven? (Check your top two.)**

   ❏ He wanted many witnesses who were convinced the resurrection was historically true.
   ❏ He wanted all of his followers empowered with the truth as they went out to spread the good news of his love.
   ❏ He wanted to give final proof that he was God almighty.
   ❏ He wanted to give overwhelming proof so that later they wouldn't think they were deceived.
   ❏ The truth of the resurrection was the foundation of all of Christianity. No resurrection and there's no forgiveness of sin.

2. **What do you think of these statements? Do you (A) agree or (D) disagree?**

   ___ We can't live for Jesus without the Holy Spirit in us.
   ___ The Holy Spirit really doesn't live in us.
   ___ We need the power of the Holy Spirit to share the gospel with others.
   ___ A benefit of becoming a Christian is receiving the Holy Spirit.
   ___ The Holy Spirit is a killjoy.
   ___ The Holy Spirit can help us pray more effectively.
   ___ The Holy Spirit is an alien life force from another planet.

3. **What is the first thing that comes to your mind when you hear the word *evangelism*?**

4. **Rank the following from the most important reason (1) to the least important reason (7) that Jesus may have had for wanting his disciples to see him ascend into heaven.**

   ___ He didn't want any lingering questions about where he was.
   ___ He liked shooting up into the skies like a rocket.
   ___ He wanted them to know that his earthly work was completed.
   ___ It was one more confirmation for the disciples that Jesus was who he said he was—God.
   ___ He wanted the disciples to know that it was up to them to spread the gospel.
   ___ He wanted to perform a final miracle to again affirm his almighty power.
   ___ Jesus wanted to show the disciples his magic disappearing trick.

5. **Jesus told his disciples to first share the gospel in Jerusalem (within their comfort zone), then in all Judea and Samaria (moving out of their comfort zone) and throughout the world (out of their comfort zone). Put an X somewhere on the line below indicating how far out of your comfort zone you're willing to go to tell others about Jesus.**

   1   2   3   4   5   6   7   8   9   10
   ◆○○○○○○○◆○○○○○○○◆○○○○○○○◆○○○○○○○◆○○○○○○◆
   Totally in   Moving out of   Totally out of
   my comfort zone   my comfort zone   my comfort zone

READ OUT LOUD

Jesus was ready to exit this world and return to the glory that was his in heaven as part of the triune Godhead. He gave last-minute instructions to his disciples. Read the story of his exit found in Acts 1:1-11.

ASK

Would you rather plan your weekend or just let things happen?

DISCUSS, BY THE NUMBERS

1. All of these are true. Talk about why each of them is important. See commentary in bold after each statement.
   - He wanted many witnesses for the truth of the resurrection. **In Christianity it's not just Peter who saw the resurrected Jesus—over 500 witnesses saw him. That's more powerful testimony.**
   - He wanted all of his followers empowered with the truth as they went out to spread the good news of his love. **A religion must be true or it is worthless. The disciples' fearless evangelism—in the face of persecution and often death—is a good proof for the resurrection.**
   - He wanted to give final proof that he was God almighty. **Again and again he proved his divinity through miracles. And the resurrection was the final proof.**
   - He wanted to give overwhelming proof so that later they wouldn't think they were deceived. **Appearing to so many people was big-time proof that Jesus rose from the dead. They saw him die a tortured death, which no one could fake. And they saw him again after his resurrection. This was proof positive.**
   - The truth of the resurrection was the foundation of all of Christianity. No resurrection and no forgiveness of sin. **Yes, without the resurrection we have no hope.**
2. See commentary in bold after each statement.
   - We can't live for Jesus without the Holy Spirit in us. **Agree. The Christian life is impossible except through the Holy Spirit's power.**
   - The Holy Spirit really doesn't live in us. **Disagree. Scripture is abundantly clear that the Holy Spirit lives in and works through believers.**
   - We need the power of the Holy Spirit to share the gospel with others. **Sharing the gospel on your**

own power will fail.
   - A benefit of becoming a Christian is receiving the Holy Spirit. **Agree. Who wouldn't want the God of the universe living in them through the Holy Spirit?**
   - The Holy Spirit is a killjoy. **Disagree. The Holy Spirit convicts of sin, for example, to protect us rather than rob us of fun.**
   - The Holy Spirit can help us pray more effectively. **Agree. See Romans 8:26.**
   - The Holy Spirit is an alien life force from another planet. **Disagree. The Holy Spirit is God—the third person of the Trinity.**
3. Listen to the words your group members considered. Break them into positive and negative. Then talk about both groups. Were there more positive than negative? Why is evangelism often seen as a negative word? Why is it often seen as the pastor's job?
4. See if there was group agreement on the top two. Discuss the importance of the 11 disciples seeing him return to heaven using these five statements.
   - He didn't want any lingering questions about where he was.
   - He wanted them to know that his earthly work was completed.
   - It was one more confirmation for the disciples that Jesus was who he said he was—God.
   - He wanted the disciples to know that it was up to them to spread the gospel.
   - He wanted to perform a final miracle to again affirm his almighty power.
5. Use this activity to see how far out of their comfort zones your group members are willing to go to share Jesus' love and forgiveness with others.

CLOSE

Use the "Jesus (plus paraphrase)" reading found in Acts 1:8 to help you close this session.

*But you will receive power (**Listen, you can do this**) when the Holy Spirit (**You don't have to do this on your own**) comes on you; and you will be my witnesses in Jerusalem, and in all Judea and Samaria (**out of your comfort zone**), and to the ends of the earth (**way out of your comfort zone**).*
—Jesus (plus paraphrase), in Acts 1:8 (NIV)

HOLY FIRE
The Holy Spirit comes at Pentecost

1. **The Day of Pentecost is considered the birthday of the church. How important is it for the church to celebrate its birthday today?**

   ❑ Not that important since it happened nearly 2,000 years ago
   ❑ Important because traditions teach lessons from the past
   ❑ Extremely important because we need to remember that the first act of the Holy Spirit was to empower the disciples to preach the gospel to people from around the world

2. **Finish this sentence—**

   I believe the fiery, sudden, noisy, out-of-heaven phenomenon that happened was...

3. **If I asked the average person in our church to explain Pentecost to me, he or she would...**

   ❑ be able to explain it
   ❑ look at me funny
   ❑ remember hearing something about it in the past
   ❑ try to explain it to me but be wrong

4. **The disciples preached in different languages to visiting Jews (or converts to Judaism). Why do you think God wanted these Jewish visitors from other countries to hear the gospel?**

   a) He was hoping they could better learn the language of their home country.
   b) He wanted these Jews who converted to Christianity (some 3,000 of them did) to go back to their home countries and tell their friends the good news of Jesus Christ.
   c) He wanted to build the self-esteem of the disciples.
   d) He wanted them to feel welcome in Jerusalem.

5. **Those listening to the disciples preach in different languages "were amazed and perplexed." What has the Holy Spirit done in your church that amazed or perplexed you the most?**

Amazed and perplexed, they asked one another, "What does this mean?"
(Acts 2:12, NIV)

READ OUT LOUD

Pentecost—also called the Festival of Weeks or the Feast of Harvest—is the Jewish holiday that first commemorated God giving the Ten Commandments to Moses and Israel. Celebrated 50 days after Passover, it was also a time when the Jewish people brought the first fruits of their harvest to the temple. For Christians, it is a celebration of the birth of the church 49 days after Easter (counting Easter gives you 50 days). Read the story of the first Christian Pentecost from Acts 2:1-13.

ASK

What is the best birthday present you've ever received?

DISCUSS, BY THE NUMBERS

1. However your congregation handles the celebration of Pentecost, it's good for you to have a talk with your group members about the importance of the church. In a world (at least the United States and Canada) that glorifies radical individualism, "I" wins out over "We." In this environment the church is often viewed as an organization that must meet my needs rather than the living organism it is—the body of Christ—which worships God and joins him in fulfilling his purposes in this world.

2. Listen to your group members' completed sentences. Use this as an opportunity to answer your group's questions about the Holy Spirit, speaking in tongues, and Pentecost.

3. Your group members' responses to this activity will give you a good picture of how much your congregation knows about the birth of the church. Use this as a time to talk about the importance of the church in today's world, including why we need each other to grow in our relationship with Jesus.

4. Why do you think God wanted these Jewish visitors from other countries to hear the gospel? The answer to this question is (b)—*He wanted these Jews who converted to Christianity (some 3,000 of them did) to go back to their home countries and tell their friends the good news of Jesus Christ.*

5. Read Acts 2:12 out loud. Then answer the question, "What has the Holy Spirit done in your church that amazed or perplexed you the most?" If your group members have blank looks on their faces, then you have the opportunity to do more teaching on the role of the Holy Spirit in your church.

Amazed and perplexed, they asked one another, "What does this mean?" (Acts 2:12, NIV)

CLOSE

Pentecost marks the birth of the church and serves to remind us that one of our jobs is to share the gospel with others. Different churches have different perspectives about speaking in tongues—something that was done on that first Pentecost—yet we're all part of the universal body of Christ. We share the same purpose—to share the gospel and make disciples of all nations.

1. **Peter stood with the other 11 apostles in order to present the gospel to the crowd. Do you like the idea of presenting the gospel by yourself or with others, as Peter did in this story?**

   ❏ I prefer to share the gospel by myself.
   ❏ I like the idea of sharing the gospel with others.
   ❏ I don't want to share the gospel.

2. **The first thing Peter did in presenting the gospel to the crowd was explain what was going on. We can do the same by telling what Jesus has done for us. What has Jesus done for you?**

   ❏ He gave me a Christian parent who helped me grow up knowing Jesus.
   ❏ He showed me he was real by answering my prayers.
   ❏ He helped me get through some tough times in life.
   ❏ He got me out of alcohol and drugs.
   ❏ He showed me what a normal life is like.
   ❏ He took away the shame I was living with because of my past.
   ❏ He gave me peace.
   ❏ He showed me unconditional love.
   ❏ He accepted me as his friend.
   ❏ He forgave me my sins and wiped away the guilt I felt.
   ❏ He gave me a purpose for living.
   ❏ He has given me a future filled with hope.

3. **The second thing Peter did in his gospel presentation was tell of the death and resurrection of Jesus. He said Jesus was sent from God, worked miracles to demonstrate he was God, and died and rose again to prove he was our Lord and our Savior. How would you describe Jesus' death and resurrection to someone who was not a Christian?**

4. **The next thing Peter talked about with the crowd was repentance and baptism.**

   • Why do you think people still need to repent of their sins today?

   • What would you tell people who want to repent of their sins?

   • What would you say about baptism?

5. **3,000 believed the message of the gospel and became Christians.**

   How many do you think flat-out rejected the message?

   ❏ **Less than 3,000**   ❏ **About 3,000**   ❏ **More than 3,000**

   How many do you think felt bad about their sins, worried about their souls, considered believing in Jesus but didn't?

   ❏ **Less than 3,000**   ❏ **About 3,000**   ❏ **More than 3,000**

READ OUT LOUD

Peter presents us with what is now a common approach to sharing the gospel of Jesus Christ. First, he explains what is happening. Then, he talks about the death and resurrection of Jesus. Next, he calls the crowd to repentance and baptism. And finally, there are some who believe and some who don't. Read the story found in Acts 2:14-41.

ASK

When was the last time you heard someone present the gospel clearly and effectively?

DISCUSS, BY THE NUMBERS

1. The point of this activity—you don't have to share the gospel alone unless you want to. But you do need to share. Address your group members' fears about sharing the gospel with others.

2. The list suggests a few things Jesus may have done in the lives of your group members. Any one of these could be shared with unbelieving friends as examples of what Jesus is doing. Your group members can also come up with their own personal examples.

3. Together with your group members answer this question, "How would you describe Jesus' death and resurrection to someone who is not a Christian?" There will be different approaches for different people and situations. There is more than one way of doing this.

4. Use these three questions to discuss repentance and baptism. This passage seems to imply it's the act of baptism that saves us. But we know from other Scriptures that Peter meant adult baptism is our recognition of God's forgiveness of sin. When you're baptized you're declaring that you're sorry for your sins and want the forgiveness Jesus offers.

5. Responses to the gospel typically include many people believing, some worried about the condition of their souls but ultimately not believing, and others flat-out rejecting the gospel message.

CLOSE

Peter gives a simple strategy for sharing the gospel that we may want to try. Talk with others about what Jesus has done in your life and what is happening now. Tell of the death and resurrection of Jesus. Give a chance for the listener to repent. Quote Scripture as Peter did when needed. And finally, give a chance for the listener to believe and be baptized. It's worth a try.

STEPHEN TALKS ABOUT JESUS AND IS KILLED

There are martyrs even today—Christians who die for their faith

1. **When you hear the word *martyr*, what's the first thing that comes to mind?**

2. **The religious leaders in Israel rejected the gospel truth shared by Stephen. Why do you think there are people who reject the truth of the gospel today?**

   ❑ They don't want anyone telling them how to live their lives.
   ❑ They can't stand the thought of a God.
   ❑ They have been hurt by a church so don't want anything to do with the gospel.
   ❑ They think that aliens brought life to this planet so they don't need God to explain why we are here.
   ❑ They like sinning.
   ❑ They wouldn't be able to tell you why.
   ❑ Other: _____

3. **Stephen presented a history of the Old Testament to the Council. He pointed out that there were times in Israel's history when God's people rejected God and his prophets. The Council members got mad when Stephen accused them of rejecting God.**

   Finish this sentence: The best way to handle people who are angry at me because of my faith in Jesus is…

4. **Georgia's homework was to find a current world event and present it in class the next day. As she looked for an article online, she came across one about people who were killed in a foreign country just for being Christians. She couldn't believe it. *Does that really still happen?* she wondered.**

   How realistic is this story?

5. **Stephen was killed for preaching the gospel of Jesus to the Jewish religious authorities. They simply would not tolerate this new sect we now call Christianity. Many Muslim countries refuse to tolerate the gospel of Jesus and the conversion of their citizens to Christianity. What do you think we should do about this? (Check your top three.)**

   ❑ Go to war with Muslim countries.
   ❑ Get jobs in these Muslim countries, like teaching English or practicing medicine, and then quietly tell Muslims about Jesus.
   ❑ Let them all go to hell.
   ❑ Support Christians in those countries as they try to tell the citizens about Jesus.
   ❑ Use radio programs to broadcast the gospel into Muslim countries.
   ❑ Share the gospel with Muslim students in our country who plan on returning to their country.
   ❑ Pray often for them.
   ❑ Ignore them because there's nothing we can do.
   ❑ Put political pressure on them to allow religious freedom.
   ❑ Other: _____

READ OUT LOUD

Stephen, a deacon of the church in Jerusalem, was the first Christian martyr. He was killed for speaking the truth of the gospel. Some were upset by what Stephen said, so they made up lies about him (see Acts 6:11-15) in order to get him in trouble with the religious authorities. Stephen was forced to defend himself before the Sanhedrin, the same council that earlier persuaded Pilate to execute Jesus. Read the story in Acts 7:1-60.

ASK

What are beliefs that people are willing to die for?

DISCUSS, BY THE NUMBERS

1. Listen to all the words. Ask, "What do these words have in common?"
2. Go through each of the statements to help your group begin talking about the reasons people reject the truth just as the Council did. Brainstorm different ways to deal with the arguments people give. Of course, the best strategy is to show them the love of Jesus (see John 13:35).
3. Listen to your group members' responses. Consider some strategies that might help your group members to act in love toward those who are angry at them because of their commitment to Jesus.
4. Use this situation to talk further about those places in the world where Christians are still in danger for their beliefs. Create a prayer list of things that need your intervention for these Christians. Take time to pray through your list.
5. See if there was a common top two or three. Talk about what the group thinks God would have them do or prepare to do.

CLOSE

Living in a country with religious freedom makes it difficult to understand why there are people who are killed for their Christian faith. But there are. And there always have been since the time of Stephen. What can we do? We can pray. We can support those who go to other countries as missionaries. And maybe, you will become a missionary…?

THE CHURCH SPREADS OUT

God wants Christians to spread his love and forgiveness around

1. **Stephen exhibited the same attitude that was in Jesus Christ. Like Jesus, Stephen prayed that God would not blame his killers for what they were doing. How can we act more like Jesus... (choose five to talk about)**

   ❏ when studying?
   ❏ doing chores?
   ❏ talking with parents?
   ❏ in a bad mood?
   ❏ at the movies?
   ❏ when babysitting?
   ❏ at sports practice?
   ❏ with teachers?
   ❏ when disciplined?
   ❏ at church?
   ❏ when surfing the Net?
   ❏ with friends?
   ❏ at the mall?
   ❏ when picking out clothes?
   ❏ when getting a bad grade?

2. **On the line scale below, indicate how much the church should emphasize the death and resurrection of Jesus.**

   1   2   3   4   5   6   7   8   9   10

   Don't talk at all about the death & resurrection

   Talk often about the death & resurrection

3. **The gospel spread because the followers of Christ were scattered throughout the Roman Empire. What do you think? Read these statements and respond with a Y (yes) or N (no).**

   ___ I need to "scatter" myself around at school so that I have more opportunities to talk about Jesus with people I don't know yet.
   ___ People I know at church talk often to others outside the church about Jesus' love and forgiveness.
   ___ My friends will make fun of me if I talk about Jesus at school.
   ___ Satan is usually involved in the persecution of Christians.
   ___ My neighbors know that I believe in Jesus.
   ___ I talk enough about Jesus when I'm at my after-school activities.

   Those who had been scattered preached the word wherever they went.
   (Acts 8:4, NIV)

4. **Two new kids showed up at church. They weren't your usual "church kids." These kids were dressed in black, had dyed black hair, and looked pretty uncomfortable.**

   "Go talk to them," Chad's mother said as she nudged him in the direction of the newcomers. Chad knew his mother meant well, but there was no way he was going over and talking to those kids.

   "That's okay, mom," he said over his shoulder as he walked toward his group of friends. "I don't think they would want to talk to me."

   How does staying in your own comfortable social group hurt the spread of the gospel?

5. **Do you agree or disagree with the following statement?**

   The best way to get Christians really excited about Jesus is to persecute them.

READ OUT LOUD

The church was growing in numbers. A severe persecution broke out in Jerusalem and grew throughout Israel. Stephen was killed because of his faith. Christians scattered throughout the land kept talking about Jesus. Read the story found in Acts 7:54-8:4.

ASK

If you could scatter seeds for any food and have them grow quickly, what would they be?

DISCUSS, BY THE NUMBERS

Note to Leader: The persecuted Christians in Jerusalem scattered not because they were persecuted, but because Jesus wanted them to move beyond Jerusalem to share the gospel. We know this because they were persecuted *wherever* they went, and they still kept sharing the gospel.

1. Stephen's prayer was the prayer Jesus prayed for those who were executing him. Stephen exemplified the character of the Lord. Choose the top five activities to discuss as a group. What does it look like when you resemble Jesus while doing these activities?

2. Use this activity to dialogue with your group about the importance the death and resurrection of Jesus plays in Christianity (REALLY IMPORTANT). Ask, "Do you think our congregation has a healthy perspective on the Christ's death and resurrection?" "Do we place too much emphasis on it?" "Not enough emphasis?"

3. Read Acts 8:4 out loud. Use these yes/no statements to talk about what it means for us to scatter and talk Jesus at school and other locations.

Those who had been scattered preached the word wherever they went. (Acts 8:4, NIV)

4. Read the situation out loud. Use this situation to talk about "scattering" at church to reach all the young people who attend rather than just your small social group.

5. Ask, "Does persecution always light a fire under followers of Christ?" "When are times that persecution doesn't work to excite Christians?" "Do we need a severe persecution in the United States and Canada to get Christians sharing the gospel?"

CLOSE

God wants us, as Christ-followers, to spread his love and forgiveness around the world. We can't do this if our world is restricted to a few friends with whom we feel comfortable. So let's get out and spread the gospel.

PHILIP TALKS ABOUT JESUS TO A STRANGER

God puts people in our lives who need to hear the good news

1. **When was the last time you talked with someone about how to become a follower of Christ?**

   ❏ I've never talked with anyone about how to become a Christian.
   ❏ I've shared the gospel once.
   ❏ I've shared the good news several times.
   ❏ I talk about the good news with others who haven't placed their faith in Christ all the time.

2. **An angel guided Philip to talk about Jesus with the Ethiopian. How might God direct you? (Check all that apply to you.)**

   ❏ God wouldn't want me to share the good news of Christ's love with anyone.
   ❏ I have no idea.
   ❏ God has given me friends who aren't Christians, and I need to talk to them about Jesus.
   ❏ God puts people in my life every day and I need to talk to them about Jesus.
   ❏ God will send an angel to tell me with whom I need to share the good news.
   ❏ I'm too scared to talk with someone about Jesus.
   ❏ I wouldn't know what to say if God did want me to talk about Jesus to someone.
   ❏ God doesn't expect us to talk with others about Jesus because everyone has already heard the gospel.
   ❏ I already witness for Christ through my actions. I don't need to talk about Jesus.
   ❏ I tried to share the gospel once, and it was a disaster. I'll never do it again.
   ❏ God could use the Bible to direct me.

3. **The Ethiopian was eager to hear about Jesus. Who do you know who hasn't put faith in Christ but is open to spiritual things?**

   ❏ Nobody I know.
   ❏ Hey, my Christianity is a private thing that I shouldn't push on anyone else.
   ❏ How would I know if they are interested?
   ❏ I know people who would be open to talk about spiritual things.
   ❏ Is this a trick question to get me to talk to my friends about Christ?

4. **The Ethiopian knew that he needed someone to explain to him the meaning of the passage from Isaiah 53. How ready are you to explain the Bible to your friends and family? What help do you need in understanding the Bible?**

5. **The Ethiopian placed his faith in Jesus Christ after Philip explained the gospel message starting with Isaiah 53. What would have happened to Philip if the Ethiopian had rejected the gospel? What would have happened to the Ethiopian?**

6. **God chased after the Ethiopian with his grace. How has God chased after you?**

READ OUT LOUD

In today's story, Philip was nudged by an angel of the Lord to head in a new direction. God intended to keep the gospel moving from Jerusalem and Judea to Samaria and then to the whole earth (see the words of Jesus in Acts 1:8). Philip was used by God to spread the gospel to Africa through an important Ethiopian official who had converted to Judaism. You can read the story of Philip and the Ethiopian in Acts 8:26-40.

ASK

How easy is it for you to talk with friends about a great new movie you enjoyed?

DISCUSS, BY THE NUMBERS

1. Unfortunately for many people it's easier to tell others about a great new movie they liked than it is to talk to others about Jesus. Draw out this point as you lead your group members into the discussion of Philip and the Ethiopian.

2. God is directing you and your group members to talk about Jesus with others. The real question is, "Are you listening to God's voice?" Philip was obedient to God's voice. He didn't hesitate or object. He went where God directed. Ask, "Are we willing to talk about Jesus to those whom God has put in our lives?"

3. Count how many people your group members know who are open to spiritual things like the Ethiopian official. Point out all the people, known by your group members, who are open to spiritual things but don't know about Christ. Ask your group members what is stopping them from telling these people about Jesus.

4. Make a list of the specific help your group members feel they need in order to explain the Bible to their friends.

5. These questions get at the responsibility Christians have to share the gospel and the responsibility the listener has to accept or reject Jesus. We need to share the good news—we are not responsible for the salvation of those with whom we share.

6. This is a concept we don't often consider. Typically we believe our faith and salvation are up to us and the choices we make. What about considering the choice God made for us before we even knew we needed him? While it's true that our choice to accept and live for Christ is vital and necessary, we also need to recognize that it is God who first offers grace and then enables us to receive that grace.

CLOSE

Just as God put the Ethiopian stranger in Philip's life, God puts people in our lives who need to hear the good news. There are many in my life whom I haven't talked with about Jesus, just as there are in your life. We often let fear stand in the way of telling others about Jesus. While there are times we shouldn't share Jesus with someone, there are many more times when we should but we don't. Let's commit together to talk with one person this week about Jesus.

NO PLAYING FAVORITES

Christ treats everyone the same

1. What do you think Cornelius did so that everyone living in his home committed themselves to God? (You can check more than one.)

❑ He hit them over the head daily with the Bible.
❑ He lived like God wanted him to live in front of his family.
❑ He prayed several times a day, both by himself and with his family.
❑ He got rid of all his idols and other items that kept him from worshiping the one true God.
❑ He paid his family members to love God.
❑ He talked often about God with his family.
❑ He spent lots of time with his family.

2. Cornelius' vision, combined with his own, finally convinced Peter that the gospel of Jesus was meant for everyone, not just the Jews. Peter realized he was wrong to think that Jesus came only to the Jews.

• If Jesus treats everyone alike, then so should I.	Agree	Disagree
• Christians were wrong to own slaves in earlier days.	Agree	Disagree
• Women and men are equal.	Agree	Disagree
• Women who have had abortions will go to hell.	Agree	Disagree
• God wants us to be concerned about social justice.	Agree	Disagree
• God views homosexuals differently than heterosexuals.	Agree	Disagree
• Those serving time in prison are just like me in God's eyes.	Agree	Disagree

3. Eddie and Samuel are Christian friends.

"Quick!" said Samuel as he grabbed Eddie's arm and pulled him down another hallway.

"Let go, Samuel! What are you doing?" said Eddie as he shook his arm out of Samuel's grip.

"I saved you," said Samuel. "That weird kid Carl was coming toward us, and I didn't want to stop and talk to him. He doesn't stop talking and he smells," Samuel continued, making a face.

"He's not so bad," said Eddie.

"You better watch out, Eddie," said Samuel. "You keep talking to weirdos, and people are going to think you're one of them."

What do you think Eddie should do?

4. What do you think? Y (yes) or N (no)—

Will God accept everyone into heaven? _____
Does God care about skin color? _____
Will you be accepted by God if your good deeds outweigh your bad? _____
Does God accept homosexuals? _____
Is the United States favored by God? _____
Will the Lord forgive anyone who asks for forgiveness of their sins? _____
Did God send the 9/11 terrorists to hell? _____

5. Peter changed his message to Cornelius from other presentations but still included the death and resurrection of Jesus. Why do you think the death and resurrection of Jesus is so critically important to Christianity? Why did Jesus have to die? Why couldn't God use reincarnation to save people? Why didn't God use good works to save people?

READ OUT LOUD

Cornelius was not Jewish but did worship the God of the Bible. He had passed his faith on to all who lived in his home—family and servants. Evidence of his relationship with God can be seen in both his prayer life and in his charity to the poor. He had a vision that you can read in the story from Acts 10:23-48.

ASK

How are the most popular kids at your school treated differently from the rest?

DISCUSS, BY THE NUMBERS

1. This item gives you a great opportunity to discuss the faith of group members' families without putting anyone, especially moms and dads, down. You can also talk about passing one's faith on to close friends. Remember, Cornelius not only invited the members of his household to hear Peter but also his close friends (see verse 24).

2. See commentary in bold after each statement:
   - If Jesus treats everyone alike, then so should I. **Agree, but you will need God's help. We all have prejudices and racism to overcome.**
   - Christians were wrong to own slaves in earlier days. **Agree. They often used the Bible to support slavery. They had a very distorted view of Scripture!**
   - Women and men are equal. **So what do you think? What is God teaching us from today's story?**
   - Women who have had abortions will go to hell. **Disagree. Hell is for those who choose it by rejecting Jesus Christ.**
   - God wants us to be concerned about social justice. **Agree. Our culture may not care about the poor, the homeless, nor anyone else who's been treated unjustly, but God does. Read the Old Testament prophets and the words of Jesus and you will see that God is a God of mercy, forgiveness, and justice.**
   - God views homosexuals differently than heterosexuals. **Disagree. People may see them differently, but God sees everyone as sinners in need of a Savior.**
   - Those serving time in prison are just like me in God's eyes. **Agree. And they need Jesus just as we do.**

3. Read the situation out loud. Use it to talk about the dilemma of young people who want to keep their circle of friends while reaching out to those outside the group—especially those considered socially disenfranchised.

4. See commentary in bold after each question.
   - Will God accept everyone into heaven? **No, only those who are forgiven of their sins.**
   - Does God care about skin color? **No. All people are equal before God.**
   - Will you be accepted by God if your good deeds outweigh your bad? **No, we can never do enough good to be made acceptable before God.**
   - Does God accept homosexuals? **Yes, if they have repented and accepted the forgiveness offered them by Christ.**
   - Is the United States favored by God? **This is an interesting one to debate. Explore the notion of a Christian nation. Can we really call the U.S. a Christian nation? Regardless of the answers discussed by your group, remind them that God does not play favorites among the nations. Grace and salvation are offered to all.**
   - Will the Lord forgive anyone who asks for forgiveness of their sins? **Yes, that's why he died and rose again.**
   - Did God send the 9/11 terrorists to hell? **No, all who end up in hell send themselves there by rejecting Jesus.**

5. Work through each of the questions as a group. These questions help you dialogue with your group about the necessity of the death and resurrection of Jesus. There is no other way to salvation. If there were, God would have done it and spared Jesus the pain and suffering.

CLOSE

Isn't it wonderful that God doesn't play favorites? If God favored some of us over others, we might be the ones not headed for heaven. And because God doesn't play favorites, we can't, either. We need to share God's love with everyone. We need to talk about Christ with everyone.

PETER MAKES A JAIL BREAK

Why are many nonbelievers afraid of Christians?

1. Which of the following groups are most afraid of Christianity?

❏ Muslims
❏ Mormons or Jehovah's Witnesses
❏ New Agers—those who believe in the god inside us
❏ Neo-satanic groups—those into astrology, chan-neling, witchcraft
❏ Atheists
❏ Hindus
❏ Religious Jews
❏ Buddhists
❏ Agnostics
❏ Other: _____

2. Why do you think God allows persecution, especially the kind in which followers of Christ like James are killed?

3. Herod Agrippa wanted Peter dead—so much so that he ordered four soldiers to guard Peter at all times. The churches had no army to rescue Peter and no money for bribes to coax his release. The church could only pray. Do you think prayer is a more powerful strategy than military strength or money?   ❏ Yes   ❏ No

Why or why not?

4. What do you think?

	Always	Sometimes	Never
• Like Peter, it takes me awhile before I realize what God is doing in my life.	❏	❏	❏
• I'm afraid of being persecuted by nonbelievers like Herod Agrippa.	❏	❏	❏
• Like the Christians at Mary's home, I'm surprised when God answers my prayers with a "Yes."	❏	❏	❏
• Peter did exactly what the angel, God's messenger, asked him to do. Like Peter, I do what God asks me to do.	❏	❏	❏
• Like Peter, I'm harassed by others for my Christian beliefs.	❏	❏	❏
• Herod Agrippa arrested Peter because it made him popular. Like Herod Agrippa, I've made fun of others for their Christian views so I could be popular with my friends.	❏	❏	❏

5. Why do you think God waited until the last minute before answering the church's prayers for Peter's release?

READ OUT LOUD
Herod Agrippa loved popularity, and the persecution of the church made him popular with his citizens. Rather than seek justice and do the right thing, he did what pleased the people he ruled. You can read the story from Acts 12:1-17.

ASK
What scares you the most?

DISCUSS, BY THE NUMBERS
1. Use this question as an opportunity to talk about various religions that are contrary to Christianity. The list gives you a good start for a discussion. Like Herod Agrippa, who fiercely opposed Christians, Muslim leaders in predominantly Muslim countries have made it illegal to convert to Christianity. Ask your group why there is such opposition toward Christianity by Muslims and other religions and cults.
2. There are many theories that attempt to answer this question, "Why do you think God allows persecution, especially when followers of Christ like James are killed?" The most popular answer is that God allowed persecution in order to spread Christianity from Jerusalem to other locations outside of Palestine so they could eventually take it throughout the world. Ask your group, "Why do you think it took persecution to spread the gospel?" "Do you think we need persecution in America today in order to spread the gospel?"
3. Herod Agrippa was both cautious and afraid of Christianity. He may have assumed if he killed both James and Peter, then their deaths would put an end to Christianity. Discuss why killing Christians, including almost all of the disciples (John was not martyred because he was commissioned by Jesus to take care of his mother, Mary), did not stop Christianity but encouraged it. Also, discuss why the continuous prayers of the church worked!
4. See commentary in bold after each statement.
   • Like Peter, it takes me awhile before I realize what God is doing in my life. **Peter thought he was just dreaming before he realized God was doing something great. We are often like Peter, dreaming that God will do something great in our lives without realizing that God is, in fact, already doing great things.**
   • I'm afraid of being persecuted by nonbelievers like Herod Agrippa. **Ask, "How often do you**

think about the persecuted Christians in other countries?"
   • Like the Christians at Mary's home, I'm surprised when God answers my prayers with a "Yes." **Though they had been praying in faith for Peter's release from prison, they were surprised about God's quick response. Ask, "Do you expect God to answer your prayers?"**
   • Peter did exactly what the angel, God's messenger, asked him to do. **Like Peter, I do what God asks me to do. Peter never questioned God's messenger but did what he was told. Ask, "How do we know when God has asked us to do something?" Discuss the importance of hearing and reading the Word of God, consulting other believers, etc. Then ask, "Why do we sometimes still hesitate to do what God asks…even when we know it is his will?"**
   • Like Peter, I'm harassed by others for my Christian stand and beliefs. **Ask, "Have you ever been hassled or made fun of for your beliefs?"**
   • Herod Agrippa arrested Peter because it made him popular. **Like Herod Agrippa, I've made fun of others for their Christian views so I could be popular with my friends. Ask, "Is it okay to stand by while other Christians are hassled for their beliefs?"**
5. God is seldom early, but never late. **God uses the circumstances in our lives to teach us total and complete reliance on him. This is but one of many situations in the Bible where God was a "just-in-time" God. Peter's faith was energized and strengthened as a result of this experience, as was the faith of his Christian friends and the whole church in Jerusalem.**

CLOSE
The persecution of the early church demonstrates the fear people had of Christians. Jesus was present with these early Christians who faced the fear and anger of those who did not believe. As a result, the greater the persecution, the greater the growth and boldness of the church! The Christian faith continued to spread despite the fears of non-believers and their subsequent attempts to wipe it out. Today, Christianity continues to spread, growing rapidly in Central and South America, Africa, and Asia.

HEROD PLAYS GOD

God is God—and you're not

1. Place C on the line before each statement that describes what's within your control. Place a P on the line before each statement that describes what you're powerless over.

___ What I eat for breakfast
___ How my teacher will treat me in math class
___ Whether or not I will die today
___ Today's weather
___ What my mom does with her money
___ How much homework I'll get done on any given night
___ When the school bus will pick me up
___ What time I wake up in the morning
___ Whether or not I will be hit by a car on the way to church
___ What happens to the people I love

2. The guards were worried, and for good reason. They ended up being executed. How is worrying like playing God? (Choose one.)

❑ You think you have control of the situation you're worrying about.
❑ Worrying is a sign that you trust in yourself rather than almighty God.
❑ You worry as if somehow worry has the power to change things.
❑ Worrying puts you at the center of your universe.
❑ Worrying gives you an illusion that you're in control of the situation.
❑ You take over God's role even though he is in charge of your life.
❑ You make yourself out to be the Creator rather than the creation.

3. The people of Tyre and Sidon, who were dependent on Herod for their food, sent a team of people to flatter him. Knowing he was angry at them, they wished to make him think he was more important than he really was. Herod, dressed in his royal outfit, gave a speech and the crowd from Tyre and Sidon pretended to worship him, saying he sounded like one of the gods. Herod, flattered by what he heard, believed their hype. And the true God of the Bible struck him dead.

• Whom do we idolize in our culture?

• Why do we idolize them?

• What does this idolization do to them?

• What does this idolization do to us?

4. Finish this sentence.
God doesn't strike down more people like Herod, who acted like he was a god, because—

5. A major project was due today in Alex's history class. The teacher had given them two weeks to research a person or event from the Civil War. They needed to include first person accounts as well as information from at least five other sources. The paper had to be at least ten pages long and have citations. It was the first big paper like this that most of the class had ever done.
Mrs. Carlyle told them that October 19 was the due date. It had to be turned in by the end of class, not a moment later. From the looks of most of the students, Alex figured that they didn't get much sleep last night. Neither did he.
Near the end of class, Trevor, the god-like captain of the football team, strolled up to the front of the room and in great detail explained to Mrs. Carlyle why he couldn't possibly turn in his paper—something about "the big game." Alex waited for Mrs. Carlyle to go ballistic, to really come apart and in that steely teacher voice tell Trevor that it was now or never. But did she do that? No, she did not! She sighed and patted Trevor on the arm and told him that she understood that the game was a priority right now, and then she gave him two more days to do his paper!
It figures, thought Alex, it just figures.

Could this have happened? How often do you see this kind of behavior at your school? At your church? In your after-school activities?

6. Herod was dead. The persecution of the church had stopped, at least for a while. But God's message of love and forgiveness kept spreading. Why?

READ OUT LOUD

Herod arrogantly killed James, one of the 12 disciples. Seeing that the people liked the execution of a Christian, he arrested Peter so he, too, could be killed. But Peter was led away from jail during the night by an angel. The soldiers guarding Peter were worried when they couldn't find Peter. You can read the story from Acts 12:18-24.

ASK

Who are more arrogant—adults or young people?

DISCUSS, BY THE NUMBERS

1. We often live with the illusion that we are in total control of our lives. This activity is designed to get your group members thinking about some of the ways we don't have control—and to remind us of our need to trust in God.

2. See which of the statements was chosen most. Each of them is a reason why worrying is like playing God.

3. Use these questions to discuss how easily we can fall into the Herod trap of thinking we are cool—so cool that we are better than others; in fact, we are God.

4. Listen to the completed sentences. The biggest reason: We would all be dead! We are so self-centered that we don't even realize it. Ask your group members to go through their day, identifying how often they considered themselves without thinking much about the interests of others.

5. This situation is an example of how people can assume the role of a god. Answer these questions with your group, "Could this have happened? How often do you see this kind of behavior at your school? At your church? In your after-school activities?"

6. Discuss the reasons your group members believe God's message kept spreading so quickly.

CLOSE

Herod became arrogant—so conceited that he thought he was more a god than a human. We can fall into the same trap if we aren't careful. Remember, God is God— and you're not. So let's let God be God, the Creator. Let's trust in him as his creation to take care of us.

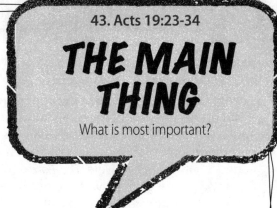

THE MAIN THING

What is most important?

1. Paul was totally dedicated to Christ and the church. And that commitment showed while he was in Ephesus. Many people's lives were changed. They gave up their idols, their evil ways, their witchcraft—and followed Jesus. What kinds of changes can we expect in ourselves when we dedicate ourselves completely to Jesus? What kinds of changes can we expect in others when we tell them about Jesus?

2. The temple of the goddess Artemis was located in Ephesus. Demetrius and his competitors worried that they would begin losing money on the silver replicas of the temple that they sold if Christianity continued to grow so rapidly. They were totally dedicated to the good living they made off the gods. Check the top five that the average person is most dedicated to.

❏ career   ❏ pleasure   ❏ car
❏ clothes   ❏ family   ❏ house
❏ travel   ❏ image   ❏ sports
❏ entertainment   ❏ Jesus   ❏ gourmet food
❏ sex   ❏ alcohol/drugs   ❏ power
❏ popularity   ❏ physical fitness

3. Do you agree or disagree with this statement?

   The main thing is to keep the main thing the main thing.

4. Jeremy thought about his friend's question for a minute. He and Brian had been talking about a question that their health teacher, Mr. Baker, had asked them. He had wanted to know what the students believed was the most important influence on their lives. Jeremy, almost without thinking, had said "Jesus."

   "I can't believe it," Brian said. "What made you say that?"

   Jeremy was pretty surprised he had said it out loud, but it was what he really believed. Now he just had to try and explain it to Brian.

   "Do you remember when my Grandpa got so sick?" asked Jeremy.

   "I remember," said Brian. He knew that his friend was really close to his grandpa. Brian liked him, too.

   "Before he died he told me how excited he was to see Jesus and that he would be waiting in heaven for me," Jeremy said. "I just knew then that I needed to get closer to Jesus. I guess that's why it just sort of popped out of my mouth in class."

   Have you come to the conclusion that Jesus is the main thing? What happened to convince you of this truth?

5. How can you keep Jesus the main thing—
   • as you get your education?

   • as you go out on dates?

   • as you participate in sports, drama, music, or other extracurricular activities?

   • as you live with your family?

   • as you look toward the future?

READ OUT LOUD

Paul traveled to Ephesus during his third missionary trip. There he found many opportunities to strengthen the few believers already living in Ephesus and to preach the gospel. Many people became followers of Christ (called *The Way*) in Ephesus. Other names were *The Lord's Way* or *God's Way*. As usual, there was opposition. Read the rest of the story found in Acts 19:23-34.

ASK

How committed are you to school?

DISCUSS, BY THE NUMBERS

1. Change always follows conversion. Use these questions to explore with your group the changes they've seen in themselves as they've become more committed to Christ. How about seeing change in others who've dedicated themselves to Jesus?

2. Explore with your group their top five. Talk about what this list would look like for a committed Christian. How about a nominal Christian?

3. Use this popular slogan to discuss how Jesus is the main thing in the lives of committed Christians. Ask, "How easy is it to forget the main thing, or to forget to keep the main thing the main thing?"

4. Talk about what circumstances led you, and then your group members, to the conclusion that Jesus is the main thing.

5. These questions help you apply the truth—Jesus is the main thing—to specific life situations. Share the struggles you've faced in keeping Jesus the main thing in each of these situations.

CLOSE

The most important thing in our lives is Jesus. Yet, keeping Jesus as our main focus is often difficult. Christians have always used simple practices to keep Jesus front and center. These include: Regular participation in church worship, daily prayer and Bible reading, faith conversations with other Christians, time in fellowship with other believers, service to others, and other spiritual disciplines.

GET GUARDED

Be alert to those who want to deceive you

1. **Paul taught and discussed everything God wanted the church to know to help them live well in Jesus Christ.**

	Yes	Maybe	No
• Do you still need to learn a lot to live well in Jesus?	❑	❑	❑
• Are you willing to put in the time to learn and grow?	❑	❑	❑
• Would you be willing to teach others what God wants them to know?	❑	❑	❑
• Has your life changed as you have learned what God wanted you to know?	❑	❑	❑
• Are you glad that you're a follower of Jesus Christ?	❑	❑	❑
• Have you asked your parents to join you in learning everything God wants you to know?	❑	❑	❑
• Has what you've learned so far excited you?	❑	❑	❑

For I have not hesitated to proclaim to you the whole will of God. (Acts 20:27, NIV)

2. **At first Krista was happy about being on the high school leadership team; it sounded exciting to be part of the group that would be making decisions for next year's high school ministry. But now that she had done it for a few weeks, some of the excitement was wearing off. The group met on Wednesday nights, which always seemed to be the night that she had the most homework. Plus, now that volleyball practice had started, she would be even busier.**

As she looked at the clock, Krista realized that she would have to leave for the meeting in thirty minutes. Ugh, she thought, I am so tired. Maybe I could stay home just this week. They won't really miss me that much.

Paul told the Ephesian church leaders to watch after themselves and those in the church. How is Krista doing this? How is Krista not doing this? How are you doing this? How are you not doing this?

Keep watch over yourselves and all the flock of which the Holy Spirit has made you overseers. Be shepherds of the church of God, which he bought with his own blood. (Acts 20:28, NIV)

3. **Do you A (agree) or D (disagree) with each of these statements?**

___ Paul's warning to be on guard against those who want to deceive Christians is no longer needed today.
___ Like Paul, I have been attacked by people who don't like Jesus.
___ The meanness of human nature hasn't changed since Paul's day.
___ The fighting and dissension that goes on in the church today also happened in Paul's day.
___ Like Paul, I have been hurt by people in the church.
___ TV preachers are the "savage wolves" Paul talked about.
___ There are beliefs in the church today that are wrong and can lead people down the wrong path.
___ What our church believes is not as important as our church members getting along.
___ The church is full of hypocrites.
___ In spite of the problems we have in our churches, Jesus is still working through the church.

So be on your guard! Remember that for three years I never stopped warning each of you night and day with tears. (Acts 20:31, NIV)

4. **Paul tells us that Jesus said, "It is more blessed to give than to receive." Acts 20:35 (CEV). Paul quotes Jesus to remind the church to help the weak. Which one of the categories of what Paul referred to as "the weak" would you want to help?**

❑ Poor   ❑ Homeless   ❑ Hungry
❑ Disabled   ❑ Alcoholics/Drug Addicts ❑ Abused
❑ Jobless

READ OUT LOUD

Paul is saying goodbye to his Christian friends. He has been called by the Holy Spirit to go to Jerusalem. He knows he probably will never see them again. He gives them parting advice, prays with them, and … you can read the story found in Acts 20:13-38.

ASK

How do some TV commercials for beer and alcohol try to tempt you to drink?

DISCUSS, BY THE NUMBERS

1. Use this activity to discuss what your group members still need to learn and how they can learn it. Also, connect this to Paul's warning to guard against false teaching. Ask, "How can learning more about God and the Bible help us guard against deception?"

   For I have not hesitated to proclaim to you the whole will of God. (Acts 20:27, NIV)

2. Read Acts 20:28 out loud. Use these questions to talk about the responsibility we have for watching out for ourselves and those God wants us to care for in our church. Krista is doing this by being part of the leadership team. Ask, "Do you think Krista is shirking her responsibility when she wants to ditch the meeting? Why or why not?"

   Keep watch over yourselves and all the flock of which the Holy Spirit has made you overseers. Be shepherds of the church of God, which he bought with his own blood. (Acts 20:28, NIV)

3. See the commentary in bold after each statement.
   - Paul's warning to be on guard against those who want to deceive Christians is no longer needed today. **Disagree. There are many people, inside and outside the church, who deceive Christians with false doctrines. This is especially true with the amount of New Age teaching making the rounds on TV and in books.**
   - Like Paul, I have been attacked by people who don't like Jesus. **Sometime in every committed Christian's life, there will be attacks from people who don't understand or respect your commitment to Jesus.**
   - The meanness of human nature hasn't changed since Paul's day. **Agree. Still sinful, human nature rears its ugly head. Just watch the news on TV.**
   - The fighting and dissension that goes on in the church today also happened in Paul's day. **Agree. It's** in everyone's church. Our job is to be like Jesus in the middle of this dissension.
   - Like Paul, I have been hurt by people in the church. **Many people have. We need to look to Jesus because people (including you) will sometimes hurt other Christians.**
   - TV preachers are the "savage wolves" Paul talked about. **There are dangerous teachers in today's church like there were in Paul's day. Some TV preachers are, and some aren't. It might be interesting to ask your group members how they can tell if a TV preacher is a "savage wolf" or not.**
   - There are beliefs in the church today that are wrong and can lead people down the wrong path. **Agree. Talk about one that is present in your community today.**
   - What our church believes is not as important as our church members getting along. **Disagree. Yes we need to learn to get along. But we also must remain faithful to orthodox beliefs.**
   - The church is full of hypocrites. **Agree. And each of us is one. That's why we need to keep going to church.**
   - In spite of the problems we have in our churches, Jesus is still working through the church. **Agree. Amazing, isn't it?**

4. Throughout the Bible we are commanded to help the poor, the homeless, the orphan, the widow, and more. Ask, "Why is it so easy for us to forget this command?"

Note: Paul tells us that Jesus said, "It is more blessed to give than to receive" (Acts 20:35, CEV). Jesus said this, but it's not recorded in the Gospels. We must rely on Paul to tell us the words of Jesus. It certainly sounds like something that could have been in the Gospels.

CLOSE

Paul's warning to guard ourselves against lies and deception is as applicable today as it was in his day. One obvious deceit in the United States is New Age teachings. New Age philosophy promotes the notion that God is you, and you are God. This New Age lie is couched in various terms: Innate wisdom, the god in you, your higher self, the higher power within. Let's continue to pray and learn all we can about the Bible so we can remain faithful to Jesus.

THE SIX-HOUR SERMON

Taking the time to "talk" Jesus
with other Christians

1. **Why do you think it was important for these first-century Christians to meet together regularly?**

   ❑ Corporate worship (that's worshiping with each other) gave everyday life meaning and purpose back in Bible times. Why?
   ❑ It made gossiping easier.
   ❑ They could best grow as Christians when they regularly met with other Christians.
   ❑ They too easily neglected their relationship with Christ if they went it alone.
   ❑ Meeting regularly made it easier to get dates.
   ❑ The coffee and donuts were worth getting out of bed for.
   ❑ They looked forward to encouraging others and receiving encouragement.
   ❑ The hymns they sang were cool.
   ❑ They wanted to celebrate Communion, the Lord's Supper, with their Christian friends.
   ❑ Living was hard back then, and they needed a weekly Holy Spirit recharge.

2. **When was the last time you were able to talk about Jesus and biblical topics for an extended period of time?**

   ❑ Retreat   ❑ Camp
   ❑ Big Event   ❑ Mission Trip
   ❑ Overnighter at church   ❑ Other: _____

3. **When Paul "spoke" or "preached" to the people gathered that Sunday nearly 2,000 years ago, the word used in the Greek was *dielegeto*, which means to talk and discuss. Paul mixed preaching with discussion about his message. How often do you get to dialogue with other Christians about faith topics?**

   ❑ Too much   ❑ Often
   ❑ Sometimes   ❑ Not often enough

4. **Eutychus fell three floors to his death after falling asleep during Paul's lengthy sermon and discussion time.**

   • How often have you fallen asleep during a church service or event?

   ❑ Never
   ❑ Once
   ❑ Several times
   ❑ On a regular basis

   • What brought you back to life?

   ❑ Nothing, I still fall asleep
   ❑ A realization that God is present within my congregation and that I need to be present with God.
   ❑ A friend jabbed me in the ribs
   ❑ My growing relationship with Christ
   ❑ Other: _____

5. **The Christians meeting together with Paul were fired up that Eutychus was brought back to life. What stories or events get you fired up when you're with your congregation?**

READ OUT LOUD

Sunday, for Christians, had taken the place of Saturday, the Jewish Sabbath. Sunday was a day to remember Christ's resurrection. And in the early church, Communion, the Lord's Supper, which is sometimes called the Eucharist, was celebrated each Sunday. Paul came to the church in Troas to celebrate the Lord's Supper with them on that Sunday. He also taught and discussed faith issues all night. You can read the story from Acts 20:1-12.

ASK

Whom could you talk with all night?

DISCUSS, BY THE NUMBERS

1. Use this item to talk about why it's also important for Christians today to meet regularly. Christianity is not an individual sport but a team sport, to use an athletic metaphor. As the body of Jesus Christ, the church is a faith community that helps every member grow to be more like Jesus. When one or more members are missing, the whole body suffers. Point out that we really do need each other to become complete in Christ.

2. Ask, "Why is it important for us to have some times during the year when we can talk Jesus and faith issues for an extended period of time?" Discuss the benefits of times like retreats, where you get extended time periods to talk about faith. Give story examples of how these times help us grow closer to each other and to Jesus Christ.

3. Talk about what your church might look like if you had more opportunities to dialogue like Paul did with the church in Troas. Ask the group for feedback on how well the faith dialogue is going using TalkSheets. Are you, as the facilitator of the discussion, talking too much? Does everyone have a chance to contribute?

4. Have some fun telling "nodding off" stories. Then, move to a more serious discussion of how the presence of God among your congregation (Jesus Christ is present where two or three are gathered—Matthew 18:20) can keep each of your group members coming back to church for more of Jesus.

5. Talk about which of the stories, events, or activities within your church have helped your group members get fired up for Christ.

CLOSE

In today's busy world, it seems as if we've no extended time to talk Jesus with other Christians. It is imperative we make time—big chunks of time—for faith conversations. Like those Christians in the early church, we too need time to think and reflect on what it means to follow Christ.

1. Paul took advantage of every opportunity to talk Jesus. In today's story he preaches to an angry mob. Name the last three opportunities you had to talk with someone about the good news of Jesus, whether you followed through or not.

    #1 _____

    #2 _____

    #3 _____

2. Laura grabbed her Bible from her desk and crawled into bed. She had been reading through the Psalms for the last month. She was really enjoying it, which was a surprise. A lot of her friends at church were able to recite a bunch of Bible verses. Somehow that never really appealed to Laura. She hadn't really ever read the Bible much, even though she had grown up in the church. Then one of her friends gave her a card that had a passage from the Psalms in it. It seemed more like poetry than anything she had ever read in the Bible before.

   Soon Laura was reading a Psalm a night before she went to bed. When she asked her mom why she found it so interesting now, her mom just smiled and said that maybe she just needed to grow into it.

   Why do you think Jesus changes you whether you grew up knowing him or just met him?

3. Paul told the story of his life both before and after he met Jesus. Use these sentence stems to tell your story.

   • I put my trust in Jesus when—

   • I'm glad I have faith in Jesus because—

   • I believe Jesus died and rose again so that—

   • I asked God to forgive my sins—

   • During this past year Jesus has—

4. Assume you're not a Christian for a minute. How would your life be different than it is right now?

5. "Then the Lord said to [Paul], "'Go; I will send you far away to the Gentiles'" (Acts 22:21, NIV). Where do you think God wants you to go?

   ❏ Stay close to home
   ❏ Go to another country as a missionary
   ❏ Get a good job where I can be a witness for Jesus at my work
   ❏ Do a summer mission trip
   ❏ I'm clueless
   ❏ I'm too scared to go where God might want me to go.

READ OUT LOUD

The apostle Paul wrapped up his third missionary trip. Agabus, a prophet of God, accurately predicted Paul's persecution that awaited him in Jerusalem. The followers of Christ who were with Paul begged him not to return to Jerusalem. Paul refused, telling them he was ready to go to jail or even die for Jesus. Back in Jerusalem a crowd attacked him for being a Jesus follower. So Paul was carried to a Roman fortress for his own safety. There he asked if he could speak to the wild mob. Pick up the story from here and read it aloud from Acts 22:1-21.

ASK

How long do you usually review for a math test?

DISCUSS, BY THE NUMBERS

1. Discuss why your group members took advantage of the opportunities to talk Jesus, as well as the opportunities that they didn't pursue. Without putting them down or on the spot, talk about fear and other roadblocks, that keep us from sharing the good news with others.

2. In this story, Laura, who grew up in the church, was changed. She went from not enjoying God's word to enjoying it. You will have group members who grew up in Christian homes and those who only recently were introduced to Jesus. The Lord changes both. Use this story as a springboard to discuss the question, "Why do you think Jesus changes you whether you grew up knowing him or just met him?"

3. Listen to these sentence stems as a strategy to review your life and your group members' lives. Ask, "How can reviewing your life with Jesus motivate you to move forward with him?"

4. Assume you're not a Christian for a minute. How would your life be different than it is right now? Without putting others down, take an honest look at how Jesus is making a difference in the lives of your group members. You go first in sharing.

5. Point out that no matter where we go or what we do we can be a witness, like Paul, for Jesus Christ.

CLOSE

Paul reviewed his life both before and after he met Jesus. He did this in order to show how his life had been changed by his encounter with Christ. We can review our lives and relationship with Jesus to help motivate us to move forward with Jesus.

PAUL ACTS CHRISTIAN

Christians who are treated unfairly act differently than nonbelievers

1. How did Paul, a Christ-follower, act differently than the others in the story?

- Paul told the truth while his accusers lied.　　I think so　I don't think so
- Paul refused to talk badly about those who accused him.　　I think so　I don't think so
- Paul stayed calm in the midst of the raging of those who accused him.　　I think so　I don't think so
- Paul secretly hated his accusers.　I think so　I don't think so
- Paul didn't bribe while Felix wanted a bribe.　　I think so　I don't think so
- Paul didn't cop an attitude like his accusers.　　I think so　I don't think so
- Paul paid a hit man to kill Ananias, the high priest.　　I think so　I don't think so
- Paul gossiped about his accusers while in jail.　　I think so　I don't think so

2. Felix, the governor, knew all about the Way, what Christianity was called at the time. What do you like about the name, the Way? What other names do you think would be cool to call Christianity?

3. Felix, knowing about the Way, had not yet become a Christian. Finish these four sentence stems.

Felix put off the decision to become a follower of Christ for another time because—

Felix was scared when Paul talked about how to live and the coming judgment because—

Even though he was afraid, Felix didn't repent of his sins because—

Felix is like some people I know because—

4. As the guard entered the cell and gave Paul his food he just stopped and stared. "How do you do it?" he asked.

"You mean eat the food?" Paul answered, assuming that the guard was referring to the slop he was handed.

"No," said the guard. "How do you just sit there patiently? You are nice to me even though I keep you prisoner. Why, as a Roman citizen you shouldn't even be in here!"

While choking down a spoonful of food Paul considered the guard's question. "I get through it," he answered, "because I know it is God's will for me. He has given me the privilege of being here to talk to you about Jesus."

"Did you do something wrong? Is that why you have to stay in this pit? I don't think I would consider this much of a privilege," the guard replied.

"No," said Paul, looking around, "this part surely isn't the privilege. It's being able to talk with you that is the gift from God."

This is a fictional account of how Paul may have handled his two-year imprisonment. How do you think he did this?

5. Paul reflected the attitude of Jesus in how he acted before Ananias, the high priest, and Felix, the governor. How do you reflect Jesus when people look at your actions? (Check all that apply to you.)

- ❏ love
- ❏ honesty
- ❏ conceit
- ❏ hope
- ❏ wisdom
- ❏ pleasure
- ❏ envy
- ❏ compassion
- ❏ joy
- ❏ strength
- ❏ revenge
- ❏ grace
- ❏ excitement
- ❏ bravery
- ❏ greed
- ❏ peace
- ❏ faith
- ❏ lust
- ❏ humor
- ❏ patience
- ❏ self-centeredness

6. This is a fictional prayer that Paul might have prayed while locked up. What can you learn from this prayer to help you become more like Jesus?

"Lord, I praise your name and thank you for loving me. I don't mean to complain, but this imprisonment is really trying my patience. The guards are really annoying, and don't get me started about the food—what there is of it. I know that I couldn't get through it at all without your presence in my life. Your strength has given me courage, and your kindness has helped me get through some very dark times. I know that all of this is somehow part of your plan, and I trust you to have my future in your hands. Thank you again for loving me. Amen."

READ OUT LOUD

Paul returned to Jerusalem in spite of the warning he was given that there would be trouble. And as predicted, trouble found him in the form of an angry mob. You can read what happened in Acts 24:1-27.

ASK

When things aren't going well, who still acts like Jesus in your church?

DISCUSS, BY THE NUMBERS

1. Paul certainly reflected the attitude of Christ when he went back to Jerusalem. And because of his bravery, God allowed Paul to go to Rome and preach the gospel there.
   - Paul told the truth while his accusers lied. **Yes.**
   - Paul refused to talk badly about those who accused him. **That's right.**
   - Paul stayed calm in the midst of the raging of those who accused him. **Yes.**
   - Paul secretly hated his accusers. **No, he loved his neighbor as Christ taught.**
   - Paul didn't bribe while Felix wanted a bribe. **Felix kept him in prison for two years hoping for financial gain. Paul continued to share the gospel with him.**
   - Paul didn't cop an attitude like his accusers. **That's right.**
   - Paul paid a hit man to kill Ananias, the high priest. **No.**
   - Paul gossiped about his accusers while in jail. **No.**
2. Have fun brainstorming all kinds of cool names for Christianity, like the "Way."
3. Listen to the completed sentence stems. Read Acts 24:25 out loud. Talk about the danger of putting off a commitment to Christ.

As Paul discoursed on righteousness, self-control and the judgment to come, Felix was afraid and said, "That's enough for now! You [Paul] may leave. When I find it convenient, I will send for you." (Acts 24:25, NIV)

4. Paul refused to complain even though he remained in prison illegally for two years. He continued to talk Jesus while he was locked up. This fictional account of how Paul may have handled his two-year imprisonment can help your group members see how he thrived during these two years. He let Christ live in him and through him.
5. Examine the list of words. Talk about those that are descriptive of Jesus in our lives. Ask, "What do we need to do in order to become more like Jesus so we can reflect Jesus?" This is also a great opportunity to discuss witnessing through actions.
6. This is a fictional prayer that Paul might have prayed while locked up in prison. What can you learn from this prayer to help you become more like Jesus?

CLOSE

In life, you will be treated unfairly like Paul. So the question is, how will you respond? We learned today from Paul that, when treated unfairly, he acted differently than those who weren't Christ-followers. Paul acted like Jesus. Let's pray that God will put us in situations where we'll be shaped to be more like Jesus.

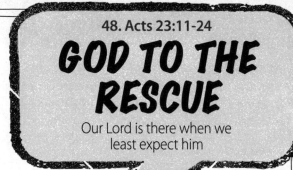

GOD TO THE RESCUE

Our Lord is there when we least expect him

1. **God had revealed to Paul that he would go to Rome to tell others of Christ's love. Yet, he had been arrested and thrown in prison, and a plot to murder him was in effect. If you were Paul, do you think you could have trusted God to work things out so that you could go to Rome?**

   ❏ Oh yeah. No problem trusting in God to work things out.
   ❏ Maybe I would trust God to work things out.
   ❏ I'm freaked out just thinking about it. No way would I trust God to work things out.

2. **Decide if you agree (A), disagree (D), or are not sure (NS) about each of these statements.**

   a) There are people who want me to fail in my relationship with Jesus.   A D NS
   b) When I face a crisis, I'm confident, like Paul, that God will get me through it.   A D NS
   c) Like Paul, I listen for God's voice to direct me.   A D NS
   d) Paul had nothing to fear because God was on his side.   A D NS
   e) The people who wanted Paul dead gossiped about him. I know gossiping is wrong, so I avoid it.   A D NS

3. **God worked through Paul's nephew in order to keep Paul alive so he could share the good news in Rome. How else could God have worked to defeat the plot to kill Paul?**

4. **How would you finish these two statements?**

   Even when I feel helpless, God—

   I need to get closer to God so that—

5. **Put an arrow by the statement that best describes how God has worked in your life during a crisis.**

   I don't think he has worked in my life during times of crisis.
   He has used people to help me in times of crisis.
   He has given me the common sense I need to act sensibly and appropriately.
   He has given me a peace that helped me get through the crisis.
   He has made his presence known to me when I have faced a crisis.

READ OUT LOUD

In today's story Paul caps off his problems in Jerusalem by landing in prison. (Oh, and it's by an assassination plot.) Paul's situation looks bleak, except for the fact that God has just told him he will be going to Rome to preach the gospel. You can read the story from Acts 23:11-24.

ASK

When have your parents shown up when you least expected them?

DISCUSS, BY THE NUMBERS

1. Things looked bleak for Paul. Yet, he knew from the promises of God in his word and from experience that God would get him to Rome. Ask, "Is God's promise to always be present in our lives true no matter what?" "Have your past experiences shown that God keeps his promises?" Tell a personal story of how God has been there for you as well as how easily you need to relearn this truth.

2. See commentary in bold after each statement.

• There are people who want me to fail in my relationship with Jesus. **Sometimes there may be friends who want to see you sin so they can say that Christianity doesn't work. Or even parents, who then call their son or daughter a hypocrite. Ask, "What can we do when we face people who want to sabotage our walk with Christ?"**

• When I face a crisis, I'm confident, like Paul, that God will get me through it. **Create a verbal scale from 1=not confident to 10=confident like Paul, and see where your group members fall within the range from 1 to 10.**

• Like Paul, I listen for God's voice to direct me. **Most, if not all, of your group members will want to know how to listen to God. They will say things like, "I never hear God speak." Take time to talk about cultivating the practice of prayer and reflection on God's word as a way to hear God's voice.**

• Paul had nothing to fear because God was on his side. **Even though God is on your side, you have plenty to fear. We can be like Paul and give our fears to Christ, or we can surround ourselves with our fears.**

• The people who wanted Paul dead gossiped about

him. I know that gossiping is wrong, so I avoid it. **Easier said than done. Gossip is harmful—for those who spread rumors, and those who are the subject of gossip. In the case of today's story, the gossip mill led to vows of assassination.**

3. List as many ways as your group can imagine. This shows that there are many ways God can work in our lives. I'm sure Paul was surprised to know that his nephew overheard the assassination plot. God is always working for our good and his glory.

4. Listen to the two completed sentence stems. Then discuss ways we can handle times when God feels far away. If this hasn't happened yet to you or your group members, it will! And yet, God is present whether we feel that presence or not. Create a list of practices (prayer in the morning while in the shower, Bible reading before homework, etc.) that can help your group members grow closer to God.

5. With a show of hands, find out which one was chosen the most and the least. Talk about the one chosen least as your first point of conversation. Point out that God uses people, his word, circumstances, and miracles to help during a crisis. In Paul's case he used Paul's nephew who overheard the assassins' conversation.

CLOSE

It's probable that Paul wondered how God was going to keep him alive long enough to get to Rome to preach the gospel. Yet, Paul walked by faith rather than by what he could see, touch, and feel. As soon as Paul heard his nephew's story, we can be fairly certain that Paul saw how God was working, but not before then. God is a God of surprises. God is a God who often waits until the last minute. God is a God who is there when we least expect him.

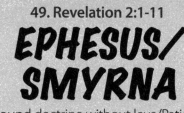

EPHESUS/ SMYRNA

Sound doctrine without love/Patient endurance of suffering and persecution

1. Here is a quiz to see how much you know about Christianity.

    a. List the Ten Commandments in order:

    b. List the six formal disciplines of systematic theology:

    c. Name the first seven ecumenical councils including dates and the primary issue addressed at each:

2. The church in Ephesus refused to compromise their beliefs. In spite of the Roman emperor worship that took place in Ephesus, they stayed true to what the Bible said. Sound doctrine (beliefs) is important and something that Jesus Christ liked about this church. What happens to your faith if—

    • you believe the resurrection never happened?

    • you don't believe in the Trinity?

    • you believe that the Ten Commandments are only nice suggestions?

3. As long as you hold the right doctrinal beliefs, you don't have to show love to others.

    ❏ I strongly agree
    ❏ I agree
    ❏ I'm not sure
    ❏ I disagree
    ❏ I strongly disagree

4. Smyrna was a church that patiently endured suffering and persecution. Jesus said they were rich even though they lived in poverty. Would you rather... (Circle one answer for each of the questions.)

    • Live in poverty with Jesus OR live in wealth without Jesus?

    • Suffer with Jesus OR live in comfort without Jesus?

    • Live with a strong faith and the threat of execution OR live without faith and grow old?

5. Jesus said nothing bad about the church in Smyrna. What would it be like to go to that kind of church? How do you think the church members in Smyrna pulled this off?

READ OUT LOUD

The church in Ephesus had all the right beliefs. They would not fall prey to false teachers, especially the Nicolaitans—a group of Christians in Ephesus who taught you could do anything you wanted because Jesus would forgive you. But they had forgotten how to love, and Jesus judged them for this.

Smyrna was a place where being a Christian was a death-defying act each and every day. If you were a member of the church in Smyrna, you lived in abject poverty—probably because committed Christians would have found it nearly impossible to make a living in a pagan culture that hated Christ-followers.

Read about both churches from Revelation 2:1-11.

ASK

What do you think the perfect church would be like?

DISCUSS, BY THE NUMBERS

1. This quiz is to show what happens when you can get the right answers but don't have love. The answers are found in bold after each letter. Ask for the answers, and then when your group members don't have them, say, "I'm disappointed that you couldn't get all the correct answers. What's wrong with you?" Point out that your attitude during this activity was like the church in Ephesus—they had all the right beliefs but had lost their love for God and neighbor.

a. List the Ten Commandments in order: **No other gods, no graven images, name in vain, Sabbath, honor your parents, don't murder, don't commit adultery, don't steal, don't lie, and don't covet.**

b. List the six formal disciplines of systematic theology: **Theology, Anthropology, Christology, Soteriology, Ecclesiology, Eschatology.**

c. Name the first seven ecumenical councils including dates and the primary issue addressed at each: **Nicea, 325—against Arianism; Constantinople, 381—finalize the creed; Ephesus 431—against Nestorianism; Chalcedon, 451—define the dual nature of Christ; Constantinople, 553—various heretics condemned; Constantinople, 680 (Council of Trullo)—affirmed Christ's human nature; Nicea, 787, 788—concerned the use of icon images.**

2. Use this time to discuss the answers to the three questions. Point out that incorrect doctrine leads you astray. Example: There are churches today that don't believe in the literal resurrection of Jesus.

3. Jesus was upset with the church in Ephesus for losing its love of God and neighbor. Read Matthew 22:35-40. Here Jesus said that all the Old Testament Law and Prophets were based on these two commandments. While they believed all the right doctrines, they forgot to love. Correct doctrine hangs on the love of God and neighbor. You must have both together. Ask, "How is it possible to believe the correct doctrine but forget love?" "How does our church sometimes do this?"

4. See where your group members stand with these three "OR" questions. These are a challenge because we want to live in comfort but also want a strong faith. Ask, "Is it possible to have a strong faith in the midst of the wealth, comfort, and religious liberty of the United States and Canada?" "Why or why not?"

5. In the midst of the suffering and persecution of the church in Smyrna, Jesus found nothing wrong with them. Ask, "Could the situation in Smyrna produce more committed Christians with the casual Christians dropping out?" "How close is your church to the church in Smyrna? What would Jesus say about your church?"

CLOSE

So what do these two churches have to say to our church today?

#1 The church in Ephesus reminds us that it's possible to be so preoccupied with our theology that we forget to love God and neighbor. We should never, ever let correct doctrine trump love, since all sound doctrine hangs on love. Both right beliefs and love are necessary for a healthy church to exist.

#2 The church in Smyrna lived in poverty and was persecuted, yet they remained faithful through it all. The message from Jesus—"Don't be afraid! Stick with me! You may have troubles now, but I will give you eternal life"— is the same for our church today.

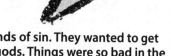

50. Revelation 2:12-29

PERGAMUM/ THYATIRA

Religious compromise never works/Good works—bad moral standards

1. The Bishop of the church in Pergamum, Antipas, was roasted to death for his faith. And still the church members continued to follow Jesus. What would it take for you to walk away from Jesus?

  • Watching our pastor roast to death for his faith would do it.
  • I don't think I would renounce my faith in Christ, but maybe I would.
  • I'm almost certain that nothing could force me to renounce my faith.
  • Nothing could force me to renounce my faith.

2. Pergamum, the church of religious compromise, tolerated all kinds of sin. They wanted to get along with the citizens of the community who worshiped false gods. Things were so bad in the city of Pergamum that Jesus said Satan lived there.

Which of the following do you think churches today tolerate when they shouldn't? Are these sins?

❏ Living together outside of marriage
❏ Neglect of the poor
❏ Littering
❏ Injustice to the homeless
❏ Divorce
❏ Flag burning

❏ Cheating in business
❏ Sex outside of marriage
❏ Racism
❏ Practicing homosexuality
❏ Listening to country music
❏ Supporting war

3. Do you think that each of these statements is T (true) or F (false)?

___ There will always be people around who try to get you to no longer care about sin.
___ Christians are supposed to be different than those who don't follow Jesus.
___ It's okay to keep sinning because of grace.
___ The church needs to be more tolerant for the world to accept her.
___ It's important for Christians not to seem weird in front of nonbelievers.
___ Christians can do what they want, whenever they want, as long as they don't get caught.
___ The church needs to throw out all the members who sin.
___ The church is too judgmental.
___ Jesus forgives us when we sin.
___ The church is to accept the sinner but not tolerate the sin.

4. The church in Thyatira enjoyed their good deeds. But it can be easy to do all kinds of good things—give to the poor, recycle, work at the food bank—and to use those good deeds to paper over our bad moral decisions. That was the problem with the church in Thyatira.

  • How do you think some Christians are able to do such good deeds but then make bad moral decisions like the church members in Thyatira?

  • How do you think some Christians are able to make good moral decisions and then not care to do any good deeds?

  • How might Christians make good moral decisions and do good deeds at the same time?

5. How can you protect yourself from false teaching?

READ OUT LOUD

Both the Pergamum church and the church at Thyatira had similar sins—they permitted false teachings, and some of their people followed them. The message given to the church at Pergamum was not to compromise theology with false teaching. The church at Thyatira's message was not to compromise morality with false teaching.

The false teachings in Pergamum were that of Balaam and the Nicolaitans—both advocating that people can sin all they want because of grace. The false teaching in Thyatira was the sin of Jezebel (a really bad person in the Old Testament)—convincing people to make bad moral choices contrary to the teachings of Jesus.

Read out loud the accounts of both churches from Revelation 2:12-29.

ASK

What do you like most about your church?

DISCUSS, BY THE NUMBERS

1. There were people who, because of persecution, walked away from Jesus. That's why Jesus commended the church in Pergamum. They still wanted to be Christians even though their faithful bishop Antipas was roasted to death. Talk about the things that get us to consider dumping Jesus. Ask, "What are the benefits of continuing to follow Jesus?"

2. It was said that Satan lived in Pergamum, probably because of the Emperor worship that took place there. This will be an interesting discussion, to see what your group members (and you) consider sinful, and not to be tolerated, versus what is okay. Remember that some of your group members' parents are divorced, living together, and the like. Handle this discussion with care.

3. See commentary in bold after each statement.
   - There will always be people around who try to get you to no longer care about sin. **True. Just like in the church in Pergamum.**
   - Christians are supposed to be different than those who don't follow Jesus. **Yes. To live the Christian life has always meant going counter to the culture.**
   - It's okay to keep sinning because of grace. **No, that's part of the reason Paul wrote the book of Romans—to correct this kind of thinking.**
   - The church needs to be more tolerant for the world to accept her. **The church needs to clearly teach the Bible and live every day for Jesus. The changing norms of the culture do not mean we change biblical teaching, if that teaching was orthodox in the first place. Using the Bible to support slavery would be an example of a wrong interpretation that needed correcting.**
   - It's important for Christians not to seem weird in front of nonbelievers. **This can lead to a great discussion about what it means for Christians to be different versus just plain weird.**
   - Christians can do what they want, whenever they want, as long as they don't get caught. **No way. Christians are freed from bondage to sin and freed to live for Christ. Freedom always has boundaries of protection.**
   - The church needs to throw out all the members who sin. **No, we must encourage each other to live for Christ.**
   - The church is too judgmental. **This one depends. We are called to bear each other's burdens—that means we help each other live holy lives.**
   - Jesus forgives us when we sin. **Yes, grace is always available.**
   - The church is to accept the sinner but not tolerate the sin. **Yes, and let's remember not to hate the sinner along with the sin.**

4. These three questions can be asked of the church today as well as of the church in Thyatira. See commentary in bold.
   - How do you think some Christians are able to do such good deeds but then make bad moral decisions like the church members in Thyatira? **Some churches boycott Chinese exports to support Tibet, adopt orphaned children, visit prisoners and shut-ins, feed the hungry, house the homeless, and then don't seem to care how members conduct their personal lives.**
   - How do you think some Christians are able to make good moral decisions and then not care to do any good deeds? **Some churches focus exclusively on morality but neglect the poor and hurting.**
   - How could Christians make good moral decisions and do good deeds at the same time? **What would a church look like that cared about both personal morality as well as social justice issues?**

5. You can answer the question, "How can you protect yourself from false teaching?" by turning to John 8:30-32. Here Jesus teaches us that we must keep obeying all that he taught, and in doing so we will know the truth and that truth will set us free.

CLOSE

So what can we learn from these two churches? I think the followers in the church in Thyatira who didn't follow the false teaching (verses 24-25) teach us much. Jesus tells them to hold on firmly to the teachings they've already received. Can we do the same?

Loving God includes obeying God. In order to obey God's Word, we must know God's word (the church at Pergamum).

How we act matters to God (the church at Thyatira).

1. Do you A (agree) or D (disagree) with the statements below?

____ There are people who say they are Christians but don't act like they are Christians.

____ If you're a member of a church, then you're a Christian.

____ Our actions reveal what our faith really looks like.

____ If you pray the sinner's prayer God will let you into heaven.

____ The church at Sardis was in trouble with Jesus for not doing the things they should do.

____ Our good works don't save us, but they do show what we believe.

2. The church in Sardis was filled with people who said they were Christians. But their actions said their faith was dead—that it wasn't really faith. Place an X on the line scale below, indicating how alive your faith really is.

```
  1      2      3      4      5      6      7      8      9      10
◆○○○○○○◆○○○○○◆○○○○○◆○○○○○◆○○○○○◆○○○○○◆
Alive &                                          Flat-lined
Energized
```

3. Imagine for a minute that you are a member of the church in Philadelphia. Jesus has promised that if you have real faith, a faith that lasts, then...

❏ you belong to God.
❏ you are a citizen of the New Jerusalem. You have eternal life.
❏ Jesus belongs to you and no one can take him away.

How can having these three things help you when you're struggling? When fear and anxiety are beating you up? When your self-image is causing you to doubt your worth?

4. The church in Laodicea was accused by Jesus of being spiritually poor (even though they were materially wealthy), spiritually blind (even though they had an excellent eye salve), and spiritually naked (even though they were known for their woolen garments). And because of their lukewarm taste, like the lukewarm water that flowed into the city, the church in Laodicea made Jesus want to puke.

When Jesus tastes our church, he wants to—

5. Jesus saw himself knocking at the door of the Laodicean church wanting back in. Place an X on the line scale below, indicating the evidence available that Jesus is inside your church.

```
  1      2      3      4      5      6      7      8      9      10
◆○○○○○◆○○○○○◆○○○○○◆○○○○○◆○○○○○◆○○○○○◆○○○○○◆
Abundance                                        Lack of
of evidence                                      evidence
```

Place an X on the line scale below, indicating the evidence available that Jesus is inside your life.

```
  1      2      3      4      5      6      7      8      9      10
◆○○○○○◆○○○○○◆○○○○○◆○○○○○◆○○○○○◆○○○○○◆○○○○○◆
Abundance                                        Lack of
of evidence                                      evidence
```

READ OUT LOUD

The church at Sardis was filled with people who had the church membership card but didn't possess a genuine faith. They could talk a good talk, but their actions defied what they said. Their faith was dead.

The church at Philadelphia was promised protection by Jesus for the intense persecution that came their way. The church was promised to be made a pillar, or permanent structure, in a permanent place called heaven (unlike the temple in Jerusalem, which had been destroyed twice). And finally, Jesus promised three inscriptions would be written upon them: The name of God, which means they belong to God; the name of the city of God, which means they are citizens of heaven; and the name of Jesus, which means they possess Jesus. Like the church in Smyrna, Philadelphia was not condemned by Jesus for doing anything wrong.

The church at Laodicea was known for three things: Their wealth, because they were at the crossroads of a major trade route; their wool that made fine clothing; and their eye salve that was thought to cure many eye problems. Laodicea was also known for the cold water that came from Colosse and the mineral-rich hot springs in the nearby city of Hierapolis. The cold water came to Laodicea via stone aqueducts and was still cold when it arrived. The hot water was a different story. By the time it flowed down to Laodicea, it had turned into a tepid, lukewarm, aluminum-tasting yuck. Take a big gulp of this water and you would puke.

ASK

What is your favorite memory of church?

DISCUSS, BY THE NUMBERS

1. See commentary in bold after each statement.
- There are people who say they're Christians but don't act like they're Christians. **Like the church at Sardis, they talk a good talk, but that's where it ends. Don't we all know Christians like this?**
- If you are a member of a church, then you are a Christian. **Church membership, just as in Sardis, is not a guarantee of anything. You don't get a pass to heaven because you are a church member.**
- Our actions reveal what our faith really looks like. **This is the message of the book of James. It is a "show me" faith. Your actions prove your faith.**
- If you pray the sinner's prayer, God will to let you into heaven. **No, it's just a prayer. The prayer does nothing. Jesus said to the church at Sardis that he was looking at the motivation behind the prayer. Many**

churches today emphasize the oral declaration of faith but have forgotten what the book of James teaches. Faith is the way we act every day. Like love, faith is more about what we do than what we say.
- The church at Sardis was in trouble with Jesus for not doing the things they should do. **Yes. Sardis didn't do anything. They were all talk.**
- Our good works don't save us, but they do show what we believe. **Agree. This, again, is the message of the book of James.**
2. Create a large line scale on flip chart paper. See if your group members bunch up in one or two areas. Ask, "Is our group more like or unlike the church in Sardis?"
3. The message to the church in Philadelphia was simple: Trust Jesus. He declared to Philadelphia, and to your church, that he has opened a door for us that no one can shut. The world can throw any silly roadblocks it wants at us. But it can never shut the door. We are God's possessions. We have been granted citizenship in his Holy city. And Jesus makes us righteous with a righteousness the world can never take away. We can live in this truth and fear nothing in the Lord.
4. Listen to the completed sentences of your group members. Talk about what your group can do to contribute to a spiritually healthy church that tastes good to Jesus.
5. Laodicea thought they were so cool because they were so rich, had such good wool to make clothes from, and made such good eye salve. Yet their faith had become meaningless—a combination of spiritual poverty, nakedness, and blindness. Their faith was no good to anyone, even to themselves. They relied so heavily on themselves they had no room for Jesus.

Talk about the evidence for Jesus' presence and work in your congregation and in the lives of your group members. Share some evidence of Jesus working in your life as an illustration of what it can look like for your group. Point out that Jesus is knocking—asking to be invited back into the church and into your life.

CLOSE

The churches from this passage experienced hardships and victories, just as our churches do today. Jesus' message to us is the same as it was to them—"follow me!" Let us strive to make our churches strong places where Jesus is trusted for everything.

1. Peter asked that we take an honest look at what Scripture teaches us. He wants to remind us of how we are to live. What do you think it means to take a serious look at Scripture?

  ❑ Memorize verses
  ❑ Rely on what someone else says the Bible says
  ❑ Read the Bible for ourselves
  ❑ Study the Bible with others
  ❑ Read books that explain the Bible
  ❑ Listen to TV preachers
  ❑ Believe what your parents believe

2. The "last days" is the period of time that began with Jesus' first coming. Since Jesus' death and resurrection, there have been people who have poked fun at a time of final judgment. They do this because…

  ❑ they are afraid of what it means if there really is a judgment.
  ❑ they don't want to be morally accountable.
  ❑ they don't believe in life after death—this is all there is.
  ❑ they live for today and don't worry about the future.
  ❑ they don't believe Jesus ever existed in the first place.
  ❑ they believe in reincarnation.
  ❑ Other: _____

3. Christ has not come back yet because…

  a) He has forgotten us.
  b) His plans have changed.
  c) He is busy doing something else in the universe.
  d) He wants to give more people a chance at salvation.
  e) He decided we aren't worth it.

4. Would you consider this to be absolutely true or false?

  We should try to figure out when Jesus will return.

5. Complete this sentence stem—

  I can make Jesus come back sooner by…

6. In the ancient world of New Testament times and earlier, it was a common belief by those who didn't follow the God of the Bible that the world would end by fire. Peter takes this picture of fire and connects it to Christ's second coming and the judgment. He foretells of a new heaven and a new earth. He calls the followers of Christ to "make every effort to be found spotless, blameless, and at peace with [God]" (2 Peter 3:14).

  ❑ I'm at peace with God because Christ is my Savior.
  ❑ I'm living a life that is pleasing to Christ because he is my Lord.
  ❑ I have no idea what you are talking about.

READ OUT LOUD

Peter, one of Christ's 12 disciples, wants us to honestly think about what the Old Testament prophets and the New Testament apostles teach us about living for Jesus. In particular, how we ought to live in light of the fact of Jesus' return. Jesus promised his followers he would return soon. It's been nearly 2,000 years, and still, no Jesus. Will he really come back? Will there really be a final judgment? Will the end come as he promised? Read about it in 2 Peter 3:1-18.

ASK

What is the longest you've been left home alone?

DISCUSS, BY THE NUMBERS

This *TalkSheet* discussion is not intended to look at the specific doctrines your church believes (such as the rapture). Rather, it is intended to help your group focus on the reality of the second coming of Christ.

1. Get a great discussion going about what it really means to take an honest look at what Scripture teaches. Ask this serious and tough question, "Why do you think Peter would want us to seriously reflect on biblical teaching before he talked about the second coming of Christ?

2. We have been in the "last days" ever since Jesus' first advent, or coming. During the early rise of the church there was a sect of Gnostics who didn't believe in the resurrection of the dead or any sort of final judgment. And skeptics like these early Gnostics have poked fun at a final judgment up through today. See which one of the reasons your group members believe is the biggest reason today.

3. We assume that if someone doesn't keep their promise after certain amount of time they forgot or changed plans, got too busy, or just lied. So it's easy to see why people would think that Christ would do the same. Yet, Peter is clear in today's story that God is on a different timetable than we are. A thousand days and one day are the same to him. He is the great "I AM" who was and is and is to come. And he is patiently waiting for more people to be saved before he sends Jesus back.

4. Scripture is clear. We won't know, so quit trying to figure out when—be it the day, the month, the year, or the century. Instead, focus on what you should be doing for Jesus *because* he will return some day.

5. Since God is patiently working out his purpose that more and more people will be saved, Peter may mean that we can help accomplish these purposes faster by cooperating with God in telling others the good news, praying that God's purposes will be achieved, and living a holy life. Another interpretation is that we don't dread the second coming but anxiously await and welcome it. Listen to the completed sentences and dialogue with your group members about the two possible meanings of this passage.

6. Peter tells us that "since everything will be destroyed in this way, what kind of people ought [we] to be?" (2 Peter 3:11) Use this item to talk about making Jesus our Savior and Lord in light of the future destruction of the world.

CLOSE

Maranatha, a term used by the early church that means "Our Lord is coming" or "Come Lord Jesus," is a word we can use today. Say the word, *Maranatha*, and remember that this word calls us to live each day in light of Jesus' promised return.

CAROLINA FOOTHILLS
SOUTH CAROLINA

90 Carolina Foothills Drive
Chesnee, SC 29323

864/461-2731

FACILITIES

ACCOMMODATIONS

- ■ Wheelchair Access
  Vacation Villas
- ■ Cabins (3)
  Rooms
- ■ Cable TV
  In-room Telephone
- ■ Trailers (1)
  - ● heated
  - ● w/bath
  - ● cooking
  Restaurant
  Lounge
  Snack Bar
- ■ Store

CAMPING

- ■ Tent Spaces (25)
- ■ R/V Spaces (13)
  - ● w/elec
  - ● w/water
  - ● w/sewer
- ■ Disposal Stations (2)
- ■ Showers
  - ● cold (1)
  - ● hot (8)
  Laundromat
- ■ Community Kitchen
- ■ Picnic Tables
- ■ Playground
- ■ Pets/Leash only

RECREATION

- ■ Swimming Pool (27' x 27')
  Lake
- ■ Whirlpool/Spa
  Sauna
- ■ Exercise Equipment
- ■ Hiking Trails
- ■ Volleyball
- ■ Shuffleboard
- ■ Horseshoes
- ■ Badminton
- ■ Meditation Gardens
- ■ Sunning Decks
  Fishing
- ■ Recreation Hall
- ■ Children's Activities
- ■ Teen Activities

■ ● denotes availability

INFORMATION

Club Personality
A cooperative club, governed by the membership, is always seeking others to join the family. Carolina Foothills is noted for its family atmosphere, teamwork, and teen activities.
E-mail: cfr@bigfoot.com

Description of Grounds
Carolina Foothills Resort's rolling beauty is just off nationally known Cherokee Foothills Scenic Highway, in the foothills of the Blue Ridge Mountains. Amenities include nature trails, a meditation garden, camping, and a mobile home park. The club serves members from the Carolinas, Tennessee and Georgia. Visitors are welcome.

Neighboring Sights and Attractions
Biltmore House, Blockbuster Pavilion, Charlotte Hornets and Panthers, Blue Ridge Parkway and Mountains, Kings Mountain, Cowpens National Battlefields, Carl Sandburg National Historic Site, and numerous colleges are within reasonable driving distance.

Honored Discounts
Discounts for AANR, TNS, ARVC, and Adventure Camping Network members.

Directions
Located in the center of the junctions of I-85, I-26, and I-40 just off South Carolina Highway 11 six miles west of Chesnee, South Carolina (by Cooley Brothers Peach Barns) on Highway 11, turn north on Mchaffey-Cooley Road. Go 1/4 mile and bear left on Rabbit-Moffett Road. Go 1 1/2 miles to Carolina Foothills Drive and turn left. If a stop sign is reached on Rabbit-Moffett Road turn around and go back 1/2 mile to Carolina Foothills Drive.

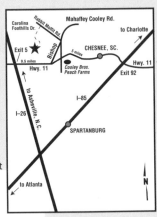

SOUTH CAROLINA

803/894-5159

CEDAR CREEK

P.O. Box 336
Pelion, SC 29123

 ACCOMMODATIONS & RECREATION

Club Personality
Located in the midlands of South Carolina, just 30 minutes west of Columbia, Cedar Creek is a friendly, family oriented club offering year-round facilities and events for all ages.
Fax: 803/894-5159
E-mail: CdrCreekSC@aol.com

Description of Grounds
Situated on 50 beautiful woodland acres, this club maintains its natural setting while offering modern and luxurious amenities including an air-conditioned clubhouse, a swimming pool, a nine-hole miniature golf course, and a children's playground. There's also a nature walk with boardwalk and sunning deck on a pristine creek.

Rental Rooms
RV Sites
Swimming Pool
Whirlpool Spa
Volleyball
Horseshoes
Deep Creek with Fishing
Recreation Hall
Playground
Nine-hole Miniature Golf Course

LOWCOUNTRY NATURIST ASSOC.

P.O. Box 40681
Charleston, SC 29423

SOUTH CAROLINA

803/552-0579

ACTIVITIES & RECREATION 🚗

Pool Parties
Theme Parties
Cookouts
Trips to Landed Clubs

General Information
A young nonlanded club with great ambitions. Members enjoy pool parties, theme parties and cookouts at members' homes, as well as get-togethers with other nonlanded groups and trips to landed clubs.

SUNAIR HEALTH PARK

SOUTH CAROLINA

RT 1, Box 126-L
Graniteville, SC 29829

803/663-6377

FACILITIES

ACCOMMODATIONS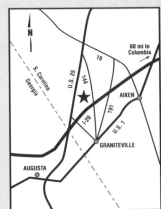

- ■ Wheelchair Access
  Vacation Villas
  Cabins
- ■ Rooms (8)
  Cable TV
  In-room Telephone
- ■ Trailers (2)
  - ● heated (1)
  - ● w/bath (2)
  - ● cooking (2)
  Restaurant
  Lounge
  Snack Bar
  Store

CAMPING

- ■ Tent Spaces
- ■ R/V Spaces
  - ● w/elec
  - ● w/water
    w/sewer
  Disposal Station
- ■ Showers
  - ● cold (2)
  - ● hot (2)
  Laundromat
- ■ Community Kitchen
- ■ Picnic Tables (5)
- ■ Playground
- ■ Small Pets/Leash only

RECREATION

  Swimming Pool
- ■ Lake (1 acre)
  Whirlpool/Spa
  Sauna
  Exercise Equipment
- ■ Tennis
- ■ Volleyball
- ■ Shuffleboard
- ■ Horseshoes
  Petanque
  Miniten
- ■ Badminton
  Fishing
- ■ Recreation Hall
  Children's Activities
  Teen Activities

■● denotes availability

INFORMATION

Club Personality
Sunair Health Park is open to membership only. Card-carrying AANR members are welcome for visits. Non-members must apply for membership.

Description of Grounds
Sunair Health Park is situated on 250 acres of wildlife habitat with a locked gate, private grounds, and a back-to-nature-with-necessary-comforts environment. Sunair does not operate as a traditional business enterprise. In an environment with no paid staff, the family feeling flourishes. Donations, only, are accepted.

Neighboring Sights and Attractions
Located in racehorse country with many historical sights nearby.

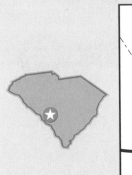

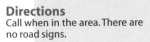

Directions
Call when in the area. There are no road signs.

SOUTH CAROLINA

803/869-1566

THE SUN STROKERS, SCN

P.O. Box 279
Edisto Island, SC 29438

ACTIVITIES & RECREATION

Group Massage
Workshops
Retreats

General Information
Sun Strokers are people who have successfully completed a Stroking Community network Esalen-style group massage workshop and who also subscribe to the AANR Code of Conduct. This special interest group promotes the benefits of safe, nurturing touch in a wholesome environment of trust and caring. Workshops, retreats, and relevant notes on body care are listed in a quarterly newsletter *In Touch* available through the above address for $7.50 per year.

TRAVELITES

P.O. Box 90836
Columbia, SC 29290

SOUTH CAROLINA

803/695-1937

ACTIVITIES & RECREATION

Theme Parties
Visits to Landed Clubs
Sailing Excursions
Community Projects
Camping
Hiking
Clothed Events

General Information
The Travelites, founded in 1987, has members ranging in age from infancy to over 65. The club hosts events at least twice a month all year long, as well as occasional impromptu get-togethers. Families, couples, and single men and women are invited to contact the club for great times and relaxation.
Fax: 803/695-2109
Web Site:
http://www.nudism.com/Travelites
E-mail: pret34B@prodigy.com or
Travelites@delphi.com

TENNESSEE

615/896-3553

ROCK HAVEN LODGE

462 Rock Haven Road
Murfreesboro, TN 37127

 ACCOMMODATIONS & RECREATION

Club Personality
Five-time winner of the AANR Visitor Appreciation Award. Located in the heart of Tennessee, just 40 miles southeast of Nashville—the perfect stopover when visiting Music City, USA. Open April through October.
Fax: 615/848-1812
Web Site: http://www.cybernude.com/rockhaven

Cabins
RV Sites with Full Hookups
Swimming Pool
Whirlpool/Sauna
Tennis, Volleyball
Shuffleboard
Petanque
Horseshoes
Recreation Hall/Darts
Snack Bar
Playground

Description of Grounds
Stroll country roads, relax poolside, or enjoy an energetic game of tennis. Whatever the choice, Rock Haven is a refreshing getaway from the stresses of everyday life.

Neighboring Sights and Attractions
Rock Haven Lodge is 40 miles from Opryland and the Grand Ole Opry, and is just minutes from the Stones River Battlefield Museum. The famous Oldtime Pottery Shop is just 20 minutes away. Shops, restaurants, churches, and motels are within 7 miles.

TIMBERLINE LODGE RESORT

RT 10, Box 153, Hwy. 70 North
Crossville, TN 38555

ACCOMMODATIONS & RECREATION

Chalets, RV and Lodge Rentals
RV Sites with Full Hookups
Swimming Pool, Lake
Whirlpool, Exercise Equipment
Volleyball
Horseshoes, Shuffleboard
Recreation Hall
Restaurant/Lounge
Snack Bar
Gift Shop
Playground
Fishing and Canoeing
Hiking Trails

TENNESSEE

800/TAN-NUDE

Club Personality
Southern hospitality at its finest. The park where friendliness abounds, quality in amenities and accommodations is beyond expectation, and visitors are always welcome.
Mailing address: P.O. Box 1173, Crossville TN 38555
Fax: 615/277-3222
Web Site: http://www.bhm.tis.net/~bottom/tmln.html

Description of Grounds
Surrounding Timberline's spacious Tree Top Inn, RV park and clubhouse are 200 acres of woodlands, mountain streams, and nature trails lined with centuries-old trees.

Neighboring Sights and Attractions
Short drive to Opryland, Dollywood, the Smokies, Big South Fork Recreation area, Tennessee's oldest winery, Fall Creek Falls, and Jack Daniels Distillery.

TEXAS

210/658-2283

BEXAR RECREATION SOCIETY

P.O. Box 13126
San Antonio, TX 78213

ACTIVITIES & RECREATION

General Information
Bexar Recreation Society is a travel club that is family oriented and welcomes singles. The group meets monthly—sometimes more often—at members' homes for pool parties, potlucks, and visits to other clubs. Bexar members are folks who enjoy getting together with like-minded friends. Some wintertime activities are also scheduled.

Swimming
Dining Out
Potlucks
Visit Other Clubs
Theme Parties

CENTRAL TEXAS NUDISTS

P.O. Box 150053
Austin, TX 78715

TEXAS

512/440-1987

ACTIVITIES & RECREATION

Pool Parties, Hot Tub Parties
Overnight Nude Campouts
Skinny Dipping at Hippie Hollow
Trips to:
Bolivar Beach, Matagorda Island,
and Nearby Nudist Resorts
Local Food Bank Volunteer
Work with City of Austin
Parks Department

General Information
Central Texas Nudists is a nonlanded family oriented club. Members include couples and singles, as well as families with children. The group is affiliated with AANR and The Naturist Society, and its members are more open than most in acknowledging their nude preferences.
E-mail: ctnudists@aol.com
Web Site:
http://rampages.onramp.net~codigest/ctn

Special Events
Host of Annual Nude Central
Texas Chili Cookoff

BLUEBONNET

TEXAS

C.R. 1180, Box 146
Alvord, TX 76225

940/627-2313

FACILITIES

ACCOMMODATIONS

- ■ Wheelchair Access
  Vacation Villas
  Cabins
  Rooms
  Cable TV
- ■ Trailers (1)
  - ● heated
  - ● w/bath
  - ● cooking
- ■ Airstream Trailers (3)
- ■ Restaurant
  Lounge
- ■ Snack Bar/Weekends
  (During High Season)

CAMPING

- ■ Tent Spaces
- ■ R/V Spaces (60)
  - ● w/elec (52)
  - ● w/water (52)
  - ● w/sewer (52)
- ■ Disposal Station
- ■ Showers
  - ● cold (2)
  - ● hot (5)
- ■ Community Kitchen
  (Off-season only)
- ■ Picnic Tables
- ■ Playground
- ■ Pets/Leash only

RECREATION

- ■ Swimming Pool
  Lake
- ■ Whirlpool/Spa
- ■ Sauna
  Exercise Equipment
- ■ Tennis
- ■ Volleyball
- ■ Shuffleboard
- ■ Horseshoes
- ■ Petanque
  Miniten
  Badminton
  Fishing
- ■ Recreation Hall
  Children's Activities
- ■ Cantina with Pool Table
  and Ping Pong

■ ● denotes availability

INFORMATION

Club Personality
Open year-round, Bluebonnet is a refuge from the pressures of urban life. Please call before visiting.

Description of Grounds
This 66$\frac{1}{2}$-acre park has rolling hills, oak trees, and meadows laced with nature walks and jogging trails. Amenities include a swimming pool, whirlpool, sauna, and clubhouse with stage and parquet dance floor.

Neighboring Sights and Attractions
Within 60 miles to the south are NASCAR racing, Six Flags and Wet 'n Wild. Just 35 miles south are Fort Worth and "Billy Bobs." Popular Log Cabin Restaurant is less than one mile from the club. Guests will find Bluebonnet surrounded by LBJ and Caddo National Grasslands. Shops, restaurants, motels and entertainment are all within 4 miles.

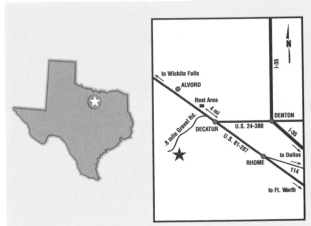

Directions
Take 287 north for approximately 4 miles north of Decatur. Take gravel road directly opposite roadside park or rest area for less than 1 mile. Please call before visiting.

TEXAS
409/297-1774

GULF COAST NUDIST YACHT CLUB
2705 Sixty-First St., Suite 212
Galveston, TX 77551

ACTIVITIES & RECREATION

General Information
A family oriented travel club with activities ranging from travel by boat to a raft-up, along with landlubber get-togethers at local clubs, the beach or members' homes for special events. You don't need a boat to join in the fun.

Boating Events in Galveston Bay
Dinner Get-togethers
Visits to Other Nudist Clubs

Special Events
Mardi Gras Celebration

HEALTHY HIDES OF HOUSTON
P.O. Box 58954
Houston, TX 77258

TEXAS
281/332-8298

ACTIVITIES & RECREATION

Hot Tubbing
Swimming
Dancing
Dining Out
Costume Parties
Body Painting
Potluck Suppers

General Information
Healthy Hides of Houston is a social, health-orientated, positive-thinking group of nudists who enjoy being together and having fun. Monthly activities include well-attended house parties with various themes, and social dinners designed to meet prospective new members. During the summer the group visits landed clubs. The newsletter *Healthy Hidelites* lists upcoming events. Write for more information.

LIVE OAK NUDIST RESORT

R#1 Box 916
Washington, TX 77880

TEXAS

409/878-2216

FACILITIES

ACCOMMODATIONS

- Wheelchair Access
- Vacation Villas
- ■ Cabins (6)
- Rooms
- Cable TV
- In-room Telephone
- ■ Trailers (2)
  - ● heated
  - ● w/bath
  - ● cooking
- ■ Restaurant (Weekends)
- Lounge
- Snack Bar
- ■ Store

CAMPING

- ■ Tent Spaces (30)
- ■ R/V Spaces (34)
  - ● w/elec (34)
  - ● w/water (34)
  - ● w/sewer (22)
- ■ Disposal Station
- ■ Showers
  - ● cold (1)
  - ● hot (15)
- ■ Laundromat
- Community Kitchen
- ■ Picnic Tables
- ■ Playground
- ■ Pets/Leash only

RECREATION

- ■ Swimming Pool (30' x 60')
- Lake
- ■ Whirlpool/Spa
- Sauna
- Exercise Equipment
- Tennis
- ■ Volleyball
- ■ Shuffleboard
- ■ Horseshoes
- Petanque
- Miniten
- Badminton
- Fishing
- ■ Recreation Hall
- Children's Activities
- Teen Activities

■ ● denotes availability

INFORMATION

Club Personality
Nestled in the heart of Texas, this family oriented club is open year-round and offers special rates to snowbirds.
Fax: 409/878-2788
Web Site: http://www.aanr.com/clubs/liveoak.html

Description of Grounds
Live Oak Ranch, with 25 acres of live oak trees and rolling green grass, offers the latest in accommodations, amenities and activities including a mobile home section, permanent RV section, and spacious lawns for lounging.

Neighboring Sights and Attractions
Within reasonable driving distance are Washington-on-the-Brazos, Historic Downtown Brenham, Blue Bell, Antique Rose Emporium and many other places of interest.

Honored Discounts
Discounts for AANR, INF, and TNS members. Special winter discounts available.

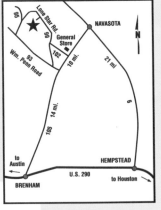

Directions
From Navasota, go west on Highway 105 approximately 10 miles. Turn right on FM 93, William Penn Road. Go 0.3 miles, turn right on FM 99, Lone Star Road. Go 3 miles to entrance. From Brenham, go east on Highway 105 approximately 14 miles. Turn left on FM 93. Go 0.3 miles, turn right on FM 99. Go 3 miles to entrance.

TEXAS

512/244-2543

HILL COUNTRY NUDISTS

P.O. Box 91802
Austin, TX 78709

ACTIVITIES & RECREATION

General Information

Hill Country Nudists is a family oriented travel club affiliated with AANR and The Naturist Society. The group meets at members' homes in the Greater Austin Area, and travels to nearby nudist resorts. Membership is open to families, couples and singles.
E-mail: hcn@aol.com
Web Site: http://www.sss.org/texnude/hcn.html

Adopt-A-Highway Cleanup
Hot Tub and Pool Parties
Floating on the Guadeloupe River
Trips to Local Nudist Resorts
Nude Swimming at a Public Park

LOST LEG CLUB

Route 2, Box 28P
Grapeland, TX 75844

TEXAS

409/544-7993

ACTIVITIES & RECREATION

Natural Lakes for Swimming and Fishing
Lake-front Beach
Horseshoes
Volleyball
Ping Pong
Playgrond
Golf Driving Range
Private Landing Strip

General Information

Lost Leg Lodge is a three-story lodge nestled in the middle of the 2,000-acre Lake Ranch, located just northeast of Crockett, Texas. Resembling an old-fashioned ranch house, the lodge sleeps 25 people, has a 40-by-40-foot activity area and two equipped kitchens for guests.

NATURAL HORISUN

11715 F.M. 442
Boling, TX 77420

TEXAS

409/657-3061

FACILITIES

ACCOMMODATIONS

- ■ Wheelchair Access
  Vacation Villas
  Cabins (2)
  Rooms
  Cable TV
  In-room Telephone
- ■ Trailers (1)
  - ● heated
  - ● w/bath
  - ● cooking
  Restaurant
  Lounge
  Snack Bar
  Store

CAMPING

- ■ Tent Spaces (60)
- ■ R/V Spaces (6)
  - ● w/elec (6)
  - ● w/water (6)
    w/sewer
- ■ Disposal Station
- ■ Showers
  - ● cold (6)
  - ● hot (6)
  Laundromat
  Community Kitchen
- ■ Picnic Tables (10)
- ■ Playground
- ■ Pets/Leash only

RECREATION

- ■ Swimming Pool (25' x 50')
  Lake
- ■ Whirlpool/Spa
  Sauna
  Exercise Equipment
  Tennis
- ■ Volleyball
- ■ Shuffleboard
- ■ Horseshoes
- ■ Recreation Hall
- ■ Dart Games
- ■ Pool Table
- ■ Ping Pong
  Fishing
- ■ Children's Activities
- ■ Teen Activities

■ ● denotes availability

INFORMATION

Club Personality
Natural Horisun is a family oriented nudist park providing a safe and pleasant environment for families and couples who enjoy the nudist lifestyle.
Toll Free: 800/NHI-NUDE
Mailing Address: P.O. Box 809, Needville, TX 77461
Web Site: http://www.phoenix.net/~mark/nhi.html or http://www.geocities.com/HotSprings/3749

Description of Grounds
Natural Horisun is nestled on a 33-acre pecan and oak orchard. Approximately one-half the property has been cleared to accommodate RVs and campers, with a clubhouse and swimming pool at the center of the complex. The remaining property retains its natural setting, with a nature trail for the adventurous.

Neighboring Sights and Attractions
Natural Horisun is 34 minutes from Houston, 75 miles from famous Galveston Island, and 60 miles from the Gulf Coast, with its swimming, boating, fishing, recreation and great seafood. 1$\frac{1}{2}$ hours from Johnson Space Center, Six Flags, Astro World and Astro Dome.

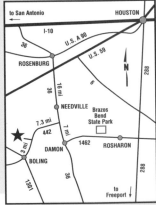

Directions
From Houston, take I-10 to Sealy. Take Highway 36 south to Needville. Go through Needville to FM442. Turn right and approximately seven and one-half miles to Natural Horisun sign on the right. Also from Houston, take Highway 59 to Rosenburg to Highway 36 south to Needville to FM 442. Turn right and go seven and one-half miles to sign.

RIVERSIDE RANCH
TEXAS

P.O. Box 14413
San Antonio, TX 78214

830/393-2387

FACILITIES

ACCOMMODATIONS

Wheelchair Access
Vacation Villas
Cabins (2)
■ Rooms (2)
■ Color TV
In-room Telephone
Trailers
    heated
    w/bath
    cooking
Restaurant
■ Lounge
■ Snack Bar
Store

CAMPING

■ Tent Spaces (10)
■ R/V Spaces (14)
  ● w/elec (10)
  ● w/water (10)
  ● w/sewer (4)
■ Disposal Station
■ Showers
  ● cold (4)
  ● hot (4)
Laundromat
Community Kitchen
■ Picnic Tables
■ Playground
■ Pets/Leash only

RECREATION

■ Swimming Pool (30' x 50')
Lake
■ Whirlpool/Spa
Sauna
■ Exercise Equipment
Tennis
■ Volleyball
■ Shuffleboard
■ Horseshoes
Petanque
Miniten
Badminton
Fishing
Recreation Hall
■ Children's Activities
Teen Activities

■
● denotes availability

INFORMATION

Club Personality
Riverside, a year-round, family oriented club serving the San Antonio area, offers visitors a tranquil, rustic setting replete with shade trees and songbirds.
Fax: 830/393-2589

Description of Grounds
Riverside Ranch is situated on 27 acres in a bend of the San Antonio River, 25 minutes southeast of San Antonio. Seventeen of those acres are river-front property dotted with trees, picnic tables and barbecue pits.

Neighboring Sights and Attractions
Shops, restaurants, churches, motels, entertainment and the airport are within 45 minutes of Riverside Ranch. Other attractions include The Alamo, Fiesta Texas, Sea World, and many museums, missions and parks.

Honored Discounts
20 percent discount on grounds fees for AANR, FCN, INF, and Naturist members, with proof of membership.

Directions
On I-37 south, 1 mile south of Loop 410, exit right onto Hwy 181. Go 7 miles to Loop 1604. Turn right, up the hill to stop sign, turn left, go 1.7 miles to the Old Corpus Christi Road exit. Turn right, down the hill to the stop sign. Turn right again, go 1.2 miles to Gillette Road. Turn right, and continue on Gillette until it dead-ends at the club gate.

SAHNOANS

P.O. Box 142233
Austin, TX 78714

TEXAS

512/273-2257

ACCOMMODATIONS & RECREATION

Rental Cabins and Rental Rooms
Camping with Water and Electric and
Pull-throughs with Full Hookups
Indoor and Outdoor Swimming Pools
Hot Tub
Covered Shuffleboard and Horseshoes
Lighted Tennis Court
2 Lighted Volleyball Courts
Covered Poolside Pavilion
Sunbathing Areas
Children's Playground

A family nudist club since 1958

Located in central Texas about 30 miles east of Austin. Approximately 112 heavily wooded acres. Open year-round. Restaurant open on weekends and holidays. Grocery store. Laundromat. Recreation room with fireplace, ping pong table, pool table, TV room, public phone, snacks, soft drinks, ice, showers, and kitchen privileges. Pets permitted on leash. Picnic areas. Alcoholic beverages at sanctioned events only. Photography not permitted.
Fax: 512/273-2025

TEXAS

713/784-0621

THE NATURAL TRAVELERS

3230 South Gessner #613
Houston, TX 77063

ACTIVITIES & RECREATION

General Information
The Natural Travelers, located in Houston, Texas, is an active travel club with activities scheduled year-round. Membership is open to families, couples and singles regardless of their geographic location. An informative and entertaining newsletter *Travelers Nude Tales* is included in club membership. Members are encouraged to submit ideas for activities and newsletter articles. Don't miss out on the fun.
Web Site: http://www.sss.org/texnude/naturaltrav.html

Day Trips to Landed Clubs
Weekend Trips to Out-of-State Resorts
Hiking, Rafting, and Biking Excursions
Nude Bus Trips to Various Locations
Private Beach/House Parties
Semimonthly Clothed Outings

Special Events
Formal Seated Dinner—The Nude Epicurean
Cap d'Agde, France
Travel to Nudist Conventions

SANDPIPERS HOLIDAY PARK

TEXAS

RT 7, Box 309
Edinburg, TX 78539

210/383-7589

FACILITIES

A C C O M M O D A T I O N S

Wheelchair Access
Vacation Villas
Cabins
Rooms
Cable TV
In-room Telephone
■ Trailers (9)
● heated
● w/bath
● cooking
■ Restaurant
Lounge
■ Snack Bar
■ Store

C A M P I N G

■ Tent Spaces (10)
■ R/V Spaces (100)
● w/elec
● w/water
● w/sewer
Disposal Station
■ Showers
● cold (7)
● hot (7)
■ Laundromat
■ Community Kitchen
■ Picnic Tables (80)
■ Playground
■ Pets/Leash only

R E C R E A T I O N

■ Swimming Pool (Olympic)
■ Kiddie Pool
Lake
■ Whirlpool/Spa
Sauna
■ Exercise Equipment
■ Tennis
■ Volleyball
■ Shuffleboard
■ Horseshoes
Petanque
Miniten
Badminton
Fishing
■ Recreation Hall
Children's Activities
Teen Activities

● ■ denotes availability

INFORMATION

Club Personality
Sandpipers Holiday Park boasts 300 days of sunshine a year. With warm winters, and summers cooled by Gulf breezes, this friendly, clothing-optional resort is an ideal spot for vacation or year-round living.

Description of Grounds
The club is nestled on 21 acres, with trees for shade and grass for sunning. Level sites and a shaded pavilion are among the amenities that make camping a relaxing treat.

Neighboring Sights and Attractions
Close to Mexico and South Padre Island Beaches.

Honored Discounts
Discounts for AANR and The Naturist Society members.

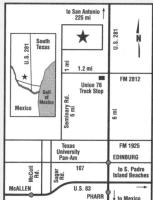

Directions
Coming from the north on U.S. Highway 281, turn west at the Union 76 truck stop 6 miles north of Edinburg. Go to the end of the road and turn north. The road dead-ends at the gate.

SUNNY PINES

P.O. Box 133
Wills Point, TX 75169

TEXAS

903/873-3311

FACILITIES

ACCOMMODATIONS

- Wheelchair Access
- Vacation Villas
- Cabins
- ■ Rooms (2)
- Cable TV
- In-room Telephone
- ■ Trailers (6)
  - ● heated (6)
  - ● w/bath (1)
  - cooking
- Restaurant
- Lounge
- ■ Snack Bar
- Store
- ■ Ice Machine

CAMPING

- ■ Tent Spaces
- ■ R/V Spaces (7)
  - ● w/elec (7)
  - ● w/water (7)
  - ● w/sewer (5)
- ■ Disposal Station
- ■ Showers
  - cold
  - ● hot (10)
- ■ Laundromat
- Community Kitchen
- ■ Picnic Tables
- Playground
- ■ Pets/Leash only

RECREATION

- ■ Swimming Pool (22' x 43')
- Lake
- ■ Whirlpool/Spa
- ■ Sauna
- Exercise Equipment
- Tennis
- ■ Volleyball
- ■ Shuffleboard
- ■ Horseshoes
- Petanque
- Miniten
- Badminton
- Fishing
- ■ Recreation Hall
- ■ Children's Activities
- Teen Activities

INFORMATION

Club Personality
Accommodations, amenities and activities for the perfect stress-free break from daily routine.

Description of Grounds
This 50-acre club has a large swimming pool, water and sand volleyball, horseshoe pits, pavilion, hot tub, sauna, tanning bed, permanent campsites, RV sites, tent camping, snack bar and a 2000-square foot clubhouse.

Neighboring Sights and Attractions
Close by are Canton's "First Monday Trades Day," Wild Willie's Mountain II, full-service restaurants, and a Super WalMart. Seventy miles from the Dallas/Fort Worth Airport.

Honored Discounts
Discounts for AANR and TNS members.

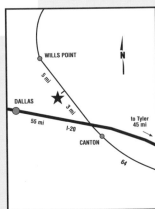

Directions
Sixty miles east of downtown Dallas on I-20. Exit Hwy 64 (Exit 523) go north 3.2 miles, main gate on left.

VISTA GRANDE RANCH

1149 FM 1885 Road
Weatherford, TX 76088

TEXAS

817/598-1312

FACILITIES

ACCOMMODATIONS

- Wheelchair Access
- ■ Vacation Villas (Bed and Bath)
- ■ Cabins (2)
- ■ Rooms (2)
- ■ Cable TV
- In-room Telephone
- ■ Trailers (4)
  - ● heated (4)
  - ● w/bath (2)
  - ● cooking (2)
- Restaurant
- Lounge
- ■ Snack Bar
- ■ Chapel, Meditation Gardens
- ■ Massage Cabin

CAMPING

- ■ Tent Spaces (100)
- ■ R/V Spaces (6)
  - ● w/elec (6)
  - ● w/water (6)
  - ● w/sewer (4)
- ■ Disposal Station
- ■ Showers
  - ● cold (2)
  - ● hot (10)
- Laundromat
- ■ Community Kitchen
- ■ Picnic Tables (25)
- ■ Playground
- ■ Pets/Leash only

RECREATION

- ■ Swimming Pool (18' x 33')
- Lake
- ■ Whirlpool/Spa (2)
- Sauna
- ■ Exercise Equipment
- Tennis
- ■ Volleyball
- ■ Shuffleboard
- ■ Horseshoes
- ■ Recreation Hall
- ■ Pool Table
- ■ Darts
- ■ Badminton
- Fishing
- ■ Children's Activities
- ■ Teen Activities

■ ● denotes availability

INFORMATION

Club Personality
A friendly park where everyone is welcome. A quiet, relaxing, scenic place to camp, swim or simply be. A fun place to enjoy Texas-style barbecue, dance, play volleyball, and meet new friends.
Web Site: http://www.flash.net/~jacklan/vistagr.html/
Alternate phone: 972/288-1104

Description of Grounds
Twenty-five beautiful acres of shaded, well-manicured camp grounds filled with trees, flowers, nature trails, birds and wildlife. The majestic view from the top of the ridge overlooking the Brazos River Valley is spectacular, as are the unforgettable sunsets.

Neighboring Sights and Attractions
A reasonable drive to Fort Worth stockyards, rodeos, Six Flags Wax Museum, botanical gardens, art museum, Health and Science Theater, Southfork Ranch, antique and craft shops, fine restaurants and hotels, historical homes and tumbleweed.

Honored Discounts
Discounts for AANR, INF, Naturist Society, veterans, military, college students, nature/travel clubs and any current card carrying naturist/nudist. Group and senior rates.

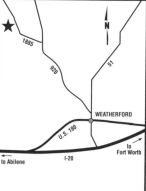

Directions
From Court House in middle of Weatherford: Go north on Hwy 51 one mile to traffic light Hwy 920 (4th Street). Turn left on 920 and go 5.6 miles to FM 1885. Turn left on 1885 and go 2.1 miles to Vista Grande (on left). Follow drive around to right and check in at farm house.

UTAH NATURISTS

P.O. Box 9058
Salt Lake City, UT 84109

UTAH

801/278-9740

ACTIVITIES & RECREATION

Camping and Hiking

Sunning and Swimming

Potluck Socials

Hot Tub and Theme Parties

Dances

General Information
This nonlanded club provides healthy naturist recreation for Utah nudists on public lands, at rented facilities and in members' homes. Year-round weekly activities are held outdoors in warm weather and indoors in cold weather. AANR singles and couples are welcomed as visitors. Call or write for information.

Special Events
Houseboat and Raft Trips
Weekend Auto Tours
Holiday Parties

Utah
Naturists

FOREST CITY LODGE

**468 Beebe Hill Road
Milton, VT 05468**

VERMONT

802/893-4513

FACILITIES

ACCOMMODATIONS

Wheelchair Access
Vacation Villas
■ Cabins (5)
Rooms
Cable TV
In-room Telephone
■ Trailers (7)
  ● heated (7)
  ● w/bath (2)
  ● cooking (7)
Restaurant
Lounge
Snack Bar
■ Store

CAMPING

■ Tent Spaces (20+)
■ R/V Spaces (17)
■ ● w/elec (17)
■ ● w/water (17)
  ● w/sewer (12)
■ Disposal Station
■ Showers
  ● cold (3)
  ● hot (3)
Laundromat
Community Kitchen
■ Picnic Tables (35)
■ Playground

RECREATION

Swimming Pool
■ Lake (³/₄ mile)
Whirlpool/Spa
Sauna
Exercise Equipment
Tennis
■ Volleyball
■ Shuffleboard
■ Horseshoes
■ Petanque (2)
Miniten
■ Badminton
■ Fishing
■ Recreation Hall
■ Children's Activities
Teen Activities
■ Adult Activities

● denotes availability

INFORMATION

Club Personality
Forest City Lodge, located in a beautiful, quiet, private setting, is a clothing-optional campground for families and couples.

Description of Grounds
The park's 50 acres provide spacious lawns and a private spring-fed lake over ³/₄ mile long with clear, 75 degree water and a sandy beach. Fishermen will find access for boat with electric motors only, or canoe to good fishing.

Neighboring Sights and Attractions
Within reasonable driving distance of Burlington and Stowe, Shelburne Farm and Museum, and the Botanical Gardens of Montreal and Plattsburgh.

Honored Discounts
Discounts on grounds fees for AANR members.

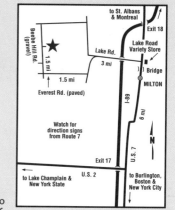

Directions
From the south and west, Interstate 87 to Exit 39, Cumberland Head Ferry to Grand Isle then Route 314 to U.S. 2 east to the junction of U.S. 7, north seven miles to the Arrowhead Variety Store. Go left 3 miles on Lake Road. 2 miles on Everest Road, go right one mile on Beebe Hill Road. From the north, take I-89 Exit 18 and from the south, take I-89 exit 17 to Lakeroad Variety Store and follow above directions.

BARE BUNS FAMILY NUDIST CLUB

VIRGINIA

P.O. Box 11
Oakton, VA 22124

703/281-7736

ACTIVITIES & RECREATION

Swim and Racquet Club Parties
Sailing on Chesapeake Bay
Canuding on the Potomac River

Special Events

Community Outreach Programs
Civic and Charitable Projects
Providing Guest Speakers

General Information

Bare Buns Family Nudist Club was founded by a small group of friends with a wealth of experience in organizing successful nudist events. Most members were attracted by the club's media and community outreach programs. Public relations efforts have resulted in an environment that is especially comfortable for singles, couples, and families with children.
Web Site: www.takeoffwithus.com
E-mail: BBFNC@erols.com

VIRGINIA

703/777-4611

NATIONAL CAPITAL SUN CLUB

P.O. Box 1894
Leesburg, VA 20177

ACTIVITIES & RECREATION

General Information

A nonlanded travel club serving the District of Columbia, Maryland, Virginia and nearby areas in Delaware, Pennsylvania and West Virginia. The club's goal is to offer a varied, all-season calendar of wholesome naturist sports and social activities for the entire family. For information, write or phone the club.
E-mail: tstokes@mnsinc.com
Web Site: http://www.mnsinc.com/tstokes/

Trips to Nearby Landed Clubs
Visits to Clothing-Optional Beaches
Volunteer Beach Cleanup
Preservation Projects

VIRGINIA

800/987-6833

WHITE TAIL PARK

39033 White Tail Drive
Ivor, VA 23866

Club Personality
With an ambience often described as "one big family,"
White Tail Park offers a wide variety of activities and
facilities for all ages.
Local Phone: 757/859-6123; Fax: 757/859-6724
E-mail: broche@gc.net ; Web Site: www.wtpnude.com

Description of Grounds
Situated on 45 beautiful acres, White Tail Park's numerous
recreational facilities are complemented by a year-round
schedule of planned activities. In addition to other
facilities and activities, children and teens enjoy their
own kid/teen center, planned activities and playground.

Neighboring Sights and Attractions
Within reasonable driving distance are Busch Gardens
Water Country USA, Virginia Beach, North Carolina's Outer
Banks, Colonial Williamsburg, Jamestown, Yorktown, Civil
and Revolutionary War battlefields, historic plantations,
and the Norfolk Naval Base.

ACCOMMODATIONS & RECREATION

Rental Cabins
RV Sites
Two Swimming Pools
Whirlpool/Spa, Sauna
Volleyball
Shuffleboard
Horseshoes
Recreation Hall
Snack Bar
Playground

FOREST MURMERS

P.O. Box 5113
Lacey, WA 98509

WASHINGTON

360/491-3171

ACTIVITIES & RECREATION

Trips to Beaches and Hot Springs
Tours of Local Tourist Sites
Visits to Landed Clubs
Barbecues, Hot Tubbing
and Socials

Special Events
Forest Murmurs Olympics
Canadian-American Gulf Island Cruise
Annual Chile Cookoff

General Information
In the mid-1950s, interested residents of the
Olympic peninsula joined together to plan,
build, develop and enjoy a comfortable setting
for nude social activities. First a landed club,
Forest Murmurs became a travel club in 1993.
The spirit of friendliness, enthusiasm,
cooperation and desire to further nude
recreation in the Northwest continues. Present
members live in an area ranging from Seattle to
Elma to Port Angeles to Olympia. The club
welcomes new members.
E-mail: QYNS85A@prodigy.com

WASHINGTON

425/392-NUDE

FRATERNITY SNOQUALMIE

P.O. Box 748
Issaquah, WA 98027

ACCOMMODATIONS & RECREATION

Club Personality
There are several fun events held annually at Fraternity Snoqualmie. The club hosts the Bare Buns Fun Run West in July, Nudestock in August and Forestiafest in September. The club is open to visitors from 11 a.m. to 4 p.m. on Saturdays, Sundays and holidays from May through September. Phone ahead to arrange visits at other times.

Description of Grounds
Nestled in the foothills of the cascades, Fraternity Snoqualmie is surrounded by a forest of stately evergreen trees. The club has 40 acres, of which about 15 are developed.

Honored Discounts
Discounts for AANR, TNS and INF members.

Rental Units, RV Sites
Solar Heated Swimming Pool
Whirlpool/Spa
Electric Sauna
Volleyball
Shuffleboard
Horseshoes
Recreation Hall/Pool Table
Store
Playground

FREE SPIRITS

WASHINGTON

15100 S.E. 38th Street, #101-759
Bellevue, WA 98006

ACTIVITIES & RECREATION

In-Home Meetings
Theme Dinners and Potlucks
Gard Games
Camping
Fishing
Swimming

General Information
Free Spirits is a tight-knit group of friends from the United States and Canada. Members enjoy get-togethers in one another's homes, as well as camping, fishing and clam digging excursions. Theme dinners place the spotlight on ethnic and regional cooking. Card games are a year-round favorite.

FACILITIES

ACCOMMODATIONS

- ■ Wheelchair Access
  Vacation Villas
  Cabins
- ■ Rooms (8)
  Cable TV
  In-room Telephone
  Trailers
  - heated
  - w/bath
  - cooking
- ■ Restaurant (Weekends)
  Lounge
  Snack Bar
  Store
- ■ Satellite TV

CAMPING

- ■ Tent Spaces (50 plus)
- ■ R/V Spaces (50)
  - ● w/elec (30)
  - ● w/water (30)
  - w/sewer
- ■ Disposal Station
- ■ Showers
  - cold
  - ● hot (7)
- ■ Laundromat
  Community Kitchen
- ■ Picnic Tables
- ■ Playground
- ■ Pets/Leash only

RECREATION

- ■ Swimming Pool (Heated)
  Lake
- ■ Whirlpool/Spa
- ■ Sauna
  Exercise Equipment
  Tennis
- ■ Volleyball
- ■ Shuffleboard
- ■ Horseshoes
  Petanque
  Miniten
- ■ Badminton
- ■ Fishing
- ■ Recreation Hall
- ■ Children's Activities
- ■ Teen Activities
- ■ Hiking Trails

■● denotes availability

INFORMATION

Club Personality
Open from May through October, Kaniksu Ranch is one of the oldest clubs in AANR. Natural tent-camping meadows and developed RV and trailer sites are nestled among tall trees, two ponds, and members' cabins.

Description of Grounds
Located in eastern Washington State at the edge of the Kaniksu National Forest, Kaniksu Ranch is composed of 240 acres of forest, meadowland, and two ponds. Eight rooms are available for guests. Campers will find more than 50 tent spaces and 50 RV sites with 30 water and electric hookups.

Neighboring Sights and Attractions
Shops, restaurants, motels, churches and entertainment are 20 miles from the grounds. Spokane, Washington is 35 miles south.

Directions
Go past Loon Lake on Highway 395 to Deer Lake North Road. Turn right. As you approach the lake, bear left at "Y" and go through developed camp area. At five miles, cross cattle guard onto gravel road. Locked gate at 6.7 miles. Go 1.75 miles past gate to Four Corners in the meadow. Turn left 1.25 miles to the Ranch. Large motor homes should contact the club for additional directions. Call for combination to locked gate.

LAKE ASSOCIATES

2174 Hwy. 9
Mt. Vernon, WA 98274

WASHINGTON

360/424-6833

FACILITIES

ACCOMMODATIONS

Wheelchair Access
Vacation Villas
Cabins
Rooms
Cable TV
In-room Telephone
Trailers
    heated
    w/bath
    cooking
Restaurant
Lounge
Snack Bar
Store

CAMPING

- Tent Spaces (15)
- R/V Spaces (50)
    - w/elec (11)
    - w/water (11)
    w/sewer
- Disposal Station
- Showers
    cold
    - hot (2)
    Laundromat
    Community Kitchen
- Picnic Tables (14)
- Playground
- Pets/Leash only

RECREATION

Swimming Pool
Lake
- Whirlpool/Spa
Sauna
Exercise Equipment
Tennis
- Volleyball
Shuffleboard
- Horseshoes
Petanque
Miniten
- Badminton
Fishing
Recreation Hall
Children's Activities
Teen Activities
- Hiking Trails

INFORMATION

Club Personality
A friendly, family oriented club where couples and singles are always welcome. Sponsor of Seattle Area Nude Swims.
Web Site: http://www.lmrr.com
E-mail: larc@sos.net

Description of Grounds
Just six and one-half miles from Interstate 5, the park is located on 65 wooded acres of rolling hills, with streams, waterfalls and walking trails.

Neighboring Sights and Attractions
Shopping, restaurants, movies, a hospital, scenic LaConner, and the San Juan Islands are nearby.

Honored Discounts
20 percent discount for AANR and TNS members.

Directions
Lake Associates Recreation Club is conveniently located mid-way between Seattle, Washington and Vancouver, British Columbia. Turn off I-5 at the Conway-Lake McMurray Exit (Exit 221), go east on State Road 534 for five miles to Highway 9 then go north (left turn) for 1.7 miles. The club is on the left side of the road.

FACILITIES

ACCOMMODATIONS

- ■ Wheelchair Access (limited)
  Vacation Villas
  Cabins
- ■ Rooms (5)
  Cable TV
  In-room Telephone
- ■ Trailers (4)
  - ● heated
    w/bath
  - ● cooking
- ■ Restaurant
  Lounge
  Snack Bar
- ■ Store

CAMPING

- ■ Tent Spaces (200)
- ■ R/V Spaces (24)
  - ● w/elec (24)
  - ● w/water (24)
    w/sewer
- ■ Disposal Station
- ■ Showers
    cold
  - ● hot (12)
- ■ Laundromat (2)
- ■ Community Kitchen
- ■ Picnic Tables (20)
- ■ Playground
- ■ Pets/Leash only

RECREATION

  Swimming Pool
- ■ Lake (7.5 acre)
- ■ Whirlpool/Spa
- ■ Sauna
  Exercise Equipment
- ■ Tennis
- ■ Volleyball
- ■ Shuffleboard
- ■ Horseshoes
  Petanque
  Miniten
- ■ Badminton
- ■ Fishing
- ■ Recreation Hall
- ■ Children's Activities
- ■ Teen Activities

■ ● denotes availability

INFORMATION

Club Personality
Open year-round, Lake Bronson Club is private and secure. It is one of the largest and most naturally beautiful family nudist parks in America, catering specifically to those who love nature and the great outdoors. Fax: 360/793-0841

Description of Grounds
This 320-acre park is surrounded by timberland and encompasses a seven-acre spring-fed lake, a spacious sunning beach and an 85-foot waterfall. There's swimming, boating, numerous hiking opportunities and winter fun. Within the rustic beauty of the forest are modern facilities, accommodations and activities suitable for everyone.

Neighboring Sights and Attractions
Shops, restaurants, motels, and churches are six miles from the park, while a wide variety of entertainment and attractions may be found in Everett, Bellevue, Seattle and Stevens Pass, all within a 50-mile radius.

Honored Discounts
Discounts for AANR, The Naturist Society, and INF members.

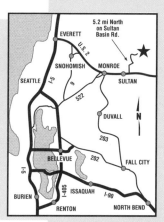

Directions
Please see map and call for entrance gate combination.

THE NATURALS CLUB OF SPOKANE

P.O. Box 75
Veradale, WA 99037

WASHINGTON

509/927-3860

ACTIVITIES & RECREATION

Nude Swims
Potlucks and Hot Tubbing
Visits to Landed Resorts
Visits to Nearby Hot Springs

Special Events
Thanksgiving Potluck and Party
Christmas Dinner and Gift Exchange
Attending Conventions and Board Meetings

General Information
The Naturals believe that recreation through exercise, relaxation and socialization is enhanced by the nudist experience. The club hosts nude swims at a local pool from October through April, and enjoys potlucks at members' homes on most major holidays.

WASHINGTON

P.O. Box 936
Snohomish, WA 98291

TANFASTICS

General Information
Tanfastics members visit landed clubs and join in the activities. Monthly meetings and cookouts are among the club's regularly scheduled events. Write for more information.

ACTIVITIES & RECREATION

Houseboat Trips
Seafood and Clambake Outing
Hot Tubbing
Visiting Landed Clubs

Special Events
Annual Birthday Party
Holiday Parties

AVALON

P.O. Box 369
Paw Paw, WV 25434

WEST VIRGINIA

304/947-5600

FACILITIES

ACCOMMODATIONS

Wheelchair Access
■ Vacation Villas (1)
Cabins
■ Rooms (18)
Cable TV
In-room Telephone
Trailers
   heated
   w/bath
   cooking
■ Restaurant
■ Lounge
Snack Bar
■ Store
■ Picnic Pavilion

CAMPING

■ Tent Spaces (20)
■ R/V Spaces (43)
  ● w/elec (43)
  ● w/water (40)
  ● w/sewer (5)
■ Disposal Station
■ Showers
  cold
  ● hot (12)
Laundromat
Community Kitchen
■ Picnic Tables (18)
■ Playground
■ Pets/Leash only

RECREATION

■ Swimming Pool (14 sq. ft.)
Lake
■ Whirlpool/Spa
Sauna
■ Exercise Equipment
■ Tennis
■ Volleyball
Shuffleboard
■ Horseshoes
Petanque
Miniten
■ Badminton
■ Fishing
■ Recreation Hall
■ Field House
■ Screen House

■ ● denotes availability

INFORMATION

Club Personality

Avalon's new, resort-like nudist park offers excellent dining, a friendly gathering lounge, and Saturday evening dances. The full-season schedule provides a variety of activities. Specializing in serenity, relaxation, and friendly atmosphere, Avalon—the natural getaway—is open year-round.
Phone: 304/947-5600
Fax: 304/947-5579
Web Site: http://www.avalon-nude.com

Description of Grounds

200-plus acres nestled in a mountain valley offering modern, clean, comfortable lodge rooms with private baths, full-service restaurant and lounge; heated swimming pool, spa; fieldhouse with indoor volleyball, ping pong, basketball, exercise equipment; two sand volleyball courts; fishing pond; horseshoes; picnic pavilion; playground; hiking trails; chapel; chalet; library; camping; and tennis courts under construction.

Neighboring Sights and Attractions

Washington, DC, is two hours away. Midway between Winchester, Virginia and Cumberland, Maryland, Avalon is close to many historic and recreational attractions. Shopping outlets and antique stores abound. An Avalon booklet is available detailing points of interest within 100 miles.

Honored Discounts

20 percent for AANR members.

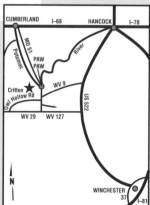

Directions

From DC, follow I-66 west to 17 north to Winchester onto I-81 north to exit 317 to 37 for 1 mile to 522 north for 12 miles to left onto 127 for 11 miles to right onto 29 for 6¼ miles to left onto 29/1 (Critton Owl Hollow Road) for 2 miles to Avalon entrance on right. From I-68 at Cumberland, MD, follow 51 south to Paw Paw where 51 becomes 9 in WV. Go another 4 miles on 9 straight onto 29 south for 1½ miles to right onto Critton Owl Hollow Road for 2 miles to Avalon entrance on right.

164

BADGER NATURISTS

P.O. Box 55346
Madison, WI 53705

WISCONSIN

608/798-1954

ACTIVITIES & RECREATION

Adopt-A-Highway
Beach Cleanups
Christmas in July
Holiday Lights by Limousine
Mardi Gras Party
Clothing Drives
Nude Cruises
Halloween & Valentines Festivities
Christmas Cookie Baking in the Buff

General Information

The Badger Naturists has been celebrating the nude lifestyle for almost two decades. In the beginning, families met at the beach seasonally, and immediately friendships grew to include get-togethers during all four seasons. The club rents appropriate facilities—health clubs, restaurants, motels and bowling alleys. The club currently mails out limited information, but the friendly folks at the phone number above will tell you the best way to get introduced to their lifestyle, and the summertime activities at the river. First time guests are sponsored by members.

WISCONSIN

414/538-4300

THE TRAVELIERS

P.O. Box 085664
Racine, WI 53408

General Information

The Traveliers meet for nudist activities at members' homes, various campgrounds, a private lake, and other recreation facilities. The group's objective is to visit and socialize while enjoying the nudist lifestyle. Members try to plan at least one social activity a month throughout the year.
Alternate phone: 414/878-1662

ACTIVITIES & RECREATION

Private Pool Parties
Nude Cruises
Dinner Dances
Lake Campouts
Visits to Campgrounds
Winter Sports Activities

VALLEY VIEW RECREATION CLUB

3080 E. Rockdale Road
Cambridge, WI 53523

WISCONSIN

608/423-3060

FACILITIES

ACCOMMODATIONS

- ■ Wheelchair Access
- Vacation Villas
- Cabins
- ■ Rooms (2)
- Cable TV
- In-room Telephone
- ■ Trailers (1)
  - heated
  - w/bath
  - cooking
- Restaurant
- ■ Lounge
- ■ Snack Bar
- ■ Store

CAMPING

- ■ Tent Spaces (48)
- ■ R/V Spaces (30)
  - ● w/elec (24)
  - ● w/water (24)
  - w/sewer
- ■ Disposal Station
- ■ Showers
  - cold
  - ● hot (4)
- Laundromat
- ■ Community Kitchen
- ■ Picnic Tables (12)
- ■ Playground
- ■ Pets/Leash only

RECREATION

- ■ Swimming Pool (40' x 22')
- Lake
- Whirlpool/Spa
- Sauna
- ■ Exercise Equipment
- Tennis
- ■ Volleyball
- ■ Water Volleyball
- ■ Horseshoes
- ■ Petanque
- Miniten
- Badminton
- Fishing
- ■ Recreation Hall
- Children's Activities
- Teen Activities

■ ● denotes availability

INFORMATION

Club Personality
Valley View, a relaxed and informal nudist facility in a rural Wisconsin setting, is known for its friendly members, frequent special events and excellent cooks. Among other activities, the club hosts an annual Nude Car Show. Mailing address: P.O. Box 605, Cambridge, WI 53523 E-mail: vvrc@juno.com

Description of Grounds
At Valley View, over 55 acres of tree-lined lawns and sun-drenched fields surround the heated pool, volleyball court and horseshoe area. The clubhouse, complete with a fireplace for cool nights, provides a perfect setting for community breakfasts, dinners, dances, and parties.

Neighboring Sights and Attractions
Nearby attractions include Wisconsin Dells, Madison, and Circus World Museum, as well as arts and crafts in downtown Cambridge.

Honored Discounts
Discounts for AANR and TNS members.

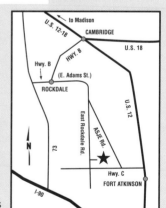

Directions
Valley View is located 25 miles east of Madison, near the town of Cambridge. At the intersection of Highway 12 and County Highway B in midtown Cambridge, turn south on County B and proceed 3 miles to the village of Rockdale. In Rockdale, turn left on East Adams Street which becomes East Rockdale Road. A few miles from town the road makes a sweeping curve to the right and passes Asje Road. Valley View entrance is the first driveway on the left at the top of the hill and the end of the woods (Fire #3080). Pass through the open road gate and continue to the main gate at the top of the rise. Register at the office.

WYOTANS

WYOMING

P.O. Box 3028, #5266
Gillette, WY 82717

ACTIVITIES & RECREATION

Camping

Hiking

Meetings

Sightseeing

Hot Tubbing at
Members' Homes

General Information

Wyotans, a family oriented club sanctioned by AANR in 1990, has members who travel long distances to meet once a month. Though small in number the club is big at heart, and members take turns hosting group events at which guests are always welcome. A monthly newsletter lists upcoming activities. Write for more information.

Special Events

Annual Balloon Rally
Annual Motorcycle Rally
Holiday Specials

Wyotans

HELIOS NUDIST ASSOCIATION

P.O. Box 8, Site 1, RR2
Tofield, AB T0B 4J0

ALBERTA

403/662-2886

FACILITIES

ACCOMMODATIONS

Wheelchair Access
Vacation Villas
Cabins
Rooms
Cable TV
In-room Telephone
Trailers
  heated
  w/bath
  cooking
Restaurant
Lounge
Snack Bar
Store

CAMPING

- Tent Spaces
- R/V Spaces
  - w/elec (5)
    w/water
    w/sewer
  Disposal Station
- Showers
    cold
  - hot (5)
  Laundromat
  Community Kitchen
- Picnic Tables
- Playground
- Pets/Leash only

RECREATION

- Swimming Pool (25 x 12 yds.)
  Lake
- Whirlpool/Spa
- Sauna
  Exercise Equipment
  Tennis
- Volleyball
  Shuffleboard
- Horseshoes
  Petanque
  Miniten
- Badminton
  Fishing
  Recreation Hall
- Children's Activities
- Teen Activities

■ ● denotes availability

INFORMATION

Club Personality
Open Good Friday to Thanksgiving Monday, this member-owned, family oriented camp offers summer and winter activities on the grounds and in Edmonton. Cellular Phone 991-2666 after 7 p.m. and weekends

Description of Grounds
Helios Nudist Association, the most northern AANR park, is situated on 22 acres of rolling, wooded land. Its rustic setting provides 50 campsites for members and ample room for guests. There are bonfires and dances on weekends, and picnic tables are available to visitors.

Neighboring Sights and Attractions
Nearby are the City of Edmonton, West Edmonton Mall, Beaverhills Wildlife Sanctuary, restaurants, motels, shops and churches.

Honored Discounts
Day Fees for AANR members: $20 for couples, $15 for singles.

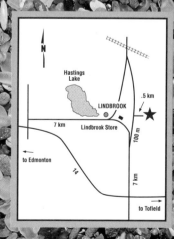

Directions
Approximately 40 kilometers east from Edmonton to the Lindbrook sign on Highway 14, turn left, then a quick right. Go seven kilometers to the Lindbrook store. Turn left, go 100 yards, turn right, then go one-half kilometer to the Helios campground.

SUNNY CHINOOKS ASSOCIATION

Box 33030, 3919 Richmond Road, S.W.
Calgary, AB T3E 7E2

ALBERTA

403/274-8166

FACILITIES

ACCOMMODATIONS

- Wheelchair Access
- Vacation Villas
- Cabins
- Rooms
- Cable TV
- In-room Telephone
- Trailers
  - heated
  - w/bath
  - cooking
- Restaurant
- Lounge
- Snack Bar
- Store
- Other

CAMPING

- ■ Tent Spaces (4 plus)
- ■ R/V Spaces (25)
  - ● w/elec (25)
  - ● w/water (25)
  - w/sewer
- Disposal Station
- ■ Showers
  - cold
  - ● hot (1)
- ■ Laundromat
- Community Kitchen
- ■ Picnic Tables (20)
- ■ Playground
- ■ Pets/Leash only

RECREATION

- Swimming Pool
- Lake
- ■ Whirlpool/Spa
- Sauna
- Exercise Equipment
- Tennis
- ■ Volleyball
- Shuffleboard
- ■ Horseshoes
- Petanque
- Miniten
- Badminton
- ■ Fishing
- ■ Clubhouse
- Children's Activities
- Teen Activities

INFORMATION

Club Personality
A small community of friendly, fun-loving campers composed of families, couples, and a few singles. As a family nudist club, Sunny Chinooks Association plans many special events from May through September.
Web Site: http://www.cadvision.com/bilko/sca/sca.html

Description of Grounds
Sunny Chinooks is located on 18 acres of land along the James River. It is 140 kilometers (90 miles) N.W. of Calgary. The grounds are rustic but well-serviced. Twenty-five developed sites, two tenting areas, and groves of poplar and pine trees are bordered on one side by the meandering river — which is accessible for fishing.

Neighboring Sights and Attractions
A town with a hospital and numerous shops, banks, and motels is just 15 minutes from Sunny Chinooks Association. The club is located in the foothills of the Rockies, near many sites for fishing, horseback riding and hiking. Banff is one and one-half hours from the camp.

Honored Discounts
Discounts for AANR members.

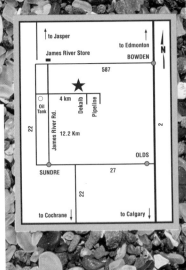

Directions
From Calgary head west to Cochrane on Highway 1A. Head north on Highway 22 to Highway 27 then west into Sundre. Turn right at the four-way stop and head approximately 12.2 kilometers. Turn right just prior to the James River bridge and head east for 4 kilometers until you see the SCA sign at the entrance. The gate is locked, so please call prior to arrival.

BRITISH COLUMBIA

250/383-5814

ARBUTUS PARK

P.O. Box 6074, Stn. C
Victoria, BC V8P 5L4

ACTIVITIES & RECREATION

General Information

Arbutus Park is a travel club based on beautiful Vancouver Island in Victoria, BC—close to Vancouver, BC and Seattle, Washington. The island is well-known for fishing, golfing, camping and boating. Arbutus Park has access during the summer to a secluded, private acreage. Call or write for more information.
Fax: 250/383-5814 (phone first)
E-mail: ub509@freenet.victoria.bc.ca

Monthly Potluck Dinners at Members' Homes
June, July, August "Picnic Site" Potlucks
Monthly Activities at Members' Homes
Travel to Other Landed and Nonlanded Clubs

OKANAGAN SHUSWAP

BRITISH COLUMBIA

Box 5149, Stn. A
Kelowna, BC V1Y 7V8

ACTIVITIES & RECREATION

Camping
Swim/Sauna/Hot Tub Evenings
Travel
House Parties

Special Events
Halloween Party
Houseboat Cruises on Shuswap Lake

General Information

Okanagan Shuswap Nudist Society (OSNS) rents public facilities in Kelowna and Kamloops for monthly swim/sauna/hot tub evenings during the winter months. The members are developing a rustic group camp located 20 minutes from Vernon. It began operating in the summer of 1996, and is expected to be AANR approved the summer of 1997. Inquire about the special park ownership program. OSNS distributes the Western Canadian Skinnydipping Guide. Write to the club for more information.

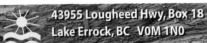

SUNNY TRAILS CLUB

BRITISH COLUMBIA

43955 Lougheed Hwy, Box 18
Lake Errock, BC V0M 1N0

604/826-3419

FACILITIES

INFORMATION

ACCOMMODATIONS

- ■ Wheelchair Access (Partial)
- Vacation Villas
- Cabins
- ■ Rooms (3)
- Cable TV
- In-room Telephone
- Trailers
  - heated
  - w/bath
  - cooking
- ■ Restaurant
- Lounge
- Snack Bar
- Store
- ■ Smoking/Nonsmoking Areas

CAMPING

- ■ Tent Spaces (50)
- ■ R/V Spaces (36)
  - ● w/elec
  - ● w/water
  - ● w/sewer
- ■ Disposal Station
- ■ Showers
  - cold
  - hot (9)
- ■ Laundromat
- Community Kitchen
- ■ Picnic Tables (20)
- ■ Playground
- ■ Pets/Leash only

RECREATION

- ■ Swimming Pool
- Lake
- ■ Whirlpool/Spa
- ■ Sauna
- Exercise Equipment
- Tennis
- ■ Volleyball
- ■ Shuffleboard
- ■ Horseshoes
- ■ Hiking Trails
- ■ Croquet/Bocce
- ■ Badminton
- ■ Table Tennis
- ■ Recreation Hall
- ■ Children's Activities
- ■ Teen Activities
- ■ Pool Table

■ ● denotes availability

Club Personality
Open 24 hours a day, all year, Sunny Trails nudist club cultivates an informal, relaxed atmosphere. Members come from all walks of life, with ages ranging from 1 to 80-plus.

Description of Grounds
The mild climate and spectacular view from anywhere on the grounds makes Sunny Trails a good place to visit any time of the year. The winterized RV sites and clubhouse are set among old growth trees and open lawn areas. Within commuting distance of the Mission/Fraser Valley. The best of country living minutes from the city.

Neighboring Sights and Attractions
Sunny Trails Club is in the center of one of BC's best known recreation areas. A ski resort, golfing, fishing and much more are 20 minutes away. Close to US/Canadian border crossing and Abbotsford AirpoRT Banks, stores and other conveniences are close by.

Honored Discounts
Discounts to members of all nudist/naturist clubs. Regular AANR discount to AANR associate members.

Directions
Take Highway #7 (Lougheed Highway) 18 miles or 28 kilometers east of Mission and 1 mile past the Lake Errock store.

171

BRITISH COLUMBIA

604/589-6848

VANCOUVER SUNBATHING ASSOC.

10185-164th Street
Surrey, BC V4N 2K4

General Information
Located in a beautiful and tranquil setting, Vancouver Sunbathing Association is a virtual Garden of Eden. Often referred to as "Elysium North," Vancouver Sunbathing Association has tenting and room for 2 or 3 RV's on its one-acre city retreat.
Fax: 604/589-1398
E-mail: GSKillen@Uniserve.com
Web Site: http://www.cadvision.com/bilko/vansun/vsa.html

ACTIVITIES & RECREATION

Hot Tubbing
Potluck Dinners
Volleyball

VAN TAN CLUB

P.O. Box 423, Stn. A
Vancouver, BC V6C 2N2

BRITISH COLUMBIA

604/980-2400

ACTIVITIES & RECREATION

Winter Social Activities
Weekend Events
Barbecues

General Information
The Van Tan Club is a rustic, relaxing, private park located on Frome Mountain, and only a 30 minute drive from downtown Vancouver. The club has a solar-heated swimming pool, sauna, sports facilities and spacious lawns for sunning. Space is available for RVs and tents.
E-mail: paula3@uniserve.com

CROCUS GROVE SUN CLUB — MANITOBA

Box 3173, R.R. 3
Beausejour, MB R0E 0C0

204/265-3469

FACILITIES

ACCOMMODATIONS

Wheelchair Access
Vacation Villas
■ Cabins (1)
Rooms
Cable TV
In-room Telephone
■ Trailers (1)
  ● heated
    w/bath
  ● cooking
Restaurant
Lounge
Snack Bar
Store

CAMPING

■ Tent Spaces (20)
■ R/V Spaces (10)
  ● w/elec (10)
  ● w/water (10)
    w/sewer
■ Disposal Station
■ Showers
  ● cold (4)
  ● hot (3)
Laundromat
■ Community Kitchen
■ Picnic Tables (15)
■ Playground
■ Pets/Leash only

RECREATION

■ Swimming Pool (45' x 20')
Lake
■ Whirlpool/Spa
■ Sauna
Exercise Equipment
Tennis
■ Volleyball
■ Shuffleboard
■ Horseshoes
Petanque
Miniten
■ Badminton
Fishing
■ Recreation Hall
■ Children's Activities
■ TV
■ Screened Gazebo

■● denotes availability

INFORMATION

Club Personality
A clothing-optional, family-atmosphere club, with weekend social events and sports, as well as an Annual Chili Cookoff in September. The club is open from May to September, with special events listed in *The Bulletin*.
E-mail: lprucyk@mb.sympatico.ca

Description of Grounds
Crocus Grove Sun Club, situated on 60 acres of woodland dotted with sandy open areas, provides serviced lots for camping and tenting, and a limited number of rental facilities. Among many other facilities are a swimming pool, a children's playground, and a recreation hall for indoor games.

Neighboring Sights and Attractions
Within reasonable driving distance are historic Stone-Walled Fort Garry, Grand Beach Provincial Park, world class catfish fishing in the Red River, parks, museums, and a zoo. There is a golf course within one mile of the club.

Honored Discounts
Standard AANR 20 percent discount for members of recognized nudist associations.

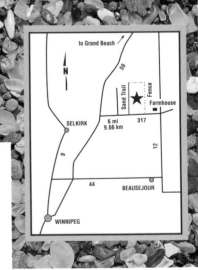

Directions
Proceed north on Highway 59 to Provincial Road 317, east 6 miles to the gate. Turn north at the sign "Private Road No Exit."

MUSQUA MEADOWS

Hwy. 201
Menisino, Manitoba

MANITOBA

204/255-5081

FACILITIES

ACCOMMODATIONS

Wheelchair Access
Vacation Villas
Cabins
Rooms
Cable TV
In-room Telephone
■ Trailers (1)
  ● heated
    w/bath
  ● cooking
Restaurant
Lounge
Snack Bar
Store

CAMPING

■ Tent Spaces
■ R/V Spaces (25)
  ● w/elec
  ● w/water
    w/sewer
■ Disposal Station
■ Showers
  ● solar (1)
  ● hot (2)
Laundromat
Community Kitchen
■ Picnic Tables (10)
Playground
■ Pets/Leash only

RECREATION

■ Above Ground Pool (18' x 33')
Lake
Whirlpool/Spa
Sauna
Tennis
■ Volleyball
Shuffleboard
■ Horseshoes
Petanque
Miniten
■ Badminton
■ Fishing
■ Recreation Hall
■ Children's Activities
■ Cross Country Skiing
■ Snowshoeing

■ ● denotes availability

INFORMATION

Club Personality
Cooperatively run, clothing-optional, family oriented club with weekend activities. Open April through October with events listed in *The Bulletin*. Winter visits, daytime only.
Mailing Address: 149 Bluewater Crescent
Winnipeg, MB R2J 2X6
E-mail: lloydec@solutions.net

Description of Grounds
Located in southeast Manitoba on 320 acres of mixed pine forest and meadows. Northern 160 acres have many trails and paths. The club offers 25 serviced sites for camping and tenting, as well as numerous unserviced areas. There is a large recreation hall with a sunken dance floor.

Neighboring Sights and Attractions
Within 45 minute drive to Warroad, Minnesota, for golf or casino. Sunset dinner flights available to various resorts. Paved airstrip 10 miles away at Piney, Manitoba.

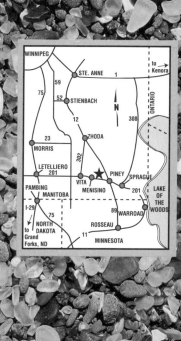

Directions
Call for directions.

PONDEROSA NATURE RESORT

Box 501, R.R. 3
Puslinch, ON N0B 2J0

ONTARIO

905/659-3410

FACILITIES

ACCOMMODATIONS

Wheelchair Access
Vacation Villas
Cabins
■ Rooms (3)
Cable TV
In-room Telephone
■ Trailers (3)
● heated (3)
w/bath
● cooking (3)
■ Restaurant
■ Lounge
■ Snack Bar
Store

CAMPING

■ Tent Spaces (30)
■ R/V Spaces (15)
● w/elec (6)
● w/water (4)
● w/sewer (5)
■ Disposal Station
■ Showers
● cold (2)
● hot (7)
Laundromat
Community Kitchen
■ Picnic Tables (50)
■ Playground
■ Pets/Leash only

RECREATION

■ Swimming Pool (Olympic)
■ Indoor Pool
■ Whirlpool/Spa
■ Sauna
■ Outdoor Hot Tub
■ Tennis (2)
■ Volleyball (2 sand, 1 paved)
■ Shuffleboard (2)
■ Horseshoes (2)
■ Petanque (2)
Miniten
Badminton
Fishing
■ Recreation Hall
■ Children's Activities
■ Library
■ Golf Pitching Green

INFORMATION

Club Personality
Experience Canadian hospitality at Ontario's loveliest resort for nudists. A family club, specializing in first-timers, where singles are also welcome. A congenial, relaxing atmosphere, and good food at reasonable prices. PNR does not accept credit cards.
Fax: 905/659-3410
E-mail: WWPOWELL@HOOKUP.NET

Description of Grounds
Ponderosa Nature Resort, open all year and fully licensed, boasts 100 idyllic acres with nature trails, spacious grounds for tenting, and fully-serviced camping sites. With an indoor pool, an outdoor pool, and a par 3, 69-yard pitching green, the club provides a full schedule of events.

Neighboring Sights and Attractions
The African Lion Safari, Royal Botanical Gardens, Pioneer Village, Mennonite markets, Kitchener Oktoberfest, race tracks, and some wonderful antique shops are all within reasonable driving distance. Only one hour away are bustling Toronto and world famous Niagara Falls.

Honored Discounts
20 percent discount on grounds fees for AANR, Naturist Society, FCN, FQN, INF and other associated naturist groups.

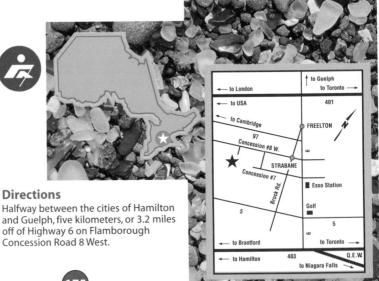

Directions
Halfway between the cities of Hamilton and Guelph, five kilometers, or 3.2 miles off of Highway 6 on Flamborough Concession Road 8 West.

GREEN HAVEN SUN CLUB

P.O. Box 3374
Regina, SK   S4P 3H1

SASKATCHEWAN

306/699-2515

FACILITIES

ACCOMMODATIONS

- ■ Wheelchair Access
  Vacation Villas
  Cabins
  Rooms
  Cable TV
  In-room Telephone
- ■ Trailers
  - ● heated
    w/bath
  - ● cooking
  Restaurant
  Lounge
- ■ Snack Bar
  Store

CAMPING

- ■ Tent Spaces
- ■ R/V Spaces
  - ● w/elec
  - ● w/water
  - ● w/sewer
- ■ Disposal Station
- ■ Showers
  - ● cold
  - ● hot
  Laundromat
  Community Kitchen
- ■ Picnic Tables
- ■ Playground
- ■ Pets/Leash only

RECREATION

- ■ Swimming Pool
  Lake
  Whirlpool/Spa
- ■ Sauna
- ■ Exercise Equipment
- ■ Tennis
- ■ Volleyball
- ■ Shuffleboard
- ■ Horseshoes
  Petanque
  Miniten
- ■ Badminton
  Fishing
- ■ Recreation Hall
- ■ Children's Activities
  Teen Activities

■ ● denotes availability

INFORMATION

Club Personality

Open May through September, Green Haven Sun Club is known for its hospitality, but asks that visitors contact the club before visiting.

Description of Grounds

Green Haven Sun Club is situated on 25 acres of gently rolling hills with large open grassy areas surrounded by trees. The club's accommodations, activities and amenities are as listed, including a snack bar and a children's playground.

Neighboring Sights and Attractions

Shops, restaurants, motels and a church are just 7 miles from the grounds. Entertainment may be found in the capital of Regina, 25 miles away.

Directions

Take Highway 1 from Regina to Balgonie. Take Highway 10, 7.2 miles to Avonhurst Grid Road, turn south one-quarter mile to the black and white gate with the large ASA and WCSA signs on the right.

ACTIVITIES & RECREATION

INFORMATION

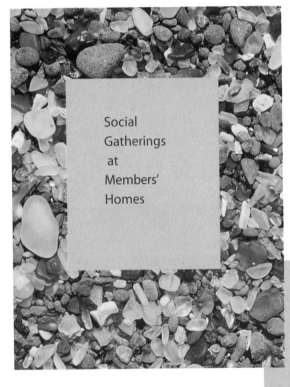

Social
Gatherings
at
Members'
Homes

General Information
Prairie Suns is a nonlanded travel club celebrating their 20th year of affiliation with the American Association for Nude Recreation.
Fax: 306/254-2102

Special Events
Halloween
and
New Year's Parties

Prairie
Suns

BARE NECESSITIES

1802 West 6th Street, Suite B
Austin, TX 78703

CARIBBEAN

800/743-0405

INFORMATION

Bare Beginnings

Bare Necessities Tour and Travel Company, Inc. was founded in 1990 by naturist travelers whose goal was to combine the option to be nude with the finest vacation experience possible. The venture has become a huge success providing travel opportunities never before available to the clothes-free vacationer. A full service travel agency, the company is accredited by the Airline Reporting Corporation, the International Association of Travel Agents, and the Cruise Line International Association.

Worldwide Acceptance

Featured on CNN Travel Log and in magazines such as *Forbes*, *New Woman*, and *Caribbean World*, Bare Necessities has received considerable media attention; convincing an ever growing number of travelers to leave their bathing suits at home. As the only clothing-optional travel agency with an international ad campaign, vacationers come together from around the world to enjoy its unique tours and resort offerings.

"A full service **travel agency** specializing in nude cruises."

Repeat Performances

Bare Necessities' thriving tour production department specializes in ship charters aboard luxury cruise and sailing vessels, producing 3–4 cruises a year to a variety of world wide destinations. Past cruises have visited the Mediterranean, French Polynesia, the Mexican Riviera and numerous ports in the Caribbean aboard shiplines such as *Holland America*, *Cunard*, and *Star Clipper*. Over fifty percent of Bare Necessities cruise ship clientele are repeat passengers.

Resort Opportunities

In addition to its unique and spectacular cruise tours, Bare Necessities represents four-star clothing optional resort properties in the U.S. and the Caribbean including the Jamaican Super Clubs, Club Orient in St. Martin, and Eden Bay in the Dominican Republic.

Fax: 512/469-0179
Web Site: www.bare-necessities.com

GRAND LIDO BRACO

CARIBBEAN

Agent: Go Classy Tours, Inc.
2676 W. Lake Road, Palm Harbor, FL 34684

800/69BRACO

INFORMATION

General Information
The newest member of the Grand Lido family (November 1, 1997), Grand Lido Braco will provide the most extensive SuperClub facilities and amenities for naturists in Jamaica. Construction on 12 acres of oceanfront property will create the ultimate luxury, super-inclusive island vacation.
Web Site: http://www.goclassy.com

"When you're ready for a different kind of all-inclusive . . ."

RECREATION

- Tennis
- Golf
- 2 Olympic-size Pools
- Fitness Center
- Volleyball
- Watersports
- Scuba
- Live Nightly Entertainment
- Shops, Beauty Salon
- 3 Restaurants, 8 Bars
- Airport Transfers

180

Go Cla
SuperClubs®

GRAND LIDO NEGRIL

Go Classy Tours, Inc.
2676 W. Lake Road, Palm Harbor, FL 34684

CARIBBEAN
800/303-LIDO

INFORMATION

General Information

Encompassing more than 22 breathtaking acres along Negril's world famous 7-mile beach, Grand Lido is one of the two most elegant Super-Inclusive resorts ever created. Three award winning restaurants. Twenty-four hour service. A private beach that seems to go on forever. Glorious sunset cruises aboard Princess Grace's honeymoon yacht. If you can dream it, you can do it at Grand Lido.
Web Site: http://www.goclassy.com

ACCOMMODATIONS

- Suite accommodations
- A world of dining experiences, from nouvelle cuisine by candlelight to burgers on the beach
- 24-hour room service
- Manicure and pedicure
- Private champagne and sunset cruises aboard Princess Grace's honeymoon yacht, the 147-foot M/Y Zein
- Virtually endless choice of bars to suit your mood, including a dreamy piano bar

RECREATION

- A secluded clothing-optional white-sand beach
- 2 Swimming Pools: one located on the clothing-optional beach
- 5 Jacuzzis, one on the clothing-optional beach
- Complimentary golf; includes greens fees and transportation (Clubs, carts and mandatory caddies not included)
- 4 Tennis courts, 2 lit for night play with resident pros
- Unlimited Watersports
- Live Nightly Entertainment

"The priceless measure of excellence."

ssy Tours, Inc.

HEDONISM II NEGRIL

Go Classy Tours, Inc.
2676 W. Lake Road, Palm Harbor, FL 34684

CARIBBEAN

888/8NEGRIL

INFORMATION

General Information

Whatever the reason, you deserve Hedonism II at least once in your life. Everything's included in one upfront price ... tipping is simply not permitted. From meals to drinks, to watersports and toga parties—unlimited possibilities for the mind, body, spirit and soul.

ACCOMMODATIONS & RECREATION

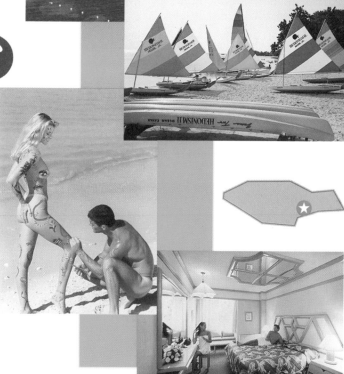

- Air-conditioned Accommodations
- All Meals Included
- Tennis
- Volleyball
- Scuba and Snorkeling
- Water Skiing
- Wind Surfing and Sailing
- Swimming Pool
- Fitness Center and Aerobics
- Indoor Game Room
- Live Entertainment
- Disco
- Piano Bar
- All Airport Transfers and Hotel Taxes

"Hedonism II Negril.
   An indulgent feast
for the senses."

Go Cla

SuperClubs®

GO CLASSY TOURS, INC.

2676 W. Lake Road
Palm Harbor, FL 34684

INFORMATION

CARIBBEAN

800/329-8145

General Information

Go Classy Tours represents many of the finest nude recreation destination in the world. In operation for 10 years, Go Classy Tours continues to be the leader in identifying and assisting in the creation of nude recreation destinations.
Web Site: http://goclassy.com

"Go Classy Tours, for the finest in nude recreation destinations."

COUPLES NEGRIL

Jamaica
An All-inclusive Resort

Separate nude facilities include:

- Swim-up Bar
- Swimming Pool
- Restrooms
- Shade Shelter
- Chaise Lounges
- Hammocks

EDEN LORETO

Baja California, Mexico
An All-inclusive Resort

- Air-conditioned Room with Patio or Balcony
- Two Swimming Pools
- Two Beaches
- Non-motorized Water Sports
- Tennis Center with 6 Courts
- Greens Fees with 18-hole Loreto Golf Course

CLUB ORIENT

St. Martin
All Nude Resort

- Air Conditioning
- Restaurant
- Shops
- Chaise Lounges
- One of the World's Finest Beaches

ssy Tours

A SAMPLING
NUDE
BEACHES

While the American Association for Nude Recreation represents organized nudist clubs and resorts, there are countless additional public and private lands used for nude recreation, some of which are listed below. While these beaches have long-standing traditions of nude use, their status could be affected at any time by real estate development or anti-nudity measures. Check with local free beach groups for current nude status before visiting. A complete guide to nude beaches—Lee Baxandall's World Guide to Nude Beaches and Resorts—is available through the AANR office, 800/879-6833, or by contacting The Naturist Society, POB 132, Oshkosh, WI 54902.

CALIFORNIA

Black's Beach

Billed as America's largest nude beach because of its nearly two miles of coastline, Black's Beach attracted up to 60,000 visitors on warm weekend days in the 1970s, outdrawing nearby attractions such as the San Diego Zoo and SeaWorld. Nudity once was condoned by the city council, but was outlawed by a narrow margin in a referendum in 1977 after religious zealots rallied support against it. But because of high cliffs, difficult access and massive public support, nude recreation continues to flourish at Black's, which is nestled below the Torrey Pines Glider Port and the University of California/San Diego campus in La Jolla. Sunbathers can enjoy breathtaking views of porpoises riding distant ocean breakers and hang gliders soaring above. Access off of I-5 from downtown San Diego is via La Jolla Village Drive. Go west one-half mile and make a right on Torrey Pines Road. Make a left at the entrance to the Salk Institute, just past UCSD, and follow the signs to the glider port's clifftop parking lot.

Baker Beach

Located just south of the Golden Gate Bridge and west of the Presidio, north Baker Beach is a popular destination for nudists—even if San Francisco's wind and cold make many days chilly. Access is from the southwest corner of the Presidio by way of Fort Point (off Lincoln Boulevard). Go west onto Bowley Street, to Gibson Road and the end of Gibson. A relatively new 40-car parking lot near the beach on Bowley Street has eased parking congestion. Nudity is at the northern end only.

Bonny Doon Beach

Arguably the most popular sunbathing spot in Santa Cruz, Bonny Doon is a model of nude beach success. Horseshoe-shaped cliffs that overlook the beach protect beachgoers from high winds. From Highway 1 go 11 miles north of Santa Cruz and look for the Bonny Doon parking lot at milepost 27.6 on the west side. Be sure to avoid parking illegally on Bonny Doon Road or the shoulder of Highway 1.

San Onofre State Beach

Besides the obvious symbolism of tanning your buns in the shadow of a nuclear power plant, nudists to San Onofre fail to miss the uncanny resemblance of the plant's twin globe facility to a pair of female breasts.

Located on the border of Orange and San Diego counties, San Onofre offers breathtaking views and a peaceful setting. San Diego police and Camp Pendleton M.P.s once issued citations and evicted nude sunbathers, but regulars have helped self-police the area from those whose sexual activities threatened the area's nude status. From I-5, exit at Basilone Road and take the crossover to the nuclear plant. Go south 2.5 miles to the park entrance ($6/car) and park near trail No. 6. Walk $^1/_2$ mile down to the beach—a much easier descent than Black's—turn left and walk $^3/_4$ mile south toward the Camp Pendleton fence.

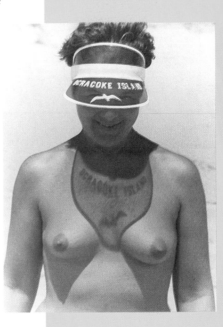

HAWAII
Honokohau Beach

A long, sandy beach on the big island of Hawaii, Honokohau Beach has mild surf due to the beach's location on the leeward side of the island and a reef 100 yards offshore. A pond behind the beach attracts ducks and other shorebirds. To reach the beach, travel 2 miles north from Kailua-Kona toward Keahole airport or south from the airport toward Kailua, and turn west on the paved road to the Honokohau Small Boat Harbor. Turn right at the marina property and follow the road counter-clockwise around the fence. Follow road to the left and into the marina, through the drydock and repair area and follow right edge of the harbor out to near the end of the road. Walk past encampment, over the rock pile to the right and follow the path through the trees to the beach. Walk north along the beach until reaching the area with the large pond behind it.

Note: A long-threatened ban on nudity at Honokohau Beach was enacted by the National Park Service on January 1, 1997. Kaloko-Honokohau National Historical Park Superintendent Francis Kuailani has claimed authority to ban mere nudity under federal and state laws, as well as under NPS regulatory mechanisms. On occasional patrols, park rangers are asking nudists to dress, but no one has been cited or arrested. The Naturist Action Committee and AANR are working with the Kona Sun Klub to reverse the superintendent's action.

Kalalua Valley—Kauai Island

The home of the original Hawaiians is now an island paradise for nude hiking, camping and sunbathing. Trekkers should be well equipped for the 11-mile hike up and down rugged coastal cliffs to a lush green valley of tropical trees, waterfalls, and no facilities. Access is from a marked trail at Kee Beach. State park permit required to enter.

Collins, then cross any of several wooden dune bridges that cut through the bushes to the beach. Lifeguards watch over the beach and vendors offer food and drinks.

Playalinda Beach

The target of anti-nudist forces, Playalinda has withstood heavy challenges and remains an active nude beach—even though beachgoers are at times cited or arrested. The clothing-optional area is located at the north end of this 25-mile pristine beach with no facilities. Take Route 406 east from Titusville to the entrance of Canaveral National Seashore. Drive north to parking lot 13 where a path leads to the nude beach. Before going, be sure to call a recorded message at 407/867-2805 to see if the beach is open. It closes whenever a space shuttle is preparing for take off at Cape Canaveral.

South Apollo Beach

Gaining popularity as an alternative to Playalinda Beach is Apollo Beach at the northern end of the Canaveral National Seashore. This pristine beach with no facilities can be accessed by I-95 or Highway 1 to the Route 44 exit. Go south approximately 10 miles to the Canaveral National Seashore entrance and park at the southernmost parking area. Walk south to at least marker #29.

FLORIDA
Haulover Beach

South Florida Free Beaches and the Dade County Parks and Recreation department worked together to establish the nude status of this quarter mile of sparkling white sands just off A1A north of Bal Harbor. Haulover Beach is a de facto nude beach, but it's unlikely that designation will change given the economic boost it has provided by attracting thousands of European visitors—to say nothing of locals, who fill the 1,000-car parking lot on weekends. Nestled less than a mile south of highrise hotels, Haulover nonetheless offers a quiet, peaceful setting and might have the easiest access of any major nude beach; it's even handicap accessible. From I-95, take State Road 826 (167th/163rd St.) and go east. Turn right at Collins Avenue (AIA) and park at Haulover County Park ($3.50) at about 150th Street. Take the north tunnel under

Makena/Little Beach

Just one mile from the Maui Prince Hotel, Little Beach is nestled away from the tourist throngs. Nudists can lounge in the shade of coconut palm trees and watch whales and nude surfers in the distance. The beach's clear waters are perfect for snorkeling. To get there, proceed exactly one mile south of the Maui Prince Hotel. Turn right and follow road to parking lot. Walk north, past Big Beach and over a lava-flow barrier. Proceed up the path to Little Beach.

Kauapea/Secret Beach

Located on the north end of Kauai, west of the Kilauea Lighthouse, Secret Beach is found at the foot of 300-foot protective cliffs covered with ferns, moss and other exotic foliage. Take Route 56 northwest to Kilauea. Beyond the 23 mile-mark, turn right at a Shell gas station, then left onto Kilauea Road and left onto Kauapea Road. Parking available near private driveway marked #2860-G.

MARYLAND
Assateague National Seashore (North Segment)

The Virginia side of Assateague National Seashore and the Assateague State Park in Maryland are off-limits to nude use. The Maryland portion of the National Seashore only is clothing-optional. About a three-hour drive from the Baltimore/Washington, D.C. area, Assateague is reachable by taking US 50 East. As you approach Ocean City, turn right on 611 and follow signs to Assateague State Park. Parking is $2. The legality of the clothing-optional area is open for debate; be sure to obey the NPS Park Rangers. Go at least to the 8.5 or 8.0 kilometer mark, well north of the State Park and into the federal section. Bug spray is recommended.

MASSACHUSETTS
Truro Beach

Despite the seemingly nudist-favorable political climate of Massachusetts, the National Park Service's only park-specific regulation banning nudity—legal on federal lands—was enacted at Cape Cod National Seashore in 1975. Such measures, however, have done little to deter nudists from pursuing nude recreation at the Cape. Many flock to Truro Beach, with its vast white sands and dunes that slope back from the sea and rise up to 80 feet in some places, effectively blocking out civilization. The beach is on the ocean side of the Cape, nearly at the tip out Route 6, between Long Nook Beach and Balston Beach. Parking permits require proof of long- or short-term residency and are available at a special office in town during the summer months. Keep in mind that there are no facilities on or near the beach.

OREGON
Rooster Rock
State Park

Located along the breathtaking Columbia River, Rooster Rock has the record for longest, continual, legal nude use in the U.S. Providing easy access, Rooster Rock State Park has its own exit off I-84 just 25 miles east of Portland. Stairs at the northeast (far right) corner of the parking area lead down to the state-designated clothing-optional section. Dams regulate the seasonal water flow of the river, creating the highest water level in May and June. In July, the water level drops, exposing more beach as well as opening the way for waders to cross to Sand Island opposite the nude shore. Rooster Rock offers full facilities and ample parking at pay lots.

Sauvie Island's
Collins Beach

Traditional for 30 years and state-designated since 1993, Collins Beach is a one-mile stretch of secluded, clothing-optional beach near the north end of Sauvie Island. The one bridge to the island is about 10 miles northwest of Portland on US-30. Collins Beach, which attracts up to 1,000 clothing-optional users per day, is one of three adjacent beaches on the Columbia River managed by the Oregon Department of Fish and Wildlife. Buy a parking permit at the store at the bottom of the bridge

NEVADA
Lake Tahoe

For nudists exercising a little discretion, beautiful Lake Tahoe offers a wealth of possibilities. The wilderness along the lake offers literally hundreds of opportunities for nude recreation. The US Forest Service permits discreet sunbathing and posts advisory signs for visitors who might otherwise be offended. The heaviest nude use occurs on the eastern shores of Lake Tahoe approximately $1^1/_2$ miles from the south of San Harbor on the Nevada side. With large granite deposits rising out of the lake and endless forest-covered mountains behind from the west, the view is breathtaking. The average weekend attendance is 50 and swells to more than 200 during holiday celebrations. There are no facilities in the area and minimal shade, so be sure to bring your own supplies.

NEW JERSEY
Sandy Hook

A nude beach mecca with a view of the New York skyline across the Hudson Bay, Sandy Hook's Gunnison Beach attracts thousands from the Mid-Atlantic states on warm weekends. The National Park Service provides lifeguards, security and maintenance and, unlike many major nude beaches, visitors do not have to trek down steep cliffs or walkways. Still, plan to arrive early as parking lots fill quickly. Located at the north end of the Gateway National Recreation Area, Sandy Hook is an hour and a half drive from Manhattan and convenient to popular Jersey Shore communities such as Red Bank, Asbury Park and Long Branch. Take the Garden State Parkway to Route 36. Follow signs to Gateway and take the road from the main gate, north, to parking lot G.

onto the island. Then drive under the bridge, and follow Gillihan Road until it ends. Turn right, and follow Reeder Road until it turns to gravel. Enter Collins Beach only via one of the five trails marked, "Collins Beach, Clothing-Optional Area, Nudity on Beach Only." You'll find a spacious beach with shallow coves, and patches of shrubs and reeds. Collins Beach has 473 parking spaces. Parking permits are required. Facilities are in the parking area, opposite each entrance trail. Sauvie Island does not receive the stiff Columbia Gorge breezes that can make Rooster Rock uncomfortable. Like Rooster Rock, Sauvie Island beaches may be under water during portions of May and June. For beach status, phone Friends of Sauvie Island Clothing Optional Beach, 503/645-2306.

TEXAS
Bolivar Beach

Although it is increasingly difficult to reach because of storm damage to the only road, Bolivar Beach remains a popular spot for recreational nudity. Remoteness is part of its allure. From Houston, travel east on I-10 to Texas 124 in the town of Winnie. Go south on 124 across the Intracoastal Waterway until 124 dead ends at Texas 87 near High Island. Highway 87 is closed to through traffic due to storm damage and is in terrible shape. Only four wheel drive vehicles can make it. Turn left (northeast) on Highway 87 and travel 4.5 miles to the unofficial nude area. You can drive on the hard packed sand of the beach during low tide. At high tide, there is very little beach at all. Check the tide tables before visiting.

South Padre Island

A haven for snowbirds and college spring breakers, the south Gulf Coast of Texas is also a premier nudist destination. The unofficial nude beach is about 8.5 miles north of the Town of South Padre Island off Route 100, the island's main road.

Padre Island National Seashore

North Beach, a protected area along the federal seashore that is a wildlife sanctuary for animals, also is a popular nudist attraction—despite occasional reports of harassment by park rangers. There are no facilities here, so come prepared. Access "PINS" from Corpus Christi via Route 358 onto Padre Island. Take the first left to the shore and park. Walk one mile south to the beach area.

WASHINGTON
Teddy Bear Cove

Located 30 miles south of the Canadian border in Bellingham, Washington, Teddy Bear Cove has been a nude beach since the 1940s. Located down a steep trail just south of Bellingham city limits, the small 500-yard wide beach looks out on Chuckanut Bay, the San Juan Islands, and the Olympic Peninsula on a clear day. To the north, there is a bluff that protects the beach from prevailing winds. Used from March through October, Teddy Bear Cove attracts as many as 300 visitors on a regular basis.

CANADA
BRITISH COLUMBIA
Wreck Beach

This nude beach haven nestled below the University of British Columbia in Pacific Spirit Park, attracts thousands of sunbathers on warm weekends, even if the chilly waters of the North Pacific keep many on shore. The three miles of nude beach are strewn with giant logs and can be found at

the base of cliffs on the west end of Vancouver. The beach extends from the Musqueam Indian reserve on the south end to West Spanish Banks on the north end. The Greater Vancouver Park Board has extended legal clothing-optional status to Wreck Beach, but offered little in way of support and facilities. Take Northwest Marine Drive toward UBC. Wreck Beach begins where the road starts to climb. Many visible trails descend to the beach, but the easy way down is a half-mile walk from a parking lot just west of the "Spanish Banks" city park sign—trail 6 across from the UBC entrance #6 descends deeply to the popular breakwater area.

LEGEND
LEGEND

The following legend is provided for the continental map on Pages 192–193. Numbered listings indicate landed parks and resorts. Non-numbered listings are clubs that have no land or facilities.

(1) **Forest City Lodge**
Milton, Vt.

● **Maine Coast Solar Bares**
Norway, Maine

(2) **Berkshire Vista Resort**
Hancock, Mass.

● **Natural High**
Dunstable, Mass.

● **Sherwood Forest**
North Reading, Mass.

● **Sunchasers**
Ludlow, Mass.

(3) **Sandy Terraces**
Marstons Mills, Mass.

(4) **Dyer Woods**
Foster, R.I.

(5) **Sun Ridge Resort**
Sterling, Conn.

(6) **Solair Recreation League**
Woodstock, Conn.

● **Garden of Eden**
Plymouth, Conn.

(7) **Hudson Valley Naturally**
Athens, N.Y.

(8) **Full-Tan Sun Club**
Sprakers, N.Y.

(9) **Empire Haven**
Moravia, N.Y.

(10) **Buckridge**
Candor, N.Y.

● **Rochester Naturist Society**
Rochester, N.Y.

● **SunFun**
Rochester, N.Y.

● **Friends of Buffalo**
Buffalo, N.Y.

● **Sun Rangers**
Blasdell, N.Y.

● **The Massage Community of New York**
Woodside, N.Y.

● **Long Island Travasuns**
Wantagh, N.Y.

● **The Skinnydippers**
Woodside, N.Y.

● **Northern Exposure Sun Club**
Clifton Park, N.Y.

(11) **Rock Lodge Club**
Stockholm, N.J.

● **Sun Airs of New Jersey**
New Milford, N.J.

● **Solaramblers**
West Caldwell, N.J.

● **Tri-State Metro Naturists**
New York, N.Y.

● **Friends of Gunnison**
Navesink, N.J.

● **The Road Warriors**
Mays Landing, N.J.

● **Tri State Sun Club**
Broadway, N.J.

(12) **Beechwood Lodge**
Ashfield, Pa.

(13) **Penn Sylvan Health Society**
Mohnton, Pa.

● **Metro Naturists**
Bensalem, Pa.

● **Hilltoppers Sun Club**
Red Lion, Pa.

● **Juvenation Naturists**
Eagleville, Pa.

● **Timber Trails**
Hersey, Pa.

● **West Penn Naturists**
East McKeesport, Pa.

(14) **Broken Arrow**
Polk, Pa.

(15) **White Thorn Lodge**
Darlington, Pa.

(16) **Pen-Mar Club**
Hancock, Md.

(17) **Pine Tree Associates**
Crownsville, Md.

(18) **Maryland Health Society**
Davidsonville, Md.

● **Delmarva Suncatchers**
Nassau, Del.

● **Potomac Rambling Bares**
Oakton, Va.

(19) **White Tail Park**
Ivor, Va.

● **Bare Buns Family Nudist Club**
Oakton, Va.

● **National Capital Sun Club**
Leesburg, Va.

(20) **Avalon**
Paw Paw, W.Va.

(21) **Cedar Trails**
Peebles, Ohio

● **Cinci Gymnos**
Cincinnati, Ohio

(22) **Paradise Gardens**
Cincinnati, Ohio

● **Have Sun Will Travel**
Marion, Ohio

(23) **Alpine Resort**
Millersburg, Ohio

(24) **Green Valley**
Bath, Ohio

● **Northcoast Naturists**
Cleveland, Ohio

● **Great Lakes Sunseekers**
Sylvania, Ohio

(25) **Turtle Lake Resort**
Union City, Mich.

(26) **Whispering Oaks**
Oxford, Mich.

● **Bares-N-Cubs**
Redford, Mich.

(27) **Forest Hills**
Saranac, Mich.

(28) **Sunshine Gardens Resort**
Battle Creek, Mich.

● **Traverse Area Naturists**
Mesick, Mich.

(29) **Valley View Recreation Club**
Cambridge, Wis.

● **Badger Naturists**
Madison, Wis.

● **The Travcliers**
Racine, Wis.

(30) **Avatan**
Minneapolis, Minn.

● **Sno-Birds**
Minneapolis, Minn.

(31) **Oakwood Club**
Coon Rapids, Minn.

● **Cornhusker Recreation Club**
Omaha, Neb.

● **Dakota Prairie Sun Club**
Estherville, Iowa

● **Camelot**
Des Moines, Iowa

(32) **Blue Lake**
Erie, Ill.

● **Chicago Sun Clubs**
Cicero, Ill.

● **Illi Mo Utopians**
Wood River, Ill.

(33) **Forty Acre Club**
Lonedell, Mo.

● **Ozark Leisure Club**
Springfield, Mo.

● **Bare Hunters**
St. Louis, Mo.

(34) **Lake O'The Woods Club**
Valparaiso, Ind.

(35) **Sunny Haven Recreation Park**
Granger, Ind.

● **Ft. Wayne Naturists**
Fort Wayne, Ind.

(36) **Sunshower Country Club**
Centerville, Ind.

(37) **Fern Hills Club**
Bloomington, Ind.

(38) **Tri-State Country Club**
Bennington, Ind.

● **Kyana Naturists**
Louisville, Ky.

● **Bluegrass Naturists**
Nicholasville, Ky.

(39) **Rock Haven Lodge**
Murfreesboro, Tenn.

(40) **Timberline Lodge**
Crossville, Tenn.

(41) **Bar-S-Ranch**
Reidsville, N.C.

● **North Carolina Naturists**
Charlotte, N.C.

(42) **Whispering Pines**
Ocean Isle Beach, N.C.

(43) **Nirvana Sun Resort**
Tabor City, N.C.

(44) **Carolina Foothills**
Chesnee, S.C.

● **ColaBares**
Columbia, S.C.

(45) **Sunair Health Park**
Graniteville, S.C.

● **Travelites**
Columbia, S.C.

● **LowCountry Naturist**
Charleston, S.C.

191

Continued on Page 194

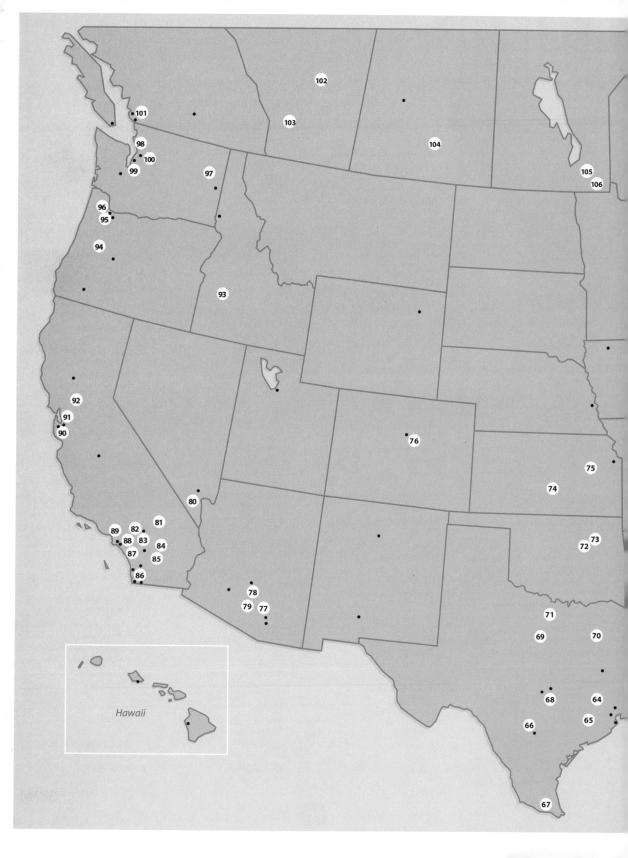

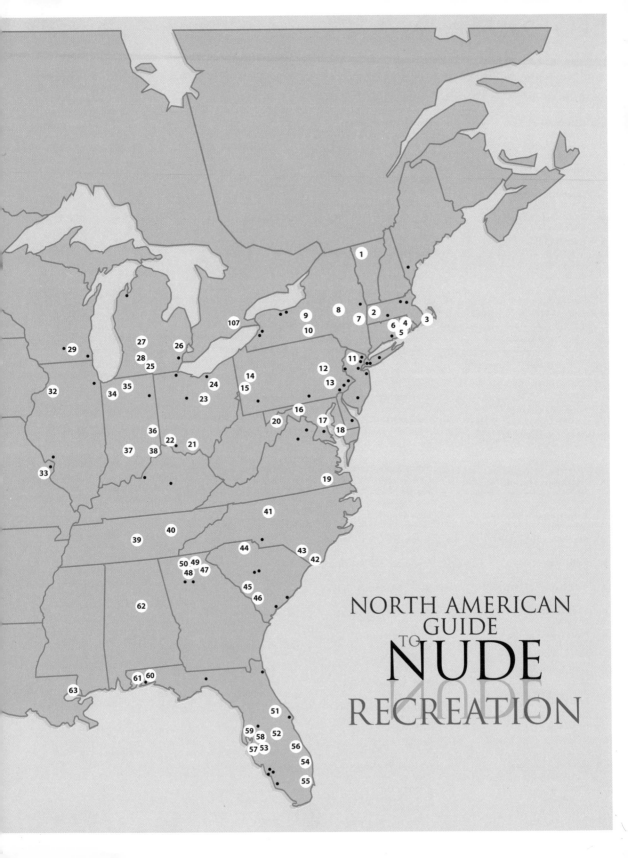

NORTH AMERICAN
GUIDE
TO
NUDE
RECREATION

LEGEND *continues...*

LEGEND *continues...*

- **The Sun Strokers, SCN**
  Edisto Island, S.C.
- (46) **Cedar Creek**
  Pelion, S.C.
- (47) **Bell Acres**
  Maysville, Ga.
- (48) **Hidden Valley**
  Dawsonville, Ga.
- (49) **Mountain Creek Grove**
  Cleveland, Ga.
- (50) **Serendipity Park**
  Cleveland, Ga.
- **SANS Travel Club**
  Lawrenceville, Ga.
- **Bare Buddies**
  Atlanta, Ga.
- (51) **Sunny Sands**
  Pierson, Fla.
- (52) **Cypress Cove**
  Kissimmee, Fla.
- **Central Florida Naturists**
  Merritt Island, Fla.
- (53) **The Island Group**
  Land O'Lakes Fla.
- (54) **Sunsport Gardens**
  Loxahatchee, Fla.
- (55) **Seminole Health Club**
  Davie, Fla.
- (56) **Sunnier Palms**
  Ft. Pierce, Fla.
- **Southern Exposure**
  Naples, Fla.
- **Sanibel Naturists**
  Ft. Myers, Fla.
- **Southwest Florida Naturists**
  Ft. Myers, Fla.
- (57) **Lake Como**
  Lutz, Fla.
- (58) **Club Paradise**
  Land O'Lakes, Fla.
- **Caliente**
  Land O'Lakes, Fla.
- **Tallahassee Bare-Devils**
  Tallahassee, Fla.
- **Panhandle Free Beaches**
  Navarre, Fla.
- **Northeast Florida Naturists**
  Jacksonville, Fla.
- (59) **Gulf Coast Resort**
  Hudson, Fla.
- (60) **Sunburst Resort**
  Milton, Fla.
- (61) **Riviera Naturist Resort**
  Pace, Fla.
- **Villages of Pine Island**
  Pineland, Fla.
- (62) **Gymno-Vita Park**
  Vandiver, Ala.
- (63) **La Pines**
  Lacombe, Lou.
- (64) **Live Oak Resort**
  Washington, Texas

- **Lost Leg Club**
  Grapeland, Texas
- **Healthy Hides of Houston**
  Houston, Texas
- **Gulf Coast Nudist Yacht Club**
  Galveston, Texas
- (65) **Natural Horisun**
  Boling, Texas
- (66) **Riverside Ranch**
  San Antonio, Texas
- **Bexar Recreation Society**
  San Antonio, Texas
- **The Natural Travelers**
  Houston, Texas
- (67) **Sandpipers Holiday Park**
  Edinburg, Texas
- (68) **Sahnoans**
  Austin, Texas
- **Central Texas Nudists**
  Austin, Texas
- **Hill Country Nudists**
  Austin, Texas
- (69) **Vista Grande**
  Weatherford, Texas
- (70) **Sunny Pines**
  Wills Point, Texas
- (71) **Bluebonnet**
  Alvord, Texas
- (72) **Oaklake Trails**
  Tulsa, Okla.
- (73) **Sun Meadow**
  Tulsa, Okla.
- (74) **Sandy Lane Club**
  Hutchinson, Kan.
- (75) **Prairie Haven**
  Scranton, Kan.
- **Heartland Naturists**
  Shawnee Mission, Kan.
- **Wyotans**
  Gillette, Wyo.
- (76) **Mountain Air Ranch**
  Indian Hills, Col.
- **Rocky Mountain Bares**
  Arvada, Col.
- **Roadrunner Naturists**
  Los Alamos, N.M.
- **SunTree Travel Club**
  Las Cruces, N.M.
- (77) **Jardin del Sol**
  Marana, Ariz.
- **Buff-A-Teers**
  Tucson, Ariz.
- **Canyon Waterway Adventures**
  Tucson, Ariz.
- (78) **Shangri La II**
  New River, Ariz.
- **Arizona Wildflowers**
  Phoenix, Ariz.
- (79) **Arizona Hidden Valley Retreat**
  Maricopa, Ariz.

- **El Dorado Hot Springs**
  Tonopah, Ariz.
- **Utah Naturists**
  Salt Lake City, Utah
- (80) **Las Vegas Sun Club**
  East Las Vegas, Nev.
- **Vegas Bares**
  Las Vegas, Nev.
- (81) **Silver Valley**
  Newberry Springs, Calif.
- (82) **Buff Creek**
  Devore, Calif.
- **Canyon Sun Club**
  San Bernardino, Calif.
- (83) **Olive Dell Ranch**
  Colton, Calif.
- (84) **The Naturist Society's Desert Shadows Inn**
  Palm Springs, Calif.
- (85) **The Terra Cotta Inn**
  Palm Springs, Calif.
- **Naked Volleyball**
  Laguna Niguel, Calif.
- (86) **Swallows**
  El Cajon, Calif.
- **Le Club**
  San Diego, Calif.
- **Golden Oaks Club**
  El Cajon, Calif.
- **Pacificans**
  Van Nuys, Calif.
- **Wee Bear**
  Santee, Calif.
- (87) **McConville**
  Lake Elsinore, Calif.
- (88) **Glen Eden Sun Club**
  Corona, Calif.
- (89) **Elysium Fields**
  Topanga, Calif.
- **The Olympian Club**
  Bellflower, Calif.
- **Natural Manner Club**
  Reedley, Calif.
- (90) **Lupin Naturist Club**
  Los Gatos, Calif.
- (91) **Sequoians Family Nudist Park**
  Castro Valley, Calif.
- (92) **Laguna del Sol**
  Wilton, Calif.
- **Sutter Buttes Sun Club**
  Yuba City, Calif.
- **Sanrobles**
  Hayward, Calif.
- **Air-A-Tans**
  Gardena, Calif.
- **Llasa**
  Los Gatos, Calif.
- (93) **Bare Backers**
  Boise, Id.
- **Running Bears**
  Moscow, Id.

- (94) **The Willamettans**
  Springfield, Ore.
- **Tumbleweeds**
  Bend, Ore.
- **The Rogue Suncatchers**
  Ashland, Ore.
- (95) **Squaw Mountain Ranch**
  Portland, Ore.
- **Sun Rovers**
  Portland, Ore.
- **Hidden Springs**
  Portland, Ore.
- (96) **Restful Haven**
  North Plains, Ore.
- (97) **Kaniksu Ranch**
  Loon Lake, Wash.
- **Free Spirits**
  Bellevue, Wash.
- **Forest Murmurs**
  Lacey, Wash.
- (98) **Lake Associates**
  Mt. Vernon, Wash.
- (99) **Fraternity Snoqualmie**
  Issaquah, Wash.
- **Tanfastics**
  Snohomish, Wash.
- (100) **Lake Bronson**
  Sultan, Wash.
- **The Naturals Club of Spokane**
  Veradale, Wash.
- (101) **Sunny Trails**
  Lake Errock, Mission, British Columbia
- **Vancouver Sunbathing Association**
  Surrey, British Columbia
- **Van Tan Club**
  Vancouver, British Columbia
- **Arbutus Park**
  Victoria, British Columbia
- **Okanagan Shuswap**
  Kelowna, British Columbia
- (102) **Helios Nudist Association**
  Tofield, Alberta
- (103) **Sunny Chinooks Association**
  Calgary, Alberta
- (104) **Green Haven Sun Club**
  Regina, Saskatchewan
- **Prairie Suns**
  Saskatoon, Saskatchewan
- (105) **Crocus Grove Sun Club**
  Beausejour, Manitoba
- (106) **Musqua Meadows**
  Menisino, Manitoba
- (107) **Ponderosa Naturist Park**
  Puslinch, Ontario
- **Kona Sun Klub**
  Kailua-Kona, Hawaii
- **Hawaii Naturist Society**
  Honolulu, Hawaii

○ Landed Clubs
● Nonlanded Clubs

INDEX

Share Your Thoughts

With the Author: Your comments will be forwarded to the author when you send them to *zauthor@zondervan.com*.

With Zondervan: Submit your review of this book by writing to *zreview@zondervan.com*.

Free Online Resources at
www.zondervan.com

Zondervan AuthorTracker: Be notified whenever your favorite authors publish new books, go on tour, or post an update about what's happening in their lives at www.zondervan.com/authortracker.

Daily Bible Verses and Devotions: Enrich your life with daily Bible verses or devotions that help you start every morning focused on God. Visit www.zondervan.com/newsletters.

Free Email Publications: Sign up for newsletters on Christian living, academic resources, church ministry, fiction, children's resources, and more. Visit www.zondervan.com/newsletters.

Zondervan Bible Search: Find and compare Bible passages in a variety of translations at www.zondervanbiblesearch.com.

Other Benefits: Register yourself to receive online benefits like coupons and special offers, or to participate in research.

ZONDERVAN.com/
AUTHORTRACKER
follow your favorite authors